Psychological Testing
for Ministerial Selection

Proceedings of the Seventh Academy Symposium
Academy of Religion and Mental Health
with the aid of
The General Service Foundation

PSYCHOLOGICAL TESTING
FOR MINISTERIAL SELECTION

edited by

WILLIAM C. BIER, S.J.

FORDHAM UNIVERSITY PRESS
New York   1970

© COPYRIGHT 1970 BY THE ACADEMY OF RELIGION AND MENTAL HEALTH
Library of Congress catalog card number: 73–79568
ISBN 0–8232–0850–8

PRINTED IN THE UNITED STATES OF AMERICA

CONTENTS

Preface

THE ACADEMY OF RELIGION AND MENTAL HEALTH consists of a group of approximately 4,000 members drawn primarily from the fields of religion and the healing professions. It provides a multi-faith and interdisciplinary approach to total health on the conviction that anything less than these combined resources is inadequate to the challenge of mental health and illness. The particular focus of the Academy is on the *relations* between religion and health, particularly mental health. It is not a treatment organization in that it does not provide religious or professional counseling to persons with emotional problems. Rather, it is concerned with the professional persons in these fields, and its efforts have been directed toward promoting mutual understanding between clergymen and other representatives of religion, on the one hand, and members of the health-related professions, on the other. To this end, the Academy holds professional meetings for its members, publishes literature appropriate to its purpose, including the quarterly *Journal of Religion and Health,* and serves as a consultant to many governmental and health organizations, both national and international.

The Academy has found that one of the most effective means at its disposal for promoting the desired mutual understanding between representatives of religion and of the health professions has been through symposia on selected topics in the area of religion and health, to which are invited representatives from several faiths and various professional disciplines. It was also found that Arden House—the Harriman, New York, conference center of Columbia

vii

University—provided an ideal setting for such symposia. The first of these, under the sponsorship of the Academy, was held in 1957. The most recent, the seventh in the series, which is reported in this volume, took place in 1966. All of them follow a similar pattern, running from a Friday afternoon to a Sunday noon, the time being chosen so as to create the minimum of conflict with the academic and professional commitments of the participants. No one, with the exception of the Rev. George C. Anderson, D.D., founder and currently honorary president of the Academy, attended all seven symposia, but the planning of them included a provision for both continuity and variety. Each time, enough people were invited who had attended a previous symposium to provide continuity, while enough new people—these being chosen by reason of special competence in the topic of the given symposium—were included to provide variety and fresh viewpoints. The topics discussed at the symposia were chosen by reason of their relevance to the relations between religion and health, as the following partial listing will indicate: Religion, Science, and Mental Health; Religion, Culture, and Mental Health; Religion in the Developing Personality; Research in Religion and Health; and Moral Values in Psychoanalysis.

The symposium reported in this volume was held at Arden House, January 14–16, 1966, and was on the topic: Psychological Testing for Ministerial Selection. The symposium was concerned with the contribution which psychological evaluation can make to the selection and, particularly when combined with appropriate follow-up counseling, to the subsequent mental health of candidates for the ministry. Quite evidently, a symposium on this topic deserved to be included in a series, sponsored by the Academy, dealing with religion and mental health.

The psychological testing of seminary applicants had been increasingly employed by each of the three major religious groups for a period of five to ten years prior to 1966. The work, however, was carried out to a surprising extent in isolation, particularly without reference to the parallel work being done by other religious groups. The work of Catholics in the field found a focus in a committee within the American Catholic Psychological Association—

the Committee for the Study of Methods in the Psychological Assessment of Candidates for the Religious Life, formed in 1960 under the chairmanship of Dr. Walter J. Coville. A similar focus was provided for Protestants engaged in this work by the Ministry Studies Board, organized in 1960 with representatives from the Department of Ministry, Vocation, and Pastoral Services of the National Council of Churches, and from the American Association of Theological Schools. In that same year, the Educational Testing Service, under the direction of Frederick R. Kling, completed the research on the Theological School Inventory, "a psychological test designed to evaluate the strength and type of motivation which attracted persons to the ministry." At the time of its organization, the Ministry Studies Board accepted responsibility for the supervision of the test, and by 1962 Dr. James E. Dittes had completed his studies on its validity and published the *Manual* for its use. Jewish workers were less active in this kind of evaluation, and their work lacked the kind of unifying organization found in the other two instances. Dr. Samuel Z. Klausner, however, made a distinct contribution to the entire field by his annotated bibliographies, which were the first to appear, in religion and psychiatry.

It was not, however, until the publication in 1965 of Menges' and Dittes' *Psychological Studies of Clergymen* that most of the workers in the field realized how much research had been done and how much they were working in isolation. Credit for the first attempt to bring together workers from the three major religious groups engaged in the psychological assessment of ministerial candidates goes to the Board of Theological Education of the Lutheran Church in America, which, under the direction of Rev. J. Victor Benson, Secretary for Psychological Services, convened a Conference on Psychological Research, November 19–20, 1962, in New York City. The time seemed ripe in 1966 for a more formal and more extended conference on the Psychological Evaluation of Ministerial Applicants, and it seemed appropriate, both in terms of its aims, as a multifaith and interdisciplinary approach to mental health, and in terms of its experience with symposia in the religion and health area, that it should be convened and sponsored by the Academy of Religion and Mental Health.

The symposium reported in this volume was organized around six position papers. In each case, the paper had been prepared beforehand, but formal presentation at the symposium was limited in order to allow sufficient time for discussion. At least one formal discussant, who had received a copy of the paper prior to the meeting, was appointed for each paper, but the major portion of each session was devoted to general discussion of the topic by the symposium participants. The general discussion has been summarized and is presented in each case.

The participants—a list of whom may be found at the end of this volume—were invited because of their involvement in the work of psychological assessment of ministerial candidates. It was a conference, therefore, of the people from each of the three major religious groups who are doing the work of psychological assessment; it did not include the church administrators who use the test results and who make the decisions on seminary admissions. This would be an appropriate topic for another conference, beamed at the administrators. By convoking the symposium, the Academy effectively brought these researchers and testers together, invited them to evaluate their work, to interact with one another, and to plan for the future.

As indicated in the table of contents, the symposium was divided into four sections. The first section was designed to focus the attention of the participants from the beginning on the problems—technical, professional, and moral—which faced them as investigators engaged in the psychological evaluation of ministerial candidates. In his paper, Dr. James E. Dittes, speaking from his considerable experience with the Theological School Inventory and his thorough knowledge of the psychological literature on clergymen, adopted an attitude of cautious but constructive skepticism with respect to the usefulness of psychological testing in ministerial selection. He challenged the participants to demonstrate more convincingly than had been done up to the present the validity of their testing procedures. He likewise raised the "criterion question," which was to recur throughout the symposium: What is the criterion of "success" in the ministry; how do we measure it and test for it?

The next section concerned itself with a presentation and evaluation of the work currently being done by the three religious groups represented at the Conference. Dr. Thomas N. McCarthy reviewed the work of Catholics, Dr. James B. Ashbrook that of Protestants, and Dr. Fred Brown that of Jews in the field. The overview was impressive. Even though working in relative independence, all three groups had much in common with respect to goals, approaches, techniques, and even tests employed. They also shared common problems, such as uncertainty with respect to the validity of their tests, concern about communicating test results to church administrators and the use made by these administrators of the results, and the criterion problem already mentioned.

The third section of the symposium directed attention to the outcomes of testing. There was general agreement among the participants that, from a research point of view, top priority should go, at the present time, to systematic follow-up studies of testing programs which would compare initial test impressions and predictions with subsequent performance in the ministry. Only in this way can the effectiveness of psychological evaluation for ministerial selection be validated. Obviously, a certain interval of time must elapse before the candidates tested are functioning in the active ministry and before such studies can be undertaken, and it is evident that an attempt of this kind runs headlong into the problem of the criterion of success in the ministry. Few testing programs have been in operation long enough to provide this kind of follow-up information. Rev. David W. Carroll, s.j., reported on one testing program which, while not following men previously tested into the active ministry, reported on them through various stages of seminary training.

Another of the papers in this section on outcomes dealt with Psychological Problems of the Clergy, presented by Rev. Edward S. Golden. The entire program of psychological evaluation of ministerial applicants has as its goal the mental health of the clergy. One of the clear generalizations emerging from the symposium was the realization that the testing of applicants needs to be combined with follow-up counseling, when and as needed, to insure the goal of a mentally healthy clergy. Dr. Golden's paper served to direct attention to the kind of psychological problems in the clergy which responsible assessment and counseling programs can help to prevent.

The final section of the symposium was devoted to a summary of Conference findings and recommendations. I think that the reader will be impressed by the candor and realism of this section. No one in the movement responsibly represents the psychological evaluation of ministerial candidates as offering a panacea for the psychological ills of the clergy, but such programs offer a more constructive contribution than any alternative approach. The conference demonstrated clearly the need for greater collaboration among those working in the field, the need for validation studies by systematic follow-ups into the active ministry, and the need for more effective communication with the church administrators who are the users of the testing results.

The delay in publishing the proceedings cannot be regarded as other than regrettable. The decision to publish despite the interval was made, however, because the conference herein reported remains unique (at least among published sources) in its multifaith approach to ministerial testing, and because much of the material included is either entirely unavailable or not readily available elsewhere. Partial amends for the delay have been made by appropriate updating of references and by the inclusion of two follow-up studies on testing outcomes, not available at the time of the conference. Father Carroll's follow-up study, which could be only partially presented at the symposium because it was still in progress, is presented in completed form in the published volume. His results show a statistically significant relationship between initial psychological prediction and subsequent evaluation by seminary faculty, despite the unavoidably restricted and attenuated nature of the sample employed. A second study of testing outcomes is provided in the paper by Rev. Charles A. Weisgerber, s.j. He was a participant at the Conference, but his study had not progressed far enough at the time of the symposium to enable him to make any report on it. Since the Conference members called for systematic follow-up studies of testing procedures as the next logical and necessary step in the responsible professional approach to the use of psychological tests in ministerial selection, these two studies provide an added and valuable dimension to the Conference in the precise direction seen by the participants as most needed.

Planning for the symposium was carried out by a Committee consisting of Dr. Fred Brown and Dr. Edgar W. Mills, with the undersigned as Chairman. It was only through the collaboration of these men that a multifaith and interdisciplinary symposium was able to be convened, which succeeded in attracting as participants the people most significantly identified with the ministerial testing movement throughout the country. I take this opportunity to express my appreciation to my colleagues on the Planning Committee for their assistance in organizing the symposium, and to the participants for their contribution of time in attending, and for their willing and spirited participation in the discussions and deliberations which formed so significant a feature of the symposium.

Without the Academy of Religion and Mental Health and its abiding interest in furthering the relations between religion and mental health, there would have been no Conference. We gladly acknowledge the guiding influence of Rev. George C. Anderson, then President, now Honorary President of the Academy, in initiating the remote planning which led to the formation of the conference, and the efficient management of Mr. Charles C. Bergman, Executive Vice-President, who attended so faultlessly to all the immediate arrangements and to the comfort of the participants at Arden House.

The Academy, as well as the participants, wishes to express its appreciation to the General Service Foundation for its financial support of the symposium.

Lastly, a particular debt of gratitude, which is gratefully acknowledged, is due to Jean W. Conti, associate editor of the *Journal of Religion and Health,* who so skillfully combined the disjointed general discussion into the smooth narrative which appears in the published volume.

November, 1969   WILLIAM C. BIER, S.J.

I

Assumptions and Goals
of Ministerial Testing

SOME BASIC QUESTIONS ABOUT TESTING MINISTERIAL CANDIDATES

JAMES E. DITTES

To ANYONE THE LEAST SOPHISTICATED about psychological testing, the questions I want to raise may seem annoyingly elementary. But elementary or not, I am not yet persuaded that they have been satisfactorily answered in connection with the use of tests among theological candidates, especially as they are used for screening and selection (cf. Dittes, 1962).*

The use of tests generates a momentum which may make it necessary for someone deliberately to blow a shrill whistle and ask for a time-out for elementary reflection. There is, first of all, the mystique of numbers and of science which too often, in our earnest, even desperate desire for more reliable information about students, makes us attribute to test scores a kind of esoteric authority in which we forget to ask too carefully where the numbers came from. Secondly, there is the massive investment of time, energy, money, even careers and reputations involved in the testing

---

* Reprints of this paper, entitled Research on Clergymen: Factors influencing decisions for religious service and effectiveness in the vocation, had been distributed to the participants prior to the symposium.—Ed.

enterprise. Even when the investments are initially intended to be exploratory and tentative, it is a psychological principle—most recently elaborated by the "dissonance" theorists (e.g., Brehm and Cohen, 1962)—that such investment tends to breed supporting conviction about the validity and worth of whatever one has committed time and effort to. So tests readily have their advocates and their willing consumers. And the voice which I think needs to be raised aloud for all of us, although it is already heard quietly within each of us, is that of the skeptic.

My skepticism is mainly that which accrues from noticing distinctions; which says, for example, that a test which may be valid for one purpose is not thereby useful for another, no matter how much our need may be for the latter rather than for the former. But it is also a skepticism tempered by a hopefulness, a hopefulness that out of reflection, research, and perhaps even new test development, we can answer our own skeptical questions and can find trustworthy guidelines for the use of particular tests in particular situations.

I have already acknowledged that such elementary skepticism as mine is, is shared by all responsible test-users. It is seen, for example, in the reluctance of almost all testers to make a definite decision about a man's career on the basis of test results. "We just describe the man with the test results and then let him or the officials decide what to do" is one common policy. Another is "Test results should be only one of many considerations"; or, "Tests should be used only for counseling on personal problems and vocational decisions, not for selection."

But if such policies betray a justified caution about trusting tests to make major decisions about a candidate, it also seems to me that they betray a less justified confidence in trusting the tests for smaller decisions and actions, which in the long run may be just as decisive. Who should be "watched"?—with what kind of reservations now planted in the mind of his supervisor? Who should be given a more probing interview or have his record scrutinized more thoroughly?—looking for evidence of what? Who should have a letter of recommendation shaded a bit by test results? Who should be counseled to reconsider what problems, to face what doubts about his vocation? Of course, it all depends on the manner of the counseling or other use of the test results, which is beyond the control of the tester; but not, I think, beyond his responsibility. A psychologist, above all, should be aware of how small suggestions, especially concerning mental health and illness, even though offered tentatively and cautiously, may still have a decisive influence. If we cannot trust tests to make overt and controlled decisions about a man's career, ought we to use them in a way that is likely to encourage more subtle and diffused but still influential decisions? Perhaps the nuclear physicist can arrive at an ethical position in which he says that his bomb-building is neutral and that the decisions about use are made by others. But the psychologist knows too much about decision-making to make such a neat separation possible.

Another example seems worth citing, of a common instance in which we acknowledge cautions but still act in violation of them. One point, to be made later more fully and systematically, is commonly accepted: this is the distinction between mental health and effective ministry. Even if tests can measure and predict health and stability, this hardly provides any basis for predicting who will become a good clergyman. With the array before us of such tormented heroes of the faith as Jeremiah, Paul, and Luther, alongside instances of present-day pastors happy, drably and faithlessly overadjusted to the suburban norms and institutional status quo in which they are embedded—with such considerations as this, no one dares to say that the usual criteria of mental health may be invoked in the selection of effective ministers. Seminary faculties, church officials, psychological testers, when pressed on the principle, will invariably accept this distinction.

Sometimes the above-mentioned persons may go even further and propose a negative correlation. Behind every earnest commitment and creative thrust we may hypothesize, for example, that there must be some animating disturbance; or perhaps the ministry needs men who are bold and visionary enough even to be called a bit paranoid; or again: only the rebel and discontent can survive the cultural pressures and remain faithful to his call. These proposals I have heard.

But the same men, even when they proclaim the negative correlation, when they are pressed by practical exigencies (as, e.g., to select among candidates for their institutions), revert to a policy of selecting out those whom testing procedures suggest to be disturbed and disturbing. The implicit reaction sometimes seems to be: since we can't detect with tests the characteristics of the good minister, we will judge by what we can measure.

FROM ANSWER SHEET TO DECISION

On the face of it, it is a daring and implausible claim that a decision about a student's future will be better made if it takes into consideration the few marks he makes or the few words he speaks in response to certain limited and particular test materials. The student may be asked to tell a story about a shadowy picture of two men and a machine (TAT *) or mark *true* or *false* after such a statement as "It takes a lot of argument to convince most people of the truth" (MMPI *). His story and his circle around T or F may be used—so the test rationale dares to claim—toward answering a question as to whether he should enter a seminary, be ordained, be assigned to a particular position rather than another, be referred for psychotherapy, etc. This is a precarious path of inference.

But it is crucially important to recognize that the path consists of many stepping stones. It is not a single outlandish jump of inference from answer sheet to decision, but a chain of inferences with many links. Many different types of evidence need to be examined in turn and many different decisions made. For a fully developed test, these steps should have been taken, or at least plotted, before the test is administered and interpreted. But the test user needs to understand these steps so that he can assess their trustworthiness and so that he can, if need be, retrace them. Recognizing that many different steps are involved may make the claim seem more plausible that test answers can aid a decision, but this process also exposes to scrutiny each of the intervening decisions.

* These abbreviations and the tests to which they refer are explained, for the benefit of those unfamiliar with them, later on in this paper.—Ed.

The chain of inferences clearly can be no stronger than its weakest link.

The accompanying chart presents a way of diagramming the major steps and the links between them. The first two links, labeled "reliability" and "validity," are the most familiar in discussion of tests and are generally the links most satisfactorily charted by test developers, although by no means entirely satisfactorily. They will be discussed briefly here. The other two links, called here "utility" and "responsibility," will be discussed at greater length, for here is where the most striking problems lie in the use of tests for screening ministerial candidates.

The following discussion of reliability and validity is intended primarily to provide a context for the later discussion of utility and responsibility. It will not raise questions about the adequacy with which existing tests commonly used with ministerial candidates meet the ordinary standards of reliability and validity. That basic questions *can* be raised concerning their adequacy can be easily seen by consulting any standard reference work on tests, such as Buros (1965) or Cronbach (1960).

From single items to a scale: reliability—"something" is there, real and discernible.

The items of a test may be correlated. That is, there may be a tendency for a student who answers one item in a particular way to answer other items in particular ways: one can predict, with some probability, a student's answer to one item by knowing his answer to another item. This inter-item correlation is one of the standard ways of assessing reliability. Like other reliability estimates (such as interobserver agreement, or consistency from one testing session to another), such a correlation may permit the inference that some underlying characteristic is being represented by these items. If several peaks of ice consistently move through the ocean together in varying currents and weather, one may suspect that they are outcroppings of a single iceberg.

Such items may be assembled into a single *scale* and regarded as a unit. The student's total score on these assembled items may be taken as an index of the magnitude of this particular under-

A CHART OF THE STEPS FROM ANSWER SHEET TO DECISION

	Test Items		Scale		Attribute		Criterion		Decision
Units of each step:									
Examples of units on MMPI:	It takes a lot of argument to convince most people of the truth: T or F		K scale		"defensiveness"		effectiveness in ministry		Admit to candidacy?
on TSI:	It will not be difficult for me to assume the responsibilities of the ministry		NL scale		strength of motivation for ministry		persistence in seminary to graduation (not drop out)		Will he be a minister?
on an ability test:	Compare "laziness" and "idleness"		Verbal aptitude		intelligence		seminary grade		Admit to seminary?
Link between steps:		*Reliability*		*Validity*		*Utility*		*Responsibility*	
Significance of making the link:		"Something" is there, real and discernible		The "something" is recognizable		The recognizable "something" is relevant		The relevant, recognizable "something" is considered	
Typical method of making the link:		Correlation among items		Correlation between scale score and independent estimate of attribute (e.g., observers' ratings)		Theoretical: analysis of attributes required by criterion. Empirical: correlation between attribute and criterion		Intuitive weighing of test's prediction to criterion, the probability of the prediction, and many non-test factors	
Who makes the link:		Test developer		Test developer		Test developer or test interpreter		Responsible official or student	

lying characteristic, so far as he is concerned. This assembling and scoring of the scale may be done even though the tester is unable to identify or characterize this underlying characteristic, nor perhaps even able to understand, simply by examining the individual items, why students' answers to them are correlated. The fact of the correlation is sufficient grounds for inferring some underlying reality, which may be deeply significant, or may be trivial. The MMPI item quoted in the chart is combined, on a purely empirical basis, with others which together are known, somewhat arbitrarily, as the K scale.

From scale to attribute: validity—the "something" is recognizable.

The underlying characteristic, which these items assembled into the scale represent, can be identified and named. The characteristic can be recognized as one which is known in some other way than by the empirical correlation of the items. It may be recognized simply by consulting the wording of the items themselves (face validity). Sometimes it is recognized by more abstract and theoretical definition (construct validity). Most often it is recognized as a characteristic observable and measurable in the student's behavior quite apart from his answers to these scale items (concurrent or predictive validity), and the validity can be empirically demonstrated by showing that scores on the scale are correlated with other measures or observations of behavior. An intelligence scale, for example, should be correlated with other estimates of intelligence, such as teachers' ratings, and with later performance to which intelligence should contribute, such as school grades. There is some evidence that the K scale of the MMPI, cited above, may be an estimate of a kind of optimistic or defensive denial of psychological weaknesses, in oneself or in others.

Attributes which are typically measured by tests of the kind here under consideration would include the following:

Particular *personality characteristics* or *motives*, such as a persistent "need for achievement" as on the Edwards Personal Preference Schedule.*

* These tests are identified and explained in a section at the end of the paper.—Ed.

Patterns of *interest* corresponding to known interests of a particular professional group—as, for example, the "ministerial" scale of the Strong Vocational Interest Blank.

Degree of *pathology* vs. mental health in correspondence with psychiatric diagnoses—as, for example, the major scales of the MMPI.

Particular *abilities* such as intelligence, or reading ability.

PROBLEMS IN INFERRING UTILITY

From attribute to criterion: utility—the recognizable "something" is relevant.

Some relationship is assumed, or theoretically argued, or empirically demonstrated between one of the attributes, such as a personality characteristic, and one of the criteria, such as effectiveness in the ministry.

This step of inference, which is here dubbed "utility," has been called by Tyler (1963) "specific validity" and by Brown (1962) "relevancy." It is an instance of the broad problem in science of "undue generalization." It is a classically acknowledged problem of test interpretation, but one too often slighted in actual practice. Once validity has been established, in the fashion described in the preceding section, a test interpreter often proceeds, with many barely recognized assumptions, to suppose that he can predict from knowledge of the attributes something about performance in particular situations. He must, for example, suppose or argue or know that particular attributes, such as strong social extraversion, or mild affiliative motives, make a man a more effective minister. To the degree that he has some general knowledge about the requirements of the situation, he may be moderately successful. But in connection with testing of theological students, this step of utility clearly seems to be the weakest link and the one requiring the most attention. We do not know, or have very good reason for supposing, what attributes are predictive of our criteria. Nor do we know even how to define or measure most of our criteria, such as effectiveness in the ministry. But this is a separate and great problem, not touched here—separate from the problem of *relating* scales and attributes to criteria.

SOME EXAMPLES OF THE WEAKNESS OF THE LINK

The supposition that a particular attribute is predictive of particular performance can never be taken for granted but needs to be established by hard labor, either empirical or theoretical. The point can perhaps be most dramatically made by considering an instance which is commonly taken for granted. It is commonly supposed that one of the ability tests, such as the Graduate Record Examination (GRE) aptitude test,* or the Miller Analogies Test (MAT),* should be predictive of grades in seminary. Yet, over a range of studies undertaking to demonstrate such a relationship, it has not been possible to demonstrate conclusively any such relationship, except when extremes are considered. That is, the tests are able to predict the extremely good and the extremely poor students, but not predict relative performance over the middle range.

Interest tests might seem to offer an easy and safe transition from attribute to criterion. If a man has the interest which ministers have, then it seems natural and legitimate to counsel him into the profession. Yet, the logic of such an inference is suspect. For this means screening or guiding men so as to perpetuate the status quo. It is entirely conceivable to suppose that most of the criteria would be better met by men who have not naturally found their way previously into the ministry and into the standardization samples for a ministry interest scale.

The use of a test intended to diagnose *pathology*, as is the intent of the MMPI, raises especially great problems about the valid utilization for predicting of the particular criteria concerning the ministry in which we are interested. Even for predicting the eventual emotional stability and health of a minister, how logical is it to suppose that the same characteristics which indicate pathology in a mental-hospital population will predict health or pathology in

* These are academic aptitude tests used quite generally in screening for admission to graduate school. The GRE has been developed by the Educational Testing Service, Princeton, N.J., and the MAT by the Psychological Corporation, New York City.—Ed.

the particular situation of the ministry? But even more dubious is the attempt to predict his effectiveness or perseverance in the ministry, or even his seminary grades, from test scores intended to diagnose pathology. By what logic is it supposed that a "normal" or "average" score on a diagnostic test is predictive of persevering or effectiveness in the ministry? If rigorous theoretical reasoning or controlled empirical data exist to support such inferences, they have not been made public.*

Dr. Fred Brown has made the same point vividly, speaking with special reference to projective tests:

> The probem of *relevancy* is a crucial one, and failure to consider it may have accounted for much loss of time, money and hopes. A case in point is the use of projective techniques (Rorschach, TAT) by clinical psychologists trained to make diagnostic evaluations in hospital and clinic settings. There is a considerable difference between a diagnostic and a predictive function, since the former is oriented toward psychopathology with prediction focused upon suitability for treatment and probable prognosis, while the latter, as in the present instance, is concerned with the future minister's susceptibility to emotional breakdown. We are interested primarily in whether the candidate will complete his training (less difficult to predict with tests and other criteria) and what kind of minister he will be when he assumes vocational responsibilities. We are not attempting to evaluate the degree of psychopathology in such individuals nor the amount of healthy psyche available for a reconstitutive response to psychiatric treatment. These are not *patients* (although they share the vicissitudes of their brothers and are just as vulnerable) and it is a gross error to evaluate projective test data within the framework of disease. Furthermore, projective tests often magnify psychopathology even when administered to what are now cautiously designated as "so-called" normals [Brown, 1962].

The above discussion is intended to illustrate that some of the most common utilizations of tests are beset with flaws or grave risks. Theory supporting alleged inferences is dubious and scant, and empirical support for the inferences is even less available. Anyone claiming to make such a link from attributes to particular criteria should acknowledge his responsibility to demonstrate the basis for

* Follow-up studies which lend support to such inferences have appeared since the Conference. Among them are: Carroll (1968) and Weisgerber (1969).—Ed.

the inference. He should argue carefully and precisely the logic and theoretical reasoning by which he supposes that the attribute is predictive of the criterion. He should make available to public scientific scrutiny any data that may demonstrate the relation between the attribute, as measured by scale scores, and the criterion, as measured by whatever index he may have devised.

SELECTED PROBLEMS OF RESPONSIBILITY

After the above technical problems are solved, there still remain the biggest, hardest, and least-well-defined dilemmas in the use of tests for ministerial selection. It generally falls to the lot, not of the psychological tester, but of the candidate himself, or an official of church or school, or of candidate and official together, to consider whatever hints the tests seem to provide about the present characteristics and future performance of the candidate, to judge the probability of the tests' certainty and accuracy, to weigh the many non-test factors which may tower far in significance over those of the tests, and to come to a decision. It is the importance of these practical, theological, and other questions, providing a context for the tests, which makes discussion here difficult to focus. Only selected topics will be discussed: a survey of the varying types of decisions to which testing may be addressed; some general considerations to be kept in mind in appraising tests; and brief attention to the theological context of testing for selection.

QUESTIONS ASKED

We present here a kind of catalogue of different questions to which psychological tests may be asked to address themselves. The purpose is chiefly just to demonstrate the point that these *are* different and independent questions, and that the ability of a test to help answer one of them does not necessarily qualify it as relevant to another.

The first distinction is between questions which are specific to the particular vocational situation of the minister or ministerial candidate and questions which are more general.

The more *general questions* assume that the minister or candidate is part of the general population for which the test is appropriate and standardized and that the same inferences from the test may be made about him as about anyone else. These general questions commonly apply to two areas, intelligence and pathology. The use of generally standardized intelligence tests assumes that effective (intellectual) performance in theological studies and in the ministry requires the general intellectual ability which the tests measure, without important specific demands on particular skills or factors of intellect because of the vocational specialization. The use of clinical tests is addressed to the common diagnostic and predictive questions, such as the assessment of degree and type of pathology, the prediction of future stability and health, indications for therapy, etc. Again, this may be without regard to any particular requirements or conditions of the vocation.

Alternatively, these same general questions may be asked with a recognition that the inferences at any stage may have to be modified because of the particular characteristics of the population of ministerial candidates and their prospective environment. Classically, Bier (1948) has demonstrated how even at the stages of reliability and validity the characteristics of the population require modification of inferences; references to sex in MMPI items must be interpreted differently for priests vowed to chastity. As another example, it is sometimes suggested that predictions of future health must consider the peculiar supports and stresses offered by the ministry.

Of *questions particularly addressed to the vocation,* there are perhaps three distinctive and independent types of decisions.

One has to do with predicting who is likely to enter the vocation. What are the particular characteristics of person and background of those who become ministers? This question is of practical interest in recruiting and in estimating who is likely to drop out of training and who is likely to persist. The question is also of theoretical and research interest and, as it happens, can be studied empirically fairly easily, so that something is now known about personality test scores typically obtained by clergy samples, compared with control groups (Menges and Dittes, 1965). But reliable information and guidance on this question should not be, though it sometimes is, confused with the empirical basis for answering the next question—who should be selected as likely to become an effective clergyman. Knowing the characteristics of those who *are* clergymen does not necessarily advance us in knowing who *should* be—even though this is the logic involved in screening on the basis of ministerial scores of the Strong Vocational Interest Blank or similar instruments. It is even possible to entertain a cynical or pessimistic hypothesis of some negative correlation between these criteria: those who withdraw from, or never enter the ministry, might conceivably have become the most effective ministers.

The second vocation-specific question is the crucial and tormenting one of selection. Who is likely to become a good minister and so should be advanced toward that objective by those responsible for making such decisions? Here, problems of prediction are dogged by the uncertainty and multiplicity of the criterion itself. The identification of excellence is difficult enough for a profession beset with norms on all sides, but none of these norms is made very specific or operational. The difficulty is multiplied by the great variety of roles and situations in which a clergyman functions. The characteristics of an effective pastor in a suburban church may be different enough from those of an effective preacher in the same church, and far different from those required for either role in a church in a city, or in Africa.

It is in the face of the virtual impasse in addressing this question that persons sometimes resort to substituting one of the other questions in this catalogue. That is, selection is made, not on the basis of prediction to effective ministry—since that is impossible—but, for example, on the basis of intelligence-test-score prediction of grades, or on the basis of clinical-test prediction of stability, or on the basis of interest-test prediction of drop-out. But there has not been, so far as I know, any demonstration of correlation among these criteria or between these and effectiveness.

The third vocation-specific question for which tests are sometimes used is the most difficult of all, because it requires some prediction of interaction between psychological and situational variables. This is the question of who can profitably be selected for particular types of training situations, so as to enhance later effectiveness—for example, who should be selected for certain types of clinical training, for internship or apprenticeship in particular kinds of situations, for a training experience in psychotherapy, etc.

QUESTIONS MODIFIED TO FIT ANSWERS

Two general comments will now be made about certain aspects of the process of using test results to aid practical decisions. The first of these is to emphasize the risk, already repeatedly mentioned, for existing tests to be used because they are available, and for test users to be content with answers which the tests are able to supply rather than answers to the questions they may originally have posed. Promiscuity with easy pick-ups is reprehensible, wherever encountered. What is needed is the greater effort to establish a firmer relationship with the sincerely intended.

If our questions originally have to do with predicting suitability for the ministry, and if we find ourselves woefully lacking, as we do, in any definition for this criterion, and equally woefully lacking, as we do, in any firm link between this criterion and any predicting attributes, too often we succumb to the easy way out of taking what is available. This means that we take tests which are able to measure with some reliability and validity some attributes, and we hope or pretend that these may be relevant and useful to our questions; or, more commonly, we become highly involved in the test and its measured attributes and lose sight of our original questions. Test users who originally talked about "good or bad ministers" find themselves now talking about "good or bad MMPI profiles."

The question may be asked: Who is master—the test user or the test?

OBVIOUS OR ESOTERIC LINKS?

If one were to shout very loudly at a telegraph key, it is conceivable that the air waves would move the key and produce a signal miles away in the reaction of the telegraph sounder. It is very unlikely, however, that this signal would bear much resemblance to the sound used to activate the key. A much more valid transmission of signals would be achieved by translating the message into Morse code and interpreting the code produced by the sounder [Myers, 1962, p. 451].

This parable, offered by Charles T. Myers, explains why the inferential links must break away from the obvious, common-sensical, and phenomenological experience, and must make use of the more abstract, analytic categories and reasoning of the scientist. Considerable psychological sophistication and precision may have to be used to understand why certain psychological attributes may be more likely to persist in the ministry, or be effective. Such understanding may invoke the language and reasoning of fairly abstract theories. If there are data in support, they may require elaborate statistical treatment to untangle the skein of complex phenomena. The theory may refer to unconscious processes. All these requirements may make the test developer's or interpreter's reasoning seem remote, perhaps even implausible.

This ought to be no more disrupting than when the physicist, for his purposes, talks about my dining room table or the light over it in terms of atoms or electrons. The test user ought not to have to apologize for a theoretically and empirically sound inferential link just because his language and reasoning may seem to the student or the administrator to be obscure or esoteric.

A problem arises, however, because students and administrators want to and ought to have more of a voice in establishing and interpreting the links than do dining-room tables in the physicist's deliberations. This arises primarily out of the lessened probability of the links which the psychological-test interpreter can establish. He feels he has done his job if he can point to any probabilities greater than chance, and he never claims to 100 percent certainty in his predictions. Therefore knowledge of this degree of uncertainty needs to be carried over into the stage which has been characterized above as "responsibility." Eventually, the lay user has to carry on from the scientist's reasoning. He can do this more intelligently if he is led into it.

Such a practice is also indicated by the principles of the common "client-centered" views of counseling and guidance, which emphasize that the final responsibility and resources for practical decisions lie in the hands of the student or the administrator.

This situation puts a special value on tests whose concepts and inferences are more apparent to a lay person. If items, scale designations, attributes, and the links among them and with the criteria are all couched in more familiar language, the test may be more useful than if not. Among the tests which are commonly used, the Edwards Personal Preference Schedule and the Theological School Inventory are far more satisfactory in this respect than is the MMPI.

THEOLOGICAL CONTEXT

Finally, some attention needs to be paid to the fact that testing for screening takes place in a theological context. The amount of prior discussion on this topic and the degree of apparent consensus makes it possible to outline fairly briefly the main lines of this consensus.

The major question concerns the seemingly presumptuous invasion by science of a supernatural matter, the call or vocation. There seem to be two broad answers, or presuppositions, which serve to establish a place for testing within this theological context.

One answer, or presupposition, is to emphasize that the supernatural has a natural referent. Much as the impetus of God may come from beyond the natural order, the meeting place of God and man is within it; and God's actions generally partake of the regularities and patterns which science knows or seeks. In principle, there is no reason to suppose that the psychological tester or researcher may not be, in his way, finding specific ways to describe some of the workings of God, rather than—as he is sometimes accused—proposing criteria and psychological processes as alternatives to an understanding of God's initiative.

The second common argument is to make quite clear that probability, even probability substantially beyond chance, is not certainty. Correlations are well enough below 1.00 to leave opportunity for a Spirit that "blows where it wills." To find patterns and consistencies, at some level of probability, leaves plenty of room for individual differences and exceptions. The hypothesis may well be entertained that some such exceptions may be the result of factors which can on some grounds be regarded as freedom or as an exceptional intrusion by God into the natural order.

Although both these positions are commonly offered as a basis for testing, they are essentially inconsistent. For the former identifies psychologically discernible processes with divine processes, and the latter position holds them as alternatives. Furthermore, the latter position adopts the precarious practice of identifying human ignorance with divine activity. Such a position leaves divine activity subject to radical curtailment, as has been the case during recent centuries, as science reduces the area of human ignorance—and correspondingly, on these premises, the arena available for divine activity.

But somewhere within the broad statement of the first position there would seem to be sufficient theological warrant for psychological testing. Doubts about its usefulness would seem to come more resoundingly, as this paper has tried to suggest, from scientific considerations themselves.

DISCUSSION OF SPECIFIC TESTS

To conclude the presentation, I will summarize the nature of several of the tests which are most commonly used, indicating how some of the special problems which have been discussed apply to them. I continue in my role as the hopeful skeptic and as the naïve observer wanting to take a close look at the clothes which others say the current emperors are wearing.

Minnesota Multiphasic Personality Inventory (*MMPI*) (Hathaway & McKinley, 1967) The MMPI was developed about 20 years ago in the line of succession of a number of venerable paper-and-pencil tests attempting to get self-reports of personality characteristics. Probably the Bell Adjustment Inventory (Bell, 1939) and the Bernreuter Personality Inventory (Bernreuter, 1938) were the most prominent predecessors. Many of the MMPI items were adapted from these earlier tests.

Several hundred items were assembled and administered to psychiatric patients and to visitors to a mental hospital. The attempt was to see whether these items would form into scales which would distinguish the visitors from the visited, and, among the visited, the various diagnostic categories into which psychiatrists had sorted the patients. This was purely an empirical arrangement of the items into scales which correlated with these particular validating criteria. There was no attempt at face validity or at prediction or at understanding why particular items were on particular scales. Because this was purely empirical, the items appear on the scales in helter-skelter fashion, with some items appearing on several scales, and some items not appearing on any scales. This is the origin of the nine basic scales of the MMPI, eight of which bear labels corresponding to psychiatric categories, the remaining one simply being a scale which distinguished males from females. A tenth scale, labeled as measuring social introversion, was soon added by the test developers. The test items have since been rearranged into literally hundreds of additional scales by various research workers. These additional scales have not been subjected to nearly as much research as the basic scales. Because response set and subject distortion are such potentially serious problems in interpreting the MMPI, several scales were developed early to try to measure the degree of such set or distortion so that this can be used as a kind of corrective in interpreting the other scales. These "validating" or "corrective" scales are those which are now listed first on MMPI profiles (L,F,K).

The popularity and the entrenchment of the MMPI is a remarkable phenomenon which seems to beg for some interpretation. My own guess is that the circumstances of the wartime and postwar periods served to elevate and to freeze the status of the MMPI, which might much earlier have been in turn succeeded by improved and new tests more suitable for many of the applications to which the MMPI has been in fact used. With the expansion of clinical psychology, sparked by the construction of Veterans Administration hospitals after the war, the role of the psychologist as a testing member of the mental-health team became established. His most available resource in paper-and-pencil tests was the MMPI, just as the Rorschach was most available among "depth" tests. Extended clinical use, in turn, encouraged more research with the MMPI to warrant and support the use (and also to provide doctoral dissertations for the new crop of clinical psychologists). In a very few years, a great deal of clinical experience and research enterprise became invested in this single instrument; such investment tended to freeze the status of the test.

If I am emphasizing the humdrum and improbable origins of this particular "emperor," it is only to insist that any claims for a higher status, in such applications as use with theological students, must be competently argued and demonstrated and cannot be taken for granted.

The multiplicity of ways in which the MMPI is adapted for interpretations of theological students is not reassuring. In consulting a number of "fully qualified and trained" clinical psychologists who use the MMPI with theological students, I have discovered the following diversity of ways in which links are made between the scales and the criteria: (1) If any four scores are 65 or more, this is regarded as evidence of some "danger"; (2) Any score over 70 is taken as reason for counseling; (3) A high score on a particular scale, such as K, is regarded as undesirable for a minister; (4) Various constellations are regarded as "danger" signs, such as high D and high Pt. "Danger" means a reference sometimes to potential drop-out, sometimes to emotional difficulty, sometimes to ineffectiveness.

Perhaps all of these are valid utilizations of the MMPI. But diversity is not reassuring, especially when no one of them seems bolstered by available data.

The MMPI raises two particular problems in *generalization,* illustrating keenly the difficulty of applying a test evolved for one purpose to another purpose. One of these problems has to do with generalizing the interpretation of one subject's response to another subject's response. The other problem has to do with a generalizing from a score of 70 (two standard deviations above the mean) to a score, say, of 55, which is commonly as "high" as some peaks go —still above the mean but not so closely.

The most obvious illustration of the first problem is the adjustment which Bier (1948) found necessary to make in adapting the MMPI for use with Catholic candidates. Denial of interest in sexual activities, for example, could hardly be construed in the same way for this population as for a more general population (unless one wants to propose the hypothesis that vows of celibacy are symptomatic of some kind of sexual distortion).

The careful scrutiny of other items on the MMPI turns up many instances in which the theological student's response is at least as likely to be determined by his prior acceptance of a particular role as by tendency toward psychological deviation. Possible examples of this may be the K and Mf scales, which are typically the highest for theological students. The high K score—if 55 is high—may represent more of a role-induced optimism and pastoral concern than it is a "defensiveness." A strong Mf score may similarly represent a pastoral solicitous concern.

The other problem of generalization is already implied in the statement by Brown (1962) about using a test diagnostic of pathology as a basis for measuring normal traits. The basic scales of the MMPI were originally derived and validated with cut-off points one or two standard deviations above the mean, represented by standard scores of 60 or 70. Yet the profiles of many theological students show no such extreme deviations. The reference to "highs" or "peaks" may often be to scores only in the 50s, within one standard deviation. An iceberg which is represented by 18 peaks above water may be very different from one which is represented by ten peaks above water.

Strong Vocational Interest Blank (*SVIB*) (Strong & Campbell, 1966) The Strong Vocational Interest Blank was also developed by an empirical matching of items with groups of persons previously sorted. But whereas the sorting, in the case of the MMPI development, was done by psychiatric diagnosis, the sorting in the case of the SVIB was done by the natural process of vocational selection. The result was a set of many scales, each of which was composed of items which tended to be correlated with each other and with a particular vocational group. Thus, one scale consisted of items which tended to discriminate ministers from other groups, and another scale consisted of items which tended to discriminate osteopaths from other groups, etc. As with the MMPI, this empirical development produced a considerable helter-skelter overlap of items on various scales. The SVIB, of course, is composed of items asking for straight-forward report of preference, tastes, and interests. The only validity claimed for it is the possibility of matching a person with a particular vocational group or groups which seem to share his interests and outlook.*

Obviously, much depends on the care with which the standardizing vocational group is selected and tested. This is a special problem in connection with the ministry scale of the SVIB, which was standardized on a sample of 250 ministers, more than 25 years ago, most of whom were Presbyterians or Methodists, and most of whom were living on the West Coast. To use this ministry scale as any serious guide for counseling of contemporary candidates for the ministry, a generation younger, would seem absurd. Contemporary theological students typically score quite "low" on the "ministry scale." Some researchers, most notably Dr. Clifford Davis (1963), have undertaken to develop more modern and representative standardizations. Davis' ministry scale shows substantial difference from that still provided by the publishers. It would not seem out of order to suggest that users prod the publishers to acknowledge their responsibility for providing a more suitable standardization.†

As with other tests, the mere existence of the test, with some semblance of objectivity and standardization, makes it seem attractive. And the test continues to be widely used, in at least 28 Protestant seminaries, as reported by the Ministry Studies Board in 1962, and in some denominational programs. One can overhear, as I have, many hypotheses, some of them apparently used in practice, about how other results with the SVIB other than the ministry scale may happen to be related to particular criteria. One sugges-

---

* The 1969 revision of the SVIB contained for the first time and for both men and women a series of Basic Interest scales, which are content-oriented rather than occupation-oriented. A major handbook on the SVIB is scheduled for publication in April, 1970.—Ed.

† Lepak (1968) has recently constructed a new priests' scale for the Strong.—Ed.

tion is that the osteopath scale is predictive of persistence and effectiveness in the ministry! So far as I know, all such notions are still awaiting empirical verification.

*Theological School Inventory (TSI)** (Dittes, 1962) The only test specifically developed for use with theological students is the Theological School Inventory. It was not, however, developed primarily in response to the type of questions posed and criteria established by prospective test users, as described earlier in this paper; the test was not developed to offer direct prediction toward such criteria as effectiveness. The TSI provides an objective and ordered record of a student's own statement of his motivations for being in the ministry. The items and scales were derived from a content analysis of ministers' statements about their motivations. It belongs most closely in the family of interest tests, along with the SVIB, and its only claim to validity is that the scores correspond to the student's own self-perception. It is intended to be primarily a kind of mirror or guide, to be an adjunct to vocational counseling. The face validity has been moderately extended by both theoretical reasoning and empirical evidence to show some relation with criteria such as persistence in seminary and subsequent decision concerning vocational assignment. These are limited and plausible extensions of the face statement of motivation: students whose motivation on entering seminary is less "pastoral" are less likely to enter a pastoral ministry, etc.

The test should not be taken as predictive of *ability* in various forms of ministry, although this confusion is already a common one, as the existence of a test provides the temptation for us to extend an inference toward answering the still-tormenting basic questions.

Edwards Personal Preference Schedule (EPPS) (Edwards, 1953) Another newer test illustrates another method of test development. The EPPS was originated not from empirical matching (as were

* The TSI is published by the Ministry Studies Board, which on March 1, 1968, merged with the Department of Ministry of the National Council of Churches, and is now located at 1717 Massachusetts Ave., N.W., Washington, D.C. 20036.—Ed.

the MMPI and SVIB) but from explicit theoretical statement of particular attributes. Edwards selected 15 of the motivations specified by Murray (1938) and allowed these definitions to generate items. By a forced choice arrangement of the items, Edwards attempted to solve one of the problems plaguing the MMPI, that of some respondents' selectively treating a response primarily for its social desirability.

The utility of the Edwards test for answering the questions concerning theological students still awaits the development of the links between the 15 motivations and such criteria as persistence or effectiveness. The fact that the motivations tend to be ones commonly recognized should encourage theoretical thinking about the relative fate of persons with varying motivations and personality characteristics. The fact that these characteristics are "normal" rather than pathological should also encourage their utility.

REFERENCES

Bell, H. M. *The Adjustment Inventory.* Palo Alto, Calif.: Consulting Psychologists Press, 1934–1939.

Bernreuter, R. G. *The Personality Inventory.* Palo Alto, Calif.: Consulting Psychologists Press, 1935–1938.

Bier, W. C. A comparative study of a seminary group and four other groups on the Minnesota Multiphasic Personality Inventory. *Studies in Psychology and Psychiatry*, 1948, 7, No. 3. Washington: Catholic University of America Press.

Brehm, J. W., & Cohen, A. R. *Explorations in cognitive dissonance.* New York: Wiley, 1962.

Brown, F. Some observations upon the use of psychological tests in the selection and assessment of candidates for ministerial training. Paper read to Conference on Psychological Research, November 20, 1962, sponsored by Board of Theological Education, Lutheran Church of America, 231 Madison Avenue, New York, N.Y.

Buros, O. K. (Ed.). *The sixth mental measurements yearbook.* Highland Park, N.J.: Gryphon Press, 1965.

Carroll, D. W. *Initial psychological prediction as related to subsequent seminary performance.* (Doctoral dissertation, Fordham University) Ann Arbor, Mich.: University Microfilms, 1968, No. 68-3682.

Cronbach, L. J. *Essentials of psychological testing* (2nd ed.). New York: Harper, 1960.

Davis, C. E. *Guide for counseling prospective church workers: Supplement I: Strong Vocational Interest Test.* Pittsburgh: United Presbyterian Church, U.S.A., Board of Christian Education, 1963.

Dittes, J. E. Research on clergymen: Factors influencing decisions for religious service and effectiveness in the vocation. In S. W. Cook (Ed.), *Review of recent research bearing on religious and character formation.*

Research Supplement to *Religious education*, 1962, *57*, No. 4. Pp. S-141–165.

Dittes, J. E. *Vocational guidance of theological students: A manual for the use of the Theological School Inventory.* Washington: Ministry Studies Board, 1964.

Edwards, A. L. *Edwards Personal Preference Schedule.* New York: Psychological Corporation, 1953.

Hathaway, S. R., & McKinley, J. C. *Minnesota Multiphasic Personality Inventory: Manual for administration and scoring.* New York: Psychological Corporation, 1967.

Lepak, R. C. Research in clergy vocational interests. *Ministry Studies,* 1968, *2* (2), 6–24.

Menges, R. J., & Dittes, J. E. *Psychological studies of clergymen: Abstracts of research.* New York: Nelson, 1965.

Murray, H. A., *et al. Explorations in personality.* New York: Oxford University Press, 1938.

Myers, C. T. Theory of scores: Review of *Studies in item analysis and prediction,* by H. Solomon (Ed.), *Contemporary Psychology,* 1962, *7,* 451–452.

Strong, E. K., Jr., & Campbell, D. P. *Manual for Strong Vocational Interest Blanks.* Stanford, Calif.: Stanford University Press, 1966.

Tyler, L. *Tests and measurements.* Englewood Cliffs, N.J.: Prentice-Hall, 1963.

Weisgerber, C. A. *Psychological assessment of candidates for a religious order.* Chicago: Loyola University Press, 1969.

DISCUSSION

Magda B. Arnold   *Joseph T. English*

Arnold: Dr. Dittes' presentation sounded a note of caution with which we would obviously all agree. We are all in full agreement, for instance, that clinical prediction is different from a prediction for effectiveness, whether it is in the ministry or anywhere else, and that it is very doubtful, actually, whether the same tests that are good for clinical predictions can be used in the same way for the prediction of effectiveness, whether in the ministry or elsewhere.

What would interest me particularly would be to open the question to discussion whether there might be some tests that do not have the assumptions that Dr. Dittes has criticized. It is true, for instance, that we have been looking for a criterion. The criterion is very difficult to find. As Dr. Dittes says, "What is a good minister? What is a good clergyman, a good priest, a good rabbi?"

It seems to me that perhaps we are asking the wrong kind of question. Maybe we might as well admit, to begin with, that a clergyman can be a good preacher, *or* a good teacher, *or* a good prophet, *or* a good organizer, and that it really depends on the individual entirely whether he excels in one or the other of these various possibilities.

Therefore, instead of saying "Is there one common denominator according to which we ought to judge every clergyman?" why could we not say "Is there a way in which we could judge the motivation of anybody who decides for the ministry?"

By "motivation" I do not mean one of the fifteen-odd motivations that have been developed for the Theological School Inventory, for instance. By "motivation" I mean the basic attitude a man has and betrays when he is asked to tell stories; his basic attitude to various goals, and the way in which he can achieve the goals; his basic attitude to right or wrong action. That is, what does he consider right? What does he consider wrong? How does he consider that the consequences of right or wrong action will affect him?

Another extremely important point, we found, is his attitude toward other human beings. What is his attitude toward women? I do not mean sexual motivation. I do mean, however, whether the minister considers women as nothing but a temptation, or considers them as just a nuisance to be somehow avoided; or whether he considers that women really are human beings, and that he has the same kind of responsibility and obligation toward them that he would have toward another man.

Again, it does not really matter whether the minister is a celibate or not. The attitude toward women in this particular respect is important; not only toward women, but toward older people and children—what he considers right or wrong in human relationships.

Finally, there is the question of how he considers that adversity ought to be countered. Does one just wait until the catastrophe has blown over or until somebody else has helped him out of it, or is he going to take steps himself?

I am sorry that I seem to be sounding my own trumpet, but we have developed (Arnold, 1962), on the basis of these categories, a scoring system for the Thematic Apperception Test, or actually for any set of ten stories. The rationale behind the test is that the imagination which goes toward making up stories is the same kind of imagination used to prepare for action of any kind, and particularly for action that the storyteller himself has in the past either engaged in, or at least approved or disapproved of. You get, then, as it were, action attitudes, which I think are in the true sense of the word "motivational."

With this type of approach what we have found is the immense importance in prediction of positive attitudes—that is, constructive attitudes, active attitudes. We have found that the kind of person who is willing to work for his success, who has goals—perhaps high goals—and is willing to go after them; the person who is responsible and friendly toward other people; the person who has a very definite sense of right and wrong; the person who is constructive in countering adversity—this kind of person is going to make a successful student, is going to make a successful teacher, and is going to make a successful minister or religious in various communities.

English: I would like to share with you some of the experiences of the Peace Corps in its selection of volunteers. Similarly to all selection programs, we try to predict who will be the successful volunteer by utilizing a variety of subjective and objective assessment methods. I suspect that your problems in determining who will be a good minister, priest, or rabbi share common ground with ours.

If we have had any success at all, much of the credit must go to the fine rapport and interaction that we, in the Medical Division, have with psychologists in the Division of Selection. I am sure that they would readily agree with the spirit of Dr. Dittes' paper— that one should take a cautious but constructive attitude toward the validity and reliability of psychological tests designed to select those who will be successful in a given role or vocation.

We use three different types of tests which should be distinguished: (1) *Aptitude tests,* e.g., vocational tests, general aptitude tests, and modern-language aptitude tests. Tests of this nature are administered to trainees at a university campus when they apply, and are quite helpful in determining the country and job most suitable for them; (2) *Diagnostic tests,* in the usual clinical sense, constitute another group. These are administered when a trainee is suspected of having a psychological disorder. Tests of this type have been extremely helpful to us, and our psychiatrists and psychologists work closely together in their administration and interpretation. These two categories of tests, i.e., aptitude measurement instruments and diagnostic tests used to determine a specific mental illness, must be distinguished from (3) the *psychodiagnostic instrument used in screening large populations*. When you realize that over 200,000 people have applied for the Peace Corps, that over 25,000 have reported for training, and that about 18,000 have gone overseas, the need for such a testing procedure is obvious. The only test that is administered to all trainees is the MMPI. Other tests in this category are administered at the discretion of the psychologist in charge of assessment.

Yet our experience has led us to become increasingly skeptical of the usefulness of these tests in dealing with the total population. The major function of the MMPI is to raise a red flag on those persons who deviate significantly from the normal population, and to enable us to examine those persons more closely. Since the Peace Corps population is quite a healthy one, the MMPI is of primary value as a screening technique. We have placed greater reliance on and have had more success with the evaluation of the trainee while he is in the actual training situation. Direct observation of behavior during the three months of training has been, perhaps, the most valuable aid to us in selection.

A second valuable source has been peer ratings that the trainees do on one another. So far, it is about the single most reliable test we have administered.

Establishing criteria of success is always a difficult task and the Peace Corps is no exception. Often "success" cannot be measured because of certain intangibles. For example, it might be relatively easy to measure the results of a construction crew by asking what they had constructed, e.g., roads, houses, etc. On the other hand how does one measure the success of a teaching program in which results might not become apparent for years? We know, however, that some research studies have shown that certain South American communities where volunteers are working have a greater rate of growth than those communities where volunteers are absent (Dobyns, Dougherty, & Holmberg, 1966).

Another parameter of success might be the number of volunteers who successfully complete two years of service. For the past five years there has been a six-percent return rate of volunteers for such reasons as resignations, dismissals, or failure to adjust to life overseas. In the last two years we have been able to reduce that six percent by 38 percent, cutting it almost in half. Of the six-percent rate, we have had a medical return of 1.4 percent—evenly split with .7 percent for organic reasons and .7 percent for psychiatric reasons. Critical to this discussion is our belief that this low rate of return is the result of factors *other* than selection alone.

We have placed tremendous emphasis on the *support* of the volunteers while they are overseas. This support is obviously dependent upon superb field leadership, and the caliber and orientation of the field staff.

Even though we feel that our results have been worthwhile, we are not at all sure what has made the difference. The challenge for psychological research is to investigate all the variables in the system that determine outcome and success. These are the kinds of questions that an exchange like this might further explore in the future.

GENERAL DISCUSSION

William G. T. Douglas: Dr. Douglas endorsed the conclusion reported by Dr. English that selection is perhaps less important on the whole than are training, programming, and support. From his own studies, beginning with his work with Episcopal clergymen, Dr. Douglas had found a good deal of misunderstanding about effectiveness (Douglas, 1957). First, there seemed to be the impression that effectiveness is a quality possessed by the person rather than something related to a total situation.

In the use of psychological appraisal with the clergy, Dr. Douglas believed that the job done best by all communions was and still is selection. The job done worst he considered to be placement. Jobs that are done somewhat better than placement but not as well as selection are those related to training and later growth opportunities, particularly the matching of a person to someone who could be an identification model, helping him to mobilize his resources.

Turning to Dr. Dittes' observations about the face validity of tests, Dr. Douglas noted his discovery that clergymen who made the highest scores on tests designed to measure administrative efficiency were rated the worst as administrators because of a compulsive perfectionism. They could not do more things less well within a given time when the situation required it. He had also discovered that men were often rated as good pastors not because of their concern for people, which might be relatively low, but because they were energetic in the performance of pastoral chores (Douglas, 1957). In other studies, including some of Howard Ham's (1960), pastors' ratings correlated positively with rather withdrawn personalities instead of with the outgoing personalities assumed to be requisite for effectiveness. Dr. Douglas also recalled some follow-ups to studies on the prediction of success in clinical psychology (Kelly & Fiske, 1951) in which it was found that people who came out of what would be considered good childhoods became administrators. Among people who had had disruptive childhoods, those with strong oedipal complexes were likely to become therapists; those from the same kind of environment but without oedipal components often became teachers.

In short, Dr. Douglas believed that selection is part of the total process; effectiveness is relational. Face validity of tests cannot be assumed. There must be empirical validity of the predictive quality. He understood Dr. Dittes to be in agreement with these statements.

Peace Corps Screening: In response to a comment about the large number of Peace Corps applicants who were screened out before the training period (175,000 out of 200,000)—an indication, apparently, of the enormously important role played by selection—Dr. English noted that the 200,000 figure was the total number who had applied to the Peace Corps, not those invited to enter training. Between the time of application and that of receiving an invitation, many applicants decide to do something else. Another factor to be considered is the case of the highly specialized applicant for whom the host country has no suitable job. Also, a number of those invited cannot meet the medical requirements. Therefore, the actual number of applicants who survive the preliminary screening done on the basis of autobiographical information is a considerably smaller one than the statistics indicate.

Asked to elaborate on his remarks about the basically healthy population with which the Peace Corps starts and which it then places and supports, Dr. English said that in the early days many people—especially ambassadors—had been skeptical, feeling that there might be a considerable number of irresponsible young people from the lunatic fringe of our society going overseas with the Peace Corps and causing international incidents all over the world. Mr. R. Sargent Shriver therefore called the National Institute of Mental Health to get psychiatric help in the selection process. Shortly afterwards, Dr. English joined the Corps staff. There was concern that beneath the dedication, commitment, and desire to serve there was likely to be a somewhat disturbed process. But in the early stages of the program the psychiatrists involved in the assessment and selection of volunteers commented frequently on the basic mental health of the population who volunteered.

"The annual premature rate of return for all reasons," Dr. English added, "has been less than eight percent. Psychiatric disqualification during training has been less than one percent. The annual rate of return from overseas for psychiatric reasons has been less than 0.7 percent."

In reply to a question about what he meant by "support" as he had used the term in connection with prediction of perseverance in the Peace Corps, Dr. English said he had been referring to the use of the total psychological resources available to the Corps throughout the entire continuum of training and field experience. In the training setting this is done by the people involved in so-called mental-health training by means of a process, a model for which has been worked out, to prepare volunteers psychologically for overseas service. The purpose is to establish the legitimacy of feelings of concern in anticipation of necessary adjustment to overseas conditions, to show that they are normal, generally experienced, and natural—not a sign of weakness. A letter from Mr.

Shriver to each trainee on his arrival at the training site says: "We expect you to have normal psychological reactions. We want them to be anticipated in training. We want you to face up to them. They are not seen as weaknesses. You can talk about them in this outfit." This is a completely different attitude from the one that is common in other agencies of the federal government.

In the training period, psychologists and psychiatrists are working with the volunteers. When they go abroad, the Corps members will be working with the staff of the Corps in the host country— the country director, deputy director, regional directors (the number depending on the size of the country), and a Public Health Service doctor assigned to the country.

"From the earliest days of the Peace Corps," Dr. English continued, "it has been the policy not to isolate anyone on the staff as a counselor. Everyone on the overseas staff is part of the counseling function. This is just good, humane, sensitive administration. All members of the professional and office staff undergo the same psychological orientation, so that the total staff structure abroad is identified with the support role, not by being amateur psychologists or psychiatrists, but by being good representative country directors, etc. Our research over the last three years allows us to tell the country directors when they may expect the principal period of difficulty with a particular volunteer or group of volunteers during the next two years in the particular cultural setting and with the particular kind of job assignment. The directors are therefore not concerned when their volunteers become depressed after four months; they are concerned if they do not. If they do not, either the volunteers are not working or the staff is not expecting enough of them. This is a support to the staff. In addition, we have now had enough experience to be able to suggest certain kinds of administrative intervention that the staff can do. Although not primarily psychological intervention, these measures have great implications for the mental health of the total Peace Corps population. Not only are the staff members sensitized to these matters before they go out, but at yearly regional meetings of country directors, doctors, and other staff in the field as well as at meetings with the volnuteers, we review their experience and learn from what we find out. We think this total supportive role of staff in relation to the volunteers is one of the most critical factors in our program."

Fred Brown: Referring to an article in the *American Psychologist* for November, 1965, in which Mr. Shriver pointed out that tests, useful as they are, represent only one factor involved in selection— a point that Dr. English also had made—Dr. Brown reported that in his research on the effect of lysergic acid diethylamide (LSD) on normal persons he had found exactly what von Felsinger had observed in his study of volunteer populations in Boston: the selection of a normal population is unpredictable. Many individuals who meet the criteria set up for normality prove to be not normal (Lasagna & von Felsinger, 1954).

In the selection of candidates for the ministry, Dr. Brown continued, there is apparently the assumption that sickness is necessarily a drawback to success. He did not consider this to be always the case. In an examination of thirteen high-ranking managers in a large industrial organization, he had found that six of them had ulcers. They were very successful. In this and another study, he had observed that psychological tests of people who were successful in large-scale planning showed a marked paranoid orientation. The word to describe this quality might be "grandiose," or perhaps it could be called "an extremely high level of aspiration."

In an evaluation of a research program carried out during the Korean war by Saul Sells (1951), Dr. Brown had found that, on the basis of the reports of the twenty or so psychologists who had studied the test material in an attempt to establish criteria for predicting success of pilots in combat, he could reasonably expect to achieve at least a seventy-percent prediction—well beyond chance—of those pilots who would function well, far beyond the pass–fail criterion. "I would do it," he said, "on the basis of those who seemed most sick—the persons who lacked inhibition, those with the grandiose point of view, who could plunge into a situation without being deterred by ethical and moral concerns, who had a rather swashbuckling attitude." The twenty evaluating psychologists had approached the test data with their middle-class, bourgeois, mental-health concept of the ideal person—one who observed all the rules of the Boy Scouts. This was a conception based on the projection of what a person should be if he was as confident, integrated, and ethical as the person making the evaluation. It did not enter into the combat situation at all.

Dr. Brown suggested that the import of what Dr. Dittes had said was along the same lines. Difficulty arises from the fact that the psychologist's conception of the careful, ethically oriented, integrated person creates a kind of matrix into which the person who conforms to this conception will fall in a given situation. It may be, however, that the person with a certain "sick" rating on the MMPI or other test, the person with a high paranoid elevation, will actually deal with a broader horizon than that of those who conform to the matrix; they will dare more, will have a bold, enterprising approach. The life history of the individual, indicating his degree of guardedness, conformity, cautiousness, etc., should be taken into account in evaluating him for any situation. In other words, what is generally considered sickness is not necessarily always unhealthy from a particular point of view.

Interpretation of tests is important in this connection, Dr. Brown continued. The tests may be absolutely right in what they show. The interpretation of them in relation to the interpreter's own biases and conceptions of what constitutes a good man, going back perhaps to St. Augustine and even to the Aristotelian conception of the symmetrical person, must be supplemented with consideration of the particular area, especially the ministry, for which the selection is being made. The cautious person is likely not to give as full a picture of himself on tests as will the more open person, whose test results may differ from the pattern that the interpreter wishes to conserve in the area, say, of the ministry. It is obligatory for the test user to get the life history of the person tested, but even more to ask himself to what extent he may be inadvertently seduced into a conception of the medical model of a disease germ that will upset the physiological homeostasis of the entire organism, rather than bearing in mind the psychosocial individual with various attitudinal factors to be considered. It may be that one sometimes has to break away from preconceived notions of the good, the true, and the beautiful.

Support for Dr. Brown's opinion about the necessity of taking into account all that can be known about the candidate's personality and life history in evaluating him for any situation came from another participant, who said that the important matter is to fit the character structure of the person to the task to be performed, whether he is to be a fighter pilot or a minister.

Walter J. Coville: Dr. Coville added an observation related to Dr. English's words about the need for an effective counseling program to aid candidates in a training program. Recently reviewing some statistics on attrition among candidates for the nursing school of St. Vincent's Hospital, New York, Dr. Coville had found that the lowest attrition rate for any class during the eleven-year period 1952–62 coincided with the period when the guidance and counseling unit was fully staffed and functioning most efficiently in meeting the students' needs. In a particularly noteworthy year, a group of 175 candidates selected out of 490 applicants remained intact during the whole year. This kind of support, Dr. Coville believed, is extremely critical in an attempt to retain qualified persons in any kind of training program.

Recent experience in his program of selection of candidates for female religious communities, Dr. Coville continued, had borne out what Dr. Brown had said about being careful not to use a stereotype as a criterion for selection. In his close follow-up of accepted candidates, he sometimes sees candidates with relatively normal personalities according to objective testing and routine clinical procedures later emerge with rather severe problems of adjustment. This happens particularly with highly intelligent but rigidly controlled candidates with an essentially passive-dependent adjustment who do well in their academic work and in adjusting to a rigidly structured and protective environment. As they are required to assume responsibility and function more independently, their stability is threatened and anxieties lead to the development of serious psychopathology. He concluded, therefore, that all kinds of personalities may qualify for the ministry and religious life provided that they meet the criteria of adequate intelligence, genuine motivation, and relatively stable emotional functioning.

Thomas N. McCarthy: Dr. McCarthy reported similar observations in relation to women developing problems after psychological clearance. With variations among groups, female applicants in their late teens have presented a smaller incidence of psychological problems than have young men of the same ages. But some of these women develop sexual problems when they reach the thirties. It is relatively common for such problems to show up in the psychological evaluations of young men at the time of application. Dr. McCarthy wondered whether this observation may not fit in with what Kinsey reported about age differences between men and women in the experience and expression of sexual desires. Possibly a woman's sexual needs are a less important component of her personality in the late teens than in the third decade of her life, with the result that trying to live a celibate life becomes more difficult for her in later years than it is for a man, whose sexual needs, according to Kinsey, reach a peak in the late teens and early twenties.

The screening program apparently presents a dual problem, Dr. McCarthy suggested: first there is the matter of identifying pathology, whatever that means. As Szasz (1961) has said, we may not know what pathology is. After the presumed pathological candidates have been eliminated, there is the problem of determining how broad the parameters for various personality and behavioral traits that can be tolerated within the ministry are. It may, of course, be open to discussion how clearly it is possible to identify seriously sick people. But the second problem is a critical one in this area. It comes back to the point Dr. Dittes had made: so many of the studies in the field are correlational. Trying to show the relation between scores on a predictive basis and criteria, psychologists also realize that there are problems with the criteria. Therefore, is the correlationship technique the proper approach?

Referring to the Strong Vocational Interest Blank research carried on by Father Paul D'Arcy (1954) and Father Brian Lhota

(1948) in measuring the interests of priests, Dr. McCarthy noted that a correlational study between scores earned by seminarians or priests on the diocesan scale of the SVIB and perseverance rates or ratings of effectiveness by peers or superiors will show a low correlation coefficient. He did not mean to say that the low correlations would be a negative comment on the usefulness of the diocesan-priest scale, because the literature shows that the majority of diocesan priests—more than ninety percent—earn scores of B, B+, or A on that scale. They are, therefore, quite different from men in general. But there is a lot of scatter within the high range into which priests fall, thus lowering the possibility of getting high correlation coefficients with criterion measures on which individual differences may exist. The scale has, nonetheless, identified a significant variable on which priests differ from the general population. Hence a lower parameter has been approximated, which is diagnostically useful. Accordingly, he thought that more attention should be given to establishing acceptable ranges of scores than to computing correlation coefficients. He proposed examining the statistical and research design methods being used so as to judge the efficiency of what is being done. The correlation coefficient he was referring to, Dr. McCarthy added, was a Pearson r.

Magda B. Arnold: Returning to Dr. Brown's comments, Dr. Arnold expressed doubt that the unconventional people would last through the seminary or the novitiate, simply because the situation is planned for a highly structured, obedient relationship of the seminarian and the novice to authority.

On another point, Dr. Arnold said that the results of testing women novices in the religious life in her experience at Loyola University, Chicago, were contrary to what Dr. Coville had reported. Over and over again in the Loyola program the passive, good-natured, pliant young people are considered the best, as long as they are in the novitiate. In testing some novices, the staff had noted some whom they judged to be likely to become serious problems in the future because they were extremely passive. The psychologists had warned the novice mistress about these girls, who were probably doing well up to that point. Their warnings were not believed. Some of the follow-up is now available. One of the girls whom the psychologists had been especially concerned about had to be sent away. The others have to see a therapist or counselor every two or three weeks and will probably need this support for years. It seemed to Dr. Arnold that such candidates—people who do well as long as they are in the highly structured situation—are frequently not revealed by many of the tests.

J. Victor Benson: Summing up what he considered to be a somewhat cynical attitude toward selection procedures verbalized during the discussion, a sort of pride in impugning the skills and techniques that the clinical psychologist has brought to the process of selection, Dr. Benson noted the following indictments of the whole method: uncertainty about what adequate criteria for health are, although psychologists are presumably experts in the determination of such criteria; disillusion with the effectiveness of tests, the instruments used to estimate the level of relative health; the rallying of pathology to the support of religion or vice versa, in a sense saying that certain apparently normal people are driven to pathology by the religious life. Would the next step, he wondered, be to say that religion sometimes blesses pathology?

Dr. Benson wished to interject a positive note by voicing the conviction that the use of testing and other selective methods has been helpful. These methods provide information that cannot be obtained in any other way. They make possible the understanding of the depths of a candidate's personality. Perhaps this information brings to light more difficult problems in selection, but the possession of this information at least makes the process of selection more exciting, and perhaps it makes more apparent the ethical responsibility involved in piecing together the various parts of information brought to light and provides the basis upon which decisions are made. The opportunities for this kind of intervention in a person's life make possible the kind of involvement that, in the long run, should result in better people in the Peace Corps and in the ministry.

Walter J. Coville: Dr. Coville thought that there was general agreement among the participants that the use of psychological instruments in the assessment of candidates for the ministry or the religious life was extremely valuable. But no instrument, he reminded his colleagues, is infallible in predicting human behavior. Instruments of measurement coupled with the acumen of a well-trained and mature psychologist provide a degree of predictive certitude that would otherwise not be available. The mature psychologist, aware of the limitations and weaknesses of his interpretations, is also confident of their value and of his interpretations. His findings will yield a dynamic profile of the personality and aid the administrator in making a decision about the candidate's suitability. But psychological testing merely to identify and eliminate the undesirable candidate represents a limited and perhaps unfair use of this procedure. Dr. Coville believed that a more important function of psychological assessment was to identify strengths and weaknesses of the person as a basis for helping him to mature and realize his fullest potential.

The psychological examination is useful also to the candidate himself, Dr. Coville added. He had often been impressed with the numbers of male and female candidates who frankly ask about the use of psychological test findings and request a discussion of the results. At the time of the examination, it may be assumed that the candidates are sincere in their vocational decision and do not want to make a mistake about it. If the evidence from the examination brings to light a basis for serious doubts about their suitability for the ministry or the religious life or shows up any need for psychological treatment, they want to know about it. Dr. Coville therefore reiterated his conviction that psychological assessment of candidates is vital and useful. He thought, however, that the focus of attention should be not on the weaknesses of the assessment techniques, but rather on research to overcome weaknesses by improving old techniques or developing new ones.

Fred Brown: Pointing out that the person who goes for diagnosis to a clinical psychologist committed to the use of tests is a sick person in need of help, whereas the candidate for ministerial training is not sick and does not consider himself so, Dr. Brown repeated his statement that one should not be too concerned at manifestations of pathology, because the same pathology appears in many of us. Like an electron microscope, the tests may magnify the pathological symptoms. What has not been done sufficiently, he believed, is to ask how effectively the person is able to cope with his pathology, to what extent it represents a dynamic force in his personality.

"I think we must always be aware," Dr. Brown said, "that what seems to be an element of sickness can result in pathology in one person, and in another, depending on the whole constellation of his defensive and adaptive techniques, can be used in the service of effective functioning. The person who accepts tests results at face value will be doing so on an unsophisticated basis, because he will not be using good clinical judgment and understanding of what a human being is within a social milieu."

Paul M. Steinberg: Dr. Steinberg said that the purpose of using psychological tests at Hebrew Union College, the center for the training of Reform rabbis, is to screen out people who show any kind of pathology. The applicant goes through an initial interview with a member of the faculty or of the staff of the dean's office, then is given a battery of tests, has a psychological interview, and then an interview with the faculty committee on admissions. It has been interesting to those concerned with selection that no one who has been rated low on the psychological or psychiatric examinations has ever been passed by the faculty committee on admissions, although that committee never sees the reports of the psychologists or psychiatrist.

One of the basic questions, Dr. Steinberg thought, was whether the person making a judgment would want a homosexual or a psychotic to serve his own parish or congregation.

Believing that the selectors of candidates for the ministry have a responsibility to those who go through the selection process as well as to the community, the Hebrew Union College refers for help those who are rejected for psychological reasons. It also encourages all students to go for therapy, "because we believe that a greater degree of self-awareness and understanding will improve their functioning, will help them to fulfill their potentialities. These are some of the reasons why we have psychological tests. These are our goals."

Frederick R. Kling: One function of psychological tests for ministerial selection that seemed to Mr. Kling to have been neglected in the discussion was the supplying of empirical evidence to substantiate various theories about who is going to make a good minister. Dr. Dittes had said that past attempts to make this explicit in the development of scales exemplifying the characteristics generally considered to be involved in effectiveness or perseverance in the ministry have not been uniformly successful. A number of ideas about other kinds of characteristics that might indicate good ministerial candidates had been brought forth in this discussion. Mr. Kling urged putting them to the test by looking for the kind of empirical evidence outlined by Dr. Dittes.

James E. Dittes: Dr. Dittes, exercising his prerogative of having the last word on the discussion of his paper, said that he had been disappointed and puzzled until Dr. Benson spoke. Knowing that a number of the participants were involved in screening procedures, he had thought he was issuing a challenge. He had meant to say that there probably was not much scientific validity—visible to him, at least—for the decisions these people were making in their selection procedures. But the discussants had not responded to his challenge until Dr. Benson picked it up. Dr. Dittes suspected that there was more enthusiasm and more confidence in the decisions being made by the members of this group engaged in selection processes than indicated by the first hour of discussion.

Dr. Dittes agreed with Mr. Kling that some alternative convictions had been exposed. "We are skeptical, and yet we announce that there are new guides that we happen to trust. They are not the values of the middle class, the bourgeoisie, as Dr. Brown suggested, but an alternate set of values that may have found lodging in some of us in one way or another. I suspect it is fair to call them a category, a set of personal preferences rather than the scientifically based norms,

"I was purposely trying to exaggerate and to use a lot of loaded statements, because I think there are still issues, even if they seem to be drawn in a loaded and exaggerated way. I still think, in other words, that there are lurking unjustified confidences in decisions we make on the basis of tests that call for further scrutiny."

REFERENCES

Arnold, M. B. *Story Sequence Analysis: A new method of measuring motivation and predicting achievement.* New York: Columbia University Press, 1962.

D'Arcy, P. F. Constancy of interest factor patterns within the specific vocation of foreign missioner. *Studies in Psychology and Psychiatry,* 1954, *9,* No. 1. Washington: Catholic University of America Press.

Dobyns, H. F., Dougherty, P. L., & Holmberg, A. R. *Peace Corps program impact in the Peruvian Andes, final report.* Ithaca: Cornell University, Department of Anthropology. Cornell Peru Project, 1966.

Douglas, W. G. T. Predicting ministerial effectiveness. Unpublished doctoral dissertation, Harvard University, 1957.

Ham, H. M. Personality correlates of ministerial success. *Iliff Review,* 1960, *17,* 3–9.

Kelly, E. L., & Fiske, D. W. *The prediction of performance in clinical psychology.* Ann Arbor: University of Michigan Press, 1951.

Lasagna, L., & von Felsinger, J. M. The volunteer subject in research. *Science,* 1954, *120,* 359–361.

Lhota, B. G. *Vocational interests of Catholic priests.* Washington: Catholic University of America Press, 1948.

Sells, S. B. *A research program on the psychiatric screening of flying personnel. I. Methodological introduction and experimental design.* USAF School of Aviation Medicine, 1951.

Szasz, T. S. *The myth of mental illness.* New York: Hoeber-Harper, 1961.

II

Testing in the Three
Major Religious Groups

TESTING FOR THE ROMAN CATHOLIC PRIESTHOOD

THOMAS N. MCCARTHY

ORIGIN AND EVOLUTION OF TESTING PROGRAMS
FOR PRIESTS

THE ORGANIZATION OF TESTING PROGRAMS for screening candidates to the priesthood grew out of four things: a recognition of the serious adjustment problems encountered in the sacerdotal life as reflected in the incidence of psychiatric problems and drop-out rates; research into the psychological characteristics of priests and other religious; the growing acceptance of clinical evaluation by society-at-large during and following World War II; and finally the positive recommendation by ecclesiastical authority that seminaries use appropriate psychological techniques in judging the qualifications of priest-candidates. The first three of these influences are intertwined with one another in the evolution of the testing programs; the fourth followed as evidence accumulated to provide solid justification for psychological evaluation. It was then that ecclesiastical authority saw fit to issue formal statements prescribing it as desirable admissions procedure (Sacred Congregation of Religious, 1957, Art. 33, p. 46).

47

Mental Illness Rates Among Priests. Psychological testing of candidates for the Catholic priesthood received its primary impetus from the pioneering work of Thomas Verner Moore in the mid-nineteen-thirties. Being priest, psychologist, and psychiatrist as well as chairman of the Department of Psychology and Psychiatry at the Catholic University of America, Moore brought a unique background to the problem of selecting candidates for the priesthood. He enjoyed the distinct advantages of being able to combine research and clinical acumen in his approach to this problem, and of having a group of productive students who have carried forward his work for the past thirty years.

Moore was initially concerned with the amount of psychopathology found among clergymen and religious, both male and female. In 1935 he carried out a national survey to determine the number of Catholic priests and religious who were then hospitalized for psychiatric reasons. His survey brought a return from well over ninety percent of the psychiatric hospitals in the country, and his figures have been accepted as definitive since that time (Moore, 1936a).

Kelley carried out a similar survey of hospitalized religious sisters in 1956, and her findings are essentially the same as those of Moore's twenty years earlier (Kelley, 1958).

Moore found that the overall incidence of psychopathology among priests was lower than was true for the American population as a whole. The reason for this was the total absence of priest-patients who were hospitalized for syphilitic-type disorders. Hospitalized priests, however, were found to have a higher incidence of schizophrenia, paranoia, manic-depression, and alcoholism than the general American male population of hospitalized patients (Moore, 1936a). These findings are summarized in Table I.

The fact that priests as a group are more intelligent and better educated than American men-in-general and presumably, therefore, more enlightened about seeking treatment for mental illness would offer reason for caution in drawing comparisons between the two groups. Samples matched for intelligence, education, social background, and similar factors that might influence hospital admission rates would clarify how much of the observed differences in rates is associated with the fact of being a priest. Interpretations of these data up to now have prescinded from concern over the appropriateness of comparing hospitalized men-in-general and hospitalized priests, however, and have instead accepted the fact of the differences in rates as a valid comment on the incidence of psychological disorder among priests. The major concern for the past thirty years has been to find reasons why priests as a group deviate from the general norm.

TABLE I. RATES OF MENTAL ILLNESS FOR PRIESTS AND MEN-IN-GENERAL*

	Priests	Men in General
Alcoholism	21%	7%
Manic-Depression	14%	10%
Paranoia	9%	1%
Schizophrenia	29%	17%

*Adapted from Moore (1936a, pp. 495–496).

Moore advanced the view that prepsychotic people are attracted to the priesthood, and he proposed that this is the major reason for the higher incidence of the particular psychological problems found among priests. Based on this view, he argued that procedures should be developed for screening out prepsychotic candidates at the time they apply for admission, and he proposed methods for detecting these people (Moore, 1936b).

Moore's students and a number of other people as well have continued to search out reasons for the observed discrepancies in mental illness between priests and men-in-general. This research has taken two major directions. One type of study has continued to test Moore's hypothesis that the priesthood attracts a special kind of person. Some of these studies have also been concerned with psychological and other differences between those who persevere and those who drop out. A second type of study has focused on the ways that training for the priesthood influences personality development.

Research on Psychological Characteristics of Priests. Moore's notion that certain types of people are likely to be attracted to the priesthood raised several questions. It would appear that his view was based primarily on his study of hospitalized priests. The question arose, therefore, about the extent to which his findings could be generalized to all priests. Research on this matter has put the issue in a broader context than the mere identification of pathology, and has been concerned with the broader question of priests' having any psychological characteristics which set them apart from men-in-general and from men with similar educational backgrounds. The psychological characteristics that have been investigated cover a broad range of personality variables including a search for pathological signs. Values, patterns of vocational interests, and personality traits have all been investigated as well as indices of pathology.

In the main the studies describing the personality of seminarians and priests have been carried out as masters' and doctoral dissertations. A few of Moore's students began this work in the early nineteen-forties. This work picked up momentum slowly after that until the last decade with a resultant torrent of dissertations from several Catholic graduate departments of psychology and education. Menges and Dittes in their 1965 review of psychological studies of clergymen list more than twenty studies describing personality characteristics of priests. Many other studies describe personality characteristics of nuns and brothers.

A review of the pertinent literature by this writer in 1957 led him to conclude that studies of the personality traits of priests and seminarians showed a consistent pattern in which the person entering religious life tends to score higher on neurotic scales than do other Catholics of the same age and the same educational and social background, the religious samples tending to be more dissatisfied with life and family, and more submissive, introspective, dependent, and self-conscious than a comparable sample drawn from the laity. The literature also indicated that priests and seminarians have a unique pattern of vocational interests which can be identified through psychometric devices (McCarthy, 1960). These conclusions were based on a review of studies done by

McCarthy (1942), Bier (1948), Lhota (1948), D'Arcy (1954), and Murray (1957). A 1962 review by D'Arcy of the literature on the measurement of interests of priests led him to support the earlier conclusion that interests of priests are unique and measurable. He pointed out further that these interests can be identified for many in their early teens. He also concluded that different kinds of interest scales are necessary for measuring interests of different types of priests, e.g. one scale for secular priests and a different one for missionary priests (D'Arcy, 1962). In 1965 Dunn reviewed ten studies of seminarians and priests that had been completed since this writer's 1957 review, and he concluded that the findings of the earlier studies were confirmed by this later work. Dunn observes that

The consistency of MMPI profiles obtained from religious samples is striking. All groups scored high on Pt and Sc. Male religious usually scored high on Mf. This pattern suggests that religious tend to be perfectionistic, worrisome, introversive, socially inept, and, in more extreme cases, perhaps isolated and withdrawn. Male religious tend to have interests and proclivities which are typically feminine [Dunn, 1965, p. 133].

Dittes in a 1962 review of several Minnesota Multiphasic Personality Inventory (MMPI) studies with Protestant and Catholic seminarians observed that both groups tend to score above standard norms on the Mf, Pt, Hs, Hy, and Sc scales (Dittes, 1962).

While there are some variations from study to study, a common core of characteristics tends to emerge that distinguishes the priest from the general population in regard to his interests and from men with comparable educational backgrounds with regard to some aspects of his personality. The question of hospitalized priests' having different rates of admission from men comparable to themselves in education, intelligence, and social background remains unanswered, but the deviant scores priest-candidates as a group earn on tests like the MMPI in comparison to other professions suggests that Moore's interpretation of his findings may be essentially correct.

One of the early questions raised in this research concerned the appropriateness of using standardized tests to describe the personality of priests. It was thought that a priest, because of his religious convictions and also because of his vows of chastity and obedience and, in the case of the order priests, poverty, might be subject to response sets which would invalidate tests standardized on general male samples as instruments suitable for research and/or selection with priests. Bier first raised this question in his study comparing seminarians to law, dental, and medical students (Bier, 1948). Having concluded that certain items on the MMPI are inappropriate for seminarians, he developed a revised form of the test in which he substituted new items for those which he believed seminarians could answer in only one way. Skrincosky then did a comparative study of seminarians' scores on the standard form of the MMPI and on Bier's revised form and found an even more deviant pattern on the latter (Skrincosky, 1953). Hence, despite a certain number of inappropriate items in the regular form of the MMPI, it does not appear that these are the main reasons for elevated profiles. Accordingly, it may be argued that at least the MMPI is appropriate for use with seminary populations as long as one recognizes that some diagnostic differentiation is lost with the regular form because of the problem with response-sets. Another possibility is that seminarians and priests may be more honest, open, and willing to reveal inadequacies. Presumably other personality tests that have been constructed and validated for the same general population from which priest-candidates are drawn could also be used, though this is something that has not been tested as yet except for the Strong Vocational Interest Blank (SVIB). This position in effect holds that personality tests have as adequate concurrent validity for clergy groups as for any other group for which the tests are intended.

A third question that has been raised by researchers in this field concerns the predictive validity of psychological tests for priest-candidates. To what extent are scores on tests related to eventual job performance, to perseverance, to emotional adjustment, and the like? Research on this point with priest-candidates up to now has mainly used perseverance as the criterion variable. In only two or three cases has a measure of adjustment been used. Predictor variables have included MMPI scores (Wauck, 1956; Barry, 1960; Weisgerber, 1962; Kobler, 1964; Sweeney, 1964) and interest test scores from the SVIB and Kuder-C. D'Arcy (1962) has reviewed five studies that have explored the extent to which interest inventories differentiate successful and unsuccessful seminarians. These studies were done by Burke (1947), Friedl (1952), Wauck (1956), Kennedy (1958), and Kenney (1959). Barry (1960) using Bier's revision of the MMPI developed a special Religious Adjustment scale (Re) which distinguishes poorly adjusted seminarians from well-adjusted seminarians.

The general conclusions that seem warranted from the studies published to date are that it is very difficult to predict who will be a successful seminarian (that is, who perseveres or who is rated well-adjusted by faculty or peers) from test scores on the MMPI, Kuder, or Strong; but it does seem possible to predict with better than actuarial expectancy who is likely to be an unsuccessful seminarian. The predictions, however, are far from perfect. Weisgerber (1962) reports the psychologist having correctly identified 45 percent of those who failed to persevere, for example; but he also points out that for every one or two persons correctly identified as a potential adjustment problem, the psychologist missed on the average two or three bad cases. The criterion of hit or miss in this case was an independent psychiatric opinion or subsequent behavior indicative of instability.

The evidence to date indicates that tests do in fact identify certain characteristics that distinguish priests as a group from others, but the presence of these characteristics cannot be used to predict success or lack of success with great accuracy. The absence of some of these traits, however, may be a negative sign—e.g., low scores on the priest scales of the SVIB. Kobler (1964) believes that this conclusion implies that a considerable amount of deviation can be tolerated in religious life. This writer has previously suggested that one reason for this may be that behavior should be evaluated in terms of its situational appropriateness rather than against some empirical norm which may not be related to the circumstances in which the behavior being judged is occurring (McCarthy, 1960). In my study of personality changes during the training of religious brothers it was found that nervous tension, irritability, and susceptibility to frustration all declined after profession of first vows. At the same time conforming behavior and withdrawal increased. These findings appear to contradict one another. On the one hand, there is evidence for increased emotional stability—the decline in tension—and on the other, there is evidence for a decrease—the withdrawal and conformity (McCarthy, 1956). The data lend themselves to several interpretations, but one that suggests itself is that, in the context of religious formation, conformance and withdrawal are situationally appropriate behavior and as such need not be construed as indicators of pathology so long as they do not interfere with the other personal and social obligations which the person's calling demands.

A fourth question that has been investigated concerns the extent to which religious training leads to personality changes. Most of these studies have been of women. Cross-sectional studies of priest-candidates at different levels of training and of priests have been done by D'Arcy (1954) and Murray (1957). D'Arcy used the SVIB and Murray used the MMPI and Guilford-Zimmerman Temperament Survey. Conclusions drawn are that candidates already have unique interest and personality characteristics at the time they apply for admission, and that further changes occur during training. In the case of interests, increased training leads to higher scores on the priest scale; in the case of personality variables, greater deviation is found with increased time in training, but with a reversion to a more normal pattern after ordination. The findings must be accepted with caution. Because of the failure to study dropouts or to follow a longitudinal research design, it may be that the group and not the individual has changed. One longitudinal study of teaching brothers does indicate that individuals change, however, and that exceptions to change do not reach the level of statistical significance (McCarthy, 1956).

One final comment about the research on priests that has been published to date is in order. For the most part these studies are mainly descriptive. One rarely finds even tentative interpretations about the dynamics implied by the data. Dunn (1965) suggests one such interpretation for the consistent finding of high Mf scores among seminarians. He wonders if the high Mf suggests a failure to identify with proper sex-roles stemming from inability to identify with the role of the like-sex parent and thus leading to the consequent need for the asexual adjustment that religious life provides. Dittes (1962) offers a less depth-oriented interpretation in suggesting that the higher Mf, Pt, and Sc scores of seminarians and their lower Ma scores as compared to law students ". . . might suggest that whereas law and seminary students share a sensitivity, solicitousness, and gentleness toward personal tribulations, these law students may respond with a somewhat greater activism and engagement with affairs of the world" (Dittes, 1962, p. 150).

Clinical Evaluation & Personnel Selection. The evolution of psychological testing of priests cannot be fully understood apart from the wide use of psychological testing methods during and following World War II in personality and job evaluations of servicemen and veterans. The acceptance of the clinical psychologist's role in examining emotionally disturbed military personnel and the dramatic reduction of washouts in pilot training that followed the use of custom-built selection tests prepared the way for a far greater role for the psychologist in civilian life than he had previously enjoyed. Added to this was the extensive clinical and counseling service offered to veterans under government sponsorship. In this milieu, and with research on the priest's adjustment and psychological make-up already underway at the university level, it was natural to hope that better selection of religious personnel might parallel the success enjoyed by the military.

By the late 1940s and early 1950s societal institutions other than the government were beginning to accept the fact that the use of psychological methods can provide a more detailed and accurate description of a person's personality and behavior than can be obtained through traditional methods. Concurrent validity was being demonstrated, though predictive validity remained more elusive. It was out of this practical success which psychology was enjoying, the growing body of psychological research on seminarians, and the substantial influence within the Church of the views of such men as Moore and Bier who were advocating psychological evaluation that screening programs began to develop. With papal approbation for judicious application of psychological methods to the study of human problems (Pius XII, 1958) added to these other factors, demand for this type service increased sharply from the middle 1950s.

PSYCHOLOGICAL ASSESSMENT PROGRAMS FOR PRIESTS

Menges and Dittes (1965) have observed that research in psychological studies of clergymen has been a flourishing field for more than a decade without the awareness of even those actively involved in the research that many others were working on similar problems. Their volume of abstracts contains more than 700 entries, over 75 percent of which is dated since 1955.

In much the same way that research with clergymen has been going on at a rapidly accelerating rate without much notice, testing programs, too, have come into a flourishing existence with rather minimal awareness of this fact even among those who offer this special service to diocesan seminaries and religious institutes. There are no records, so far as I know, when the first testing program for priest-candidates was begun; nor am I aware of information about the nature and extent of the kind of early testing that was done. Even now it is difficult to ascertain with much precision the nature and extent of psychological services being offered in the evaluation of priest-candidates.

In 1960 the American Catholic Psychological Association's Committee for the Study of Methods in the Psychological Assessment of Religious Candidates conducted a survey of ACPA members and received replies from 153 members who indicated *an interest* in psychological services to seminaries and religious institutes. A follow-up survey in 1962 to those 153 respondents plus 4 new members who were known to be active in the work provided the first attempt to describe what was actually being done nationally by Catholic psychologists, at least those Catholics who were members of ACPA.

The 1962 ACPA survey provided a relatively gross picture of the nature and scope of psychological services then being extended to seminaries and religious institutes. The survey did not request a description in depth of an actual testing program, however. As a matter of fact, this writer has never seen such a description in the literature. Accordingly, in the belief that this would be useful information for those interested and/or involved in this type of work to share, a description of an actual testing program for candidates to the priesthood is given here following a summary of the 1962 ACPA survey findings.

1962 American Catholic Psychological Association Survey of Services to Seminaries and Religious Institutes. In 1962 the ACPA Committee for the Study of Methods in the Psychological Assessment of Religious Candidates conducted a survey of 157 ACPA members who had indicated an interest in psychological services to seminaries and religious institutes. The purpose of the survey was to determine the number of ACPA psychologists involved in this work, their geographical location, the nature of the services they rendered, and their felt need for special training in the work of candidate assessment (Coville, 1962a, 1962b).

A total of 58 members, or 37 percent of the 157 who were sent questionnaires, responded. The number of them who were priests, religious, and lay persons is indicated in Table II.

Most of the respondents (37) held a doctoral degree in psychology; four listed doctorates in guidance, counseling, or medicine; 17 listed master's degrees in psychology.

TABLE II. NUMBER OF RELIGIOUS, CLERICAL, AND LAY
RESPONDENTS GIVING PSYCHOLOGICAL SERVICE
TO DIOCESES AND RELIGIOUS INSTITUTES IN 1962

Respondents	N
Female Religious	14
Male Religious	22
Secular Priests	4
Laywomen	3
Laymen	15
TOTAL	58

Seventeen states, one territory, and two foreign countries were represented among the respondents. The Northeast—Maryland (2), Massachusetts (3), New Jersey (1), New York (12), Pennsylvania (8), and Rhode Island (1)—had the heaviest concentration of respondents (the figure in parentheses indicates the number of respondents from each state). Several midwestern states also had respondents: Illinois (5), Indiana (2), Kentucky (2), Iowa (1), Michigan (4), Missouri (1), Ohio (3), and Wisconsin (3). On the West Coast there were 7 respondents: California (5), Oregon (1), and Washington (1).

The services offered by the respondents could be classified into two broad categories: testing, and psychotherapeutic or counseling consultation. Some of the respondents (N = 34) offered what might be called relatively complete assessment programs—i.e., the program made use of tests of ability, interests, and personality, personal documents, and interviews; and all candidates to a given community or seminary were examined on a regular basis. Much of this testing was done in groups. Some of the respondents (N = 10) offered testing services but not as a regular program. In this case some but not all candidates to a given community or seminary were examined on referral to the psychologist. Most of the testing was concerned with personality and basic intelligence and was done individually. The remaining respondents (N = 14) described their services as being in counseling or psychotherapy rather than in testing. This information is summarized in Table III according to the type of religious institute served.

The survey pointed out that in 1960 a total of 42,629 men were studying for the priesthood in 387 diocesan and religious seminaries in the United States. Allowing for the foreign respondents, about ten percent of the seminaries in the United States were receiving some type of psychological service from one or more of the respondents in this 1962 survey. About eight percent were receiving regular assessment services for all candidates. How many seminaries were then receiving services from non-respondents and from non-ACPA members is not known, but it does not seem likely that they would have totalled more than those receiving assistance from the survey respondents. It should also be pointed

TABLE III. THE NUMBER OF TESTING PROGRAMS—REGULAR AND ON REFERRAL
—AND CONSULTING SERVICES EXTENDED TO MALE AND FEMALE
RELIGIOUS INSTITUTES AND DIOCESAN SEMINARIES BY THE 58 RE-
SPONDENTS.

| | | Type Institute | | | |
Service	Respondents	Male Religious	Female Religious	Diocesan Seminary	TOTAL
Testing					
Regular	34	28	44	2	74
Referral	10	7	9	3	19
Consulting	14	3	5	0	8
TOTAL	58	38	58	5	101

out that some of the male religious institutes included are orders
of brothers. Hence the figures overestimate services to seminaries.

It will be seen from Table IV that one form of the MMPI,
either the regular form or the Bier revision, was the most commonly used test. Twenty-seven of the 34 respondents used a group-
testing approach in their programs with individually administered
tests being used only when special need arose.

Of the 34 respondents, 28 submitted an integrated, written report of their findings; 4 submitted merely a profile of test scores,
and 2 presented their findings orally.

The kinds of information included in the reports of the 34 respondents are listed in Table V.

The final question in the survey asked what kind of assistance
those engaged in the work would find useful. Most of the respondents indicated interest in participating in workshops concerned
with problems of assessment. A smaller number requested short
training institutes for direction in organizing and administering an
assessment program.

Description of a Testing Program. The ACPA survey showed that
the assessment programs for priests are varied in character. Some
offer very minimal testing; some rely exclusively on tests and use
no interview; some have a short battery of tests for preliminary

TABLE IV
TESTS EMPLOYED BY THE 34 CONSULTANTS WHO OFFER
74 REGULAR ASSESSMENT PROGRAMS

INTELLIGENCE TESTS

GROUP Name of Test	No. Using	INDIVIDUAL Name of Test	No. Using
College Qualification Tests (CQT)	8	Wechsler Adult Intelligence Scale (WAIS)	18
School & College Ability Tests (SCAT)	8	Wechsler Intelligence Scale for Children (WISC)	1
Otis	5		
American Council on Education (ACE)	5	Stanford-Binet	1
Ohio State Psychological Test	3	Raven Progressive Matrices	1
Henmon-Nelson	3		
College Entrance Exam. Board (CEEB)	3		
Army General Classification Test	2		
California Test of Mental Maturity	2		
Terman-McNemar	1		
SRA Primary Mental Abilities (PMA)	1		
Ammons Full-Range Picture Vocabulary	1		

PERSONALITY TESTS

GROUP Name of Test	No. Using	INDIVIDUAL Name of Test	No. Using
Minnesota Multiphasic (MMPI)	18	Rorschach	14
MMPI (Bier revision)	8	Thematic Apperception Test (TAT)	11
Guilford-Zimmerman Temperament Survey (GZTS)	7	Sentence Completion	8
		Draw-a-Person Test (DAP)	5
California Test of Personality	3	Draw-a-Boy (or a Girl)	3
Cattell 16 Personality Factor Questionnaire	2	House-Tree-Person Projective Technique (H-T-P)	2
Edwards Personal Preference Schedule	3	Minnesota Multiphasic (MMPI)	3
Bell Adjustment Inventory	1	Szondi Test	1
Cornell Index	1	Cornell Index	1
Neuroticism Schedule	1	Edwards Personal Preference Schedule	1
Personality Inventory for Seminarians	1		
Bernreuter Personality Inventory	1		
Sentence Completion	12		
Draw-a-Person Test (DAP)	10		
Rorschach	6		
Thematic Apperception Test (TAT)	6		

INTEREST AND OTHER TESTS—PERSONAL DOCUMENTS

GROUP Name of Test	No. Using	INDIVIDUAL Personal Documents	No. Using
Kuder Preference Record	13	Academic Record	3
Strong Vocational Interest Blank	4	Application Blank	3
Brainard Occupation Preference Inventory	1	Reference Letters	2
SRA Diagnostic Reading Tests	1	Health Records	5
Iowa Silent Reading Tests	1	Personal or Life History Data	9
Davis Reading Test	2	Autobiography	6
Nelson-Denny Reading Test	1	Teacher Rating Scale	2
Cooperative English	1	Essays	6
Flanagan Aptitude Classification Tests (FACT)	1		

screening followed by more extensive testing and interviewing—
sometimes including a psychiatric evaluation—when need for this
is indicated; others consist in lengthy testing and interviews as
routine procedure for all candidates. The program to be described
here is of the last-named type.

A. *Purposes and Areas Covered.* Most seminaries are concerned primarily with screening-out candidates who would be unfit for the priestly life. Included among those considered unqualified
would be psychotics, neurotics, individuals with character disorders, homosexuals, and those with insufficient ability to manage

TABLE V. ITEMS INCLUDED IN REPORTS
OF THE 34 RESPONDENTS

Report Content	No. Using
Behavior and Appearance	21
Motivation	23
Interests	18
Intelligence	28
Academic Performance	19
Personality Traits	28
Modes of Adjustment	23
Quality of Interpersonal Relations	22
Family Background	15
Health History	9
Diagnosis	14
Prognosis	17
Recommendation for Suitability	24

the lengthy scholastic training for the priesthood. Beyond merely
screening out unwanted candidates, some seminaries also utilize
the results of the assessment to aid in counseling the seminarian
in his educational and personal development. When both of these
objectives are being sought, the assessment program normally
covers the areas of ability, interests, and personality in some depth.

Included in the assessment of ability is an evaluation of the
candidate's aptitude for college and theological studies. Usually
an attempt is made to determine relative strengths and weaknesses
along verbal and numerical lines in reading skills. While the pri-

mary aptitude required for seminary studies is verbal, many priests eventually function as teachers of various secular subjects and some engage in scientific research. Sometimes preparation for these kinds of work can begin during the seminarian's training provided he has the aptitude and inclination for it. In my own assessment programs for priests, college ability—as indicated by both achievement and aptitude—is evaluated through tests such as the College Qualifying Tests or College Entrance Examination Boards and through past performance. A transcript of prior academic work is requested to aid in making the diagnosis of ability. Despite increased sophistication in testing procedures, past performance as indicated by rank in class, overall academic average, the ratio of college certifying grades to total grades carried, and similar indices, remains the best single predictor of future scholastic work. General intelligence is evaluated on the Wechsler Adult Intelligence Scale (WAIS). Reading skills are evaluated by a standard test such as the Nelson-Denny or Davis Reading Tests.

Interests of the candidate are assessed in three ways: from a report of the kinds of activities in which he regularly engages, from a statement of what he feels he would like to do, and through an interest inventory. The SVIB is taken by all candidates and it is scored on Lhota's Diocesan Priest Scale as well as on all occupational and non-occupational scales provided by an electronic scoring service. Interest scores are thus received on more than fifty occupations falling into eleven different areas—e.g., science, social welfare, business, and linguistic. Scores on the non-occupational scales provide measures of interest maturity, occupational level, masculinity–femininity, and specialization.

The personality assessment includes a description of the candidate's temperamental and behavioral traits, his concept of himself, his typical ways of relating to others, and his motivation. The objective is to describe those aspects of the candidate's behavior and personality which are thought to be relevant to the priestly vocation. The procedures used to determine these things are direct observations of his behavior during the examination period, an interview, personal documents, and personality tests. The latter include standardized questionnaires such as the MMPI, Cattell 16 P-F

Questionnaire, and the Edwards Personal Preference Schedule; and projective tests such as the TAT, sentence completion, figure drawings, and Rorschach. The personal documents include an autobiographical statement, a six-page personal-data form, and an essay modified from one developed by Gordon Allport for Protestant ministers in which the person describes his views of the priestly life, who has influenced his thinking, and what he hopes to contribute to the Church through his ministry.

B. *Administration of the Program.* Normally candidates are examined before they enter the seminary. In some cases, however, this is not practicable, and the evaluation is then done shortly after entry, generally just before college preparation has started or shortly thereafter. Rarely is this kind of testing done before senior year of high school.

Candidates are examined in groups over a two-day period, approximately four three-hour sessions being required for the testing which is then followed by private interviews.

Prior to assembling for the evaluation, candidates are requested to sign a release-of-information form permitting the psychologist to carry out the testing and to submit a report of his findings to a designated ecclesiastical authority for the latter's discretionary use. Candidates under twenty-one years of age are asked to have their parents or legal guardians authorize the examination and release of the report to this official. A copy of one release-of-information form currently being used is reproduced here.

(Name of Seminary)

PSYCHOLOGICAL TESTING PROGRAM

A psychological evaluation is a requirement for admission to this seminary.

The evaluation, which requires two days, includes an assessment of abilities, interests, and personality. A summary report of the psychological evaluation is submitted to the provincial and becomes a part of the candidate's confidential file. Reports are not given to the candidate, nor to his parents or guardian. Information in the report is used by the provincial and at his discretion by those responsible for the candidate's religious, educational, and personal formation.

The report will be released to a professional person outside the seminary only if both the candidate and the provincial request this in writing.

The psychologist for this seminary is _____, a certified psychologist in the State of _____.

_____   _____
(Candidate's Signature)   (Parents' Signatures)

_____   _____
(Date)   (Date)

At the beginning of the first testing session candidates are informed of: (1) the kinds of tests they will be taking: tests of ability, interests, and personality; (2) the way in which the results of the tests will be used: that a confidential report will be submitted to an official of the diocese or institute, usually a seminary rector or a provincial, for his discretionary use in evaluating their qualifications for the priesthood and in guiding them during their training; (3) the fact that if they find difficulty in answering any items on personal forms or personality questionnaires they may circle the item number to signify that they want to discuss their answer in private, either to qualify or to extend it. The latter practice is followed to reduce the sense of coercion that examinees sometimes feel in being asked to answer questions in all-or-nothing terms. Such qualifications are, of course, also helpful diagnostically.

Each candidate is assigned a code number for identifying his test materials and for use in submitting the evaluation report. This is used to protect the privacy of the candidate and also to promote greater freedom of expression in completing the various tests and forms.

A report is submitted which describes the findings from the evaluation; inferences are drawn from the findings regarding the kind of adjustment that could be expected of the candidate in religious life; and recommendations are made about a course of action. In the latter case this would include a recommendation for acceptance or rejection, and it might also include a recommendation about providing counseling, psychotherapy, remedial work, or whatever might be deemed appropriate in helping the candidate to make a successful adjustment to the seminary.

The development of local norms on ability, interest, and personality tests, and follow-up of candidates—almost always only of those accepted, not of those rejected—is standard practice. Perseverance rates and descriptions of behavior during training given by immediate superiors are the usual kinds of information obtained.

CONCERNS ABOUT TESTING PRIEST-CANDIDATES

A variety of concerns has been expressed by ecclesiastical authorities and by clergymen generally about requiring priest-candidates to undergo a psychological evaluation as a condition for admission to a seminary. Some of these concerns are those which have been voiced generally about using tests in personnel selection, and some are peculiar to the priesthood because of the specific canons of the Church governing that vocation, and the teachings related to the theology of the religious vocation.

Perhaps the earliest and strongest objection to testing priest-candidates was raised over the place of grace in the calling to the priesthood. The teaching of the Church on this point is clear: the vocation is a response to a special call from God and as such involves a special grace. Many of those who have opposed testing priest-candidates have done so on the grounds that the psychologist is restricted to the natural order of things and consequently misses the very thing that gives life to the true vocation—the grace that flows from God to the candidate through the supernatural relationship that exists between them. Two interrelated answers have been given to this objection. The first is the view that grace builds on nature and that if the raw material is not present to begin with— i.e., if the person lacks the intellectual, physical, or psychological requisites for the life—the grace of the calling would not be given. Working backward, therefore, one may infer to the absence of a special call from the absence of the required personal credentials.

The second answer that has been given to this objection is based on the recognition of the principle that behavior is generally the resultant of a multitude of factors. For any pattern of behavior, social, physical, psychological, and spiritual factors may be intertwined and interacting with one another in a variety of ways. The argument goes on to hold that because a clinical psychologist is trained to untangle the dynamics that lie behind behavior he sometimes can offer insights into the extent to which abnormal and/or unconscious factors may be playing a significant part in the choices and conduct of an individual. The assumption is then made that, to the extent that abnormal and unconscious factors are contributing to a religious calling, there is less likelihood of its being a genuine one.

It would appear that a consensus has formed regarding this matter, and now most would not view psychological assessment as a violation of grace so long as the inferences drawn from personality descriptions are based on sufficiently sound premises.

Unanimous consensus has not formed regarding the issue of invasion of privacy. This matter continues to be a source of concern to the public-at-large as indicated by Congressional hearings on psychological testing (American Psychological Association, 1965), and it also has occupied the attention of thoughtful churchmen in regard to testing candidates for the seminary (Ristuccia, 1962; Ford, 1964). A complicating factor so far as the Church is concerned is that the issue of psychic privacy is tied up with canonical definitions of manifestation of conscience. Religious superiors are strictly forbidden by Canon 520 of the Code of Canon Law to induce those persons subject to them to make a manifestation of conscience to them. The term manifestation of conscience has three different meanings in Canon Law: (1) a manifestation of sins, imperfections, and moral failures; (2) a manifestation of temptations, propensities to evil, improper attractions, personal repugnances, interior acts of virtue, and good intentions; (3) knowledge about spiritual and religious life as obtained from lectures and conferences. It is the first two types of manifestation which superiors are forbidden to induce their subjects to give. Clearly, the type of material included in this definition is the object of scrutiny in a psychological evaluation.

Ristuccia (1962) holds that the proscription against a manifestation of conscience applies for all religious and clerics who are under vows. He points out that there is some disagreement about postulants' being included, but candidates seeking admission are not included in it. Nonetheless, the person's right to privacy is held to be basic, regardless of his status, and the psychologist is obliged to safeguard it. Bier (1962) has argued that religious institutes also have rights that must be respected in this matter. One of these rights is to have sufficient knowledge of candidates so that correct judgments about their qualifications for the priesthood can be made. It is his view that the mere fact of requiring a psychological evaluation of candidates prior to entry is not an abridgment of the candidates' rights to psychic privacy since candidates have a balancing obligation to demonstrate their qualifications. On the other hand, Bier recognizes limits on the extent of the testing that may be done. He and most writers follow the principles outlined by Pope Pius XII in his 1958 allocution on moral limits in the application of psychology to human problems (Pius XII, 1958). The principle generally invoked to justify testing priest-candidates is that the motive for doing so is proportionate to any danger involved for the person being tested.

Vexing problems about a candidate's rights to psychic privacy are not abrogated merely by invoking this principle, however. Questions about the kind of information to be presented in the psychologist's report, about who is to see the report, and about how long the report should be retained in the person's dossier are some of those that need to be clarified in the actual operation of an assessment program. Bier has urged that a conservative practice be followed and that the information be limited strictly to those who must pass judgment for admission. It is my view, on the other hand, that limits on the use of the psychological report may be altered by the objectives for which candidates understand they are being tested. If candidates understand beforehand that they are being tested for the dual objectives of screening and counseling during training, I believe that a less restrictive practice in the use of the report can be justified. This, however, raises further practical considerations about safeguarding confidential information, and about how long such information remains reliable, considerations that call for greater attention than they have received up till now.

Seminaries and religious institutes have shown some apprehension about who should conduct the evaluation of priest-candidates. Should the psychologist be a priest? Should he be a member of the same diocese or institute? May a lay person function effectively in this role? If so, must he be a Catholic? Will the lay person need special training to understand the nature of the priest's life? To a lesser extent questions are asked about involving psychiatrists and social workers in the screening evaluation. There are differences of opinion about recommended procedures in these matters. Some dioceses and religious institutes have trained their own priests to do the evaluations or they have other religious psychologists do them. Others employ outside lay consultants, generally Catholic psychologists but sometimes non-Catholics as well. Most would agree today that the primary criterion is that the evaluator be a competent psychodiagnostician, and that other considerations are secondary to this. It is my view that he should also be thoroughly versed in research that has been done on clergymen and that he should be competent in carrying out independent research in his own assessment work.

There are questions, too, about the range of abilities and personality characteristics which priests may possess and still function effectively in their personal and sacerdotal lives. It is generally agreed that the priest-candidate must possess at least the minimal ability necessary for college studies; but in the personality realm, research indicates a broad range of personality characteristics among seminarians and priests, including what appears to be a high degree of pathological-type traits. Are characteristics such as introversion, compulsiveness, dependency, and submissiveness detrimental to effective functioning as a priest? Many seminaries would find themselves with greatly depleted ranks if the psychologist's personality descriptions were rigorously employed as selection criteria, and there is genuine concern about how much reliance should be placed on the reports of candidates who are not suffering clear pathology but who have personal characteristics such as those listed in the foregoing. The concurrent validity of the tests is not so much in question in this matter; the predictive validity is.

SOME QUESTIONS REQUIRING STUDY IN TESTING PROGRAMS FOR PRIESTS

It is evident from the research which has been done as testing programs for priest-candidates have evolved, and from the forthright manner in which the concerns of those who have had serious reservations about testing have been faced, that a substantial amount of progress has been achieved in this work. This has been especially true during the last decade when research efforts multiplied at a rapid rate and when problems peculiar to testing priests and religious came under special study. Still, there are a number of important questions that call for serious consideration. Included among these are questions related to research problems, to problems of extending diagnostic service to a larger number of seminaries, and to improving communication among those who are working in the research and/or service aspects of this field.

Research problems. Of all the matters that require intensive research, none is more difficult or more essential than the criterion problem of specifying what constitutes being a good priest, an effective priest, a well-adjusted priest, or whatever it is that one wants to predict. As stated previously, the most common criterion of success in the studies done on priests is perseverance rate. That this criterion leaves much to be desired from a research-design viewpoint is generally acknowledged, but genuine concern about attrition and the ease of obtaining attrition data have conspired to give it pre-eminence in research. Several attempts have been made to use rating scales as measures of adjustment. Both faculty ratings (McCarthy, 1942; Wauck, 1956; Barry, 1960; Quinn, 1961) and peer ratings (Quinn, 1961) have been used. Quinn's sample, it should be noted, was comprised of teaching-brother candidates while the other samples were seminarians.

The criterion problem admittedly is one of the most difficult in all personnel-selection research, and, as Dittes has observed, ". . . many studies [of clergymen] are really correlating two different types of predictor variables (for example, test results and faculty ratings of promise) rather than a predictor and criterion variable" (Dittes, 1962, p. 158). He goes on to note that Kling (1958) has done substantial work on measures of actual performance for ministers. Similar work has not yet been done in research on priests so far as I know. Until this task is accomplished in a satisfactory way, it will be difficult to expect much progress in predictive validity studies. The work of Davis (1964) in deriving empirical scales to describe the "effective student" is one example of a possible approach to the problem. He had professors list all the behavior which they believe is identified with the notion of being a good student. From several of these lists he was able to derive a number of factors on which ratings could be obtained. This procedure apparently is similar to one used by Stern in his attempt to establish a criterion for the ideal theology student (Dittes, 1962).

While much work is still needed on criterion definition if predictive validity is to be improved, work on new ways of describing personality and behavior is also needed to improve construct validity. There has been a tendency in research on priests to rely heavily on standardized tests such as the MMPI or SVIB for personality descriptions. One problem with the scales of such tests is the fact that they have been empirically derived in a nose-counting way, often without concern for the ways in which items within the scales might be interrelated or for the intrinsic meaning of the items. O'Connor and Stefic (1959), for example, factor-analyzed the Hs scale of the MMPI and identified three primary factors (asthenic reaction, vague somatic complaints, and gastrointestinal reaction) and one second-order factor (poor physical health). Several other MMPI scales have been factored and they also are shown to be functionally complex. In view of these findings, how is one to interpret the meaning of elevated MMPI scores for seminarians? It is one thing to know that seminarians resemble certain clinical groups, but it is quite another matter to know if these high scores are a function of one variable or another within a given scale. In brief, personality descriptions of more factorially pure traits are needed for a fuller understanding of personality characteristics of priest-candidates as compared to others.

Arnold's (1962) ingenious method for measuring motivation through a sequence analysis of TAT themes is an example of a new approach to describing this important aspect of the seminarian's personality. The work of Combs and Soper (1963) in measuring the perceptions and attitudes of effective counselors as compared to less effective counselors is another example of the kind of improvement that is needed in assessment work with priest-candidates.

In effect what Arnold and Combs and Soper have done is to identify and measure variables that have been shown to have a high degree of relevance in understanding behavior. Much more of this innovative kind of work is needed if assessment programs are to be improved.

Another problem that calls for attention is the need to move from the descriptive level to an interpretive level. As noted previously, Dittes and Dunn have proposed psychodynamic interpretations of what the elevated MMPI scores for seminarians might mean. Tentative interpretations about the meaning of the high Mf interest scores and high scores on social-welfare scales that go along with the submissiveness, dependency, and a tendency to be somewhat threatened by people—traits typically found among seminarians—would be useful and enlightening. It is my impression, though not a documented one, that among seminarians there is a much higher proportion of sons of widows than one would find in the general population. If this is true, it might account for the high Mf and social-service scores as a function of identification with the mother.

In this same vein, studies are needed to assess dynamics involved in living the communal life of seminarians and of order priests. Meissner (1965) has highlighted a number of problems that call for study within the framework of group dynamics. Among them are: interpersonal relationships and group solidarity of religious, communication and feedback as necessities for spiritual development, modalities for the discharge of tension, the structuring of group goals, and the dissociative effects of excessive demands.

Service problems. The 1962 ACPA survey of psychologists serving Catholic seminaries made it evident that there is great need to find ways to extend psychological-assessment services to a substantially larger number of dioceses and religious institutes. Some seminaries have responded to this need by training one of their own priests in clinical or counseling psychology. Others have turned to lay psychologists. To the extent that the 1962 survey figures can be accepted as reasonably accurate, it seems safe to surmise that a great many seminaries which might like to initiate or improve candidate-assessment procedures would be hampered by lack of qualified people. At the very least, a new survey probably should be taken now to ascertain the current status of this service to Catholic seminaries and of the qualified manpower available and interested in rendering this service.

The survey also pointed out the need for short training conferences and longer workshops for psychologists interested in learning how to organize and administer candidate-assessment programs. Similar kinds of institutes would be desirable for religious superiors who are responsible for selecting and training seminarians. Research questions and concerns about issues like the right to psychic privacy have occupied the major positions of importance in conferences and publications to date. One important need now is for attention to the practical problems of providing needed service.

Communication problems. Menges and Dittes in their *Psychological Studies of Clergymen* (1965) wrote: ". . . neither is it difficult to demonstrate the relative isolation of researchers within this field. . . . Regrettably and more significantly, examination of almost any of the research reports abstracted here supplied unfortunate evidence of the relative isolation in which each worker has proceeded" (Menges & Dittes, 1965, pp. 11–12). Thus, as they observe, the field as a whole has had no identification within the psychological-research community nor have those carrying out studies been well informed about what others were doing in the same area. Their book of abstracts goes a long way toward remedying that situation, but much more needs to be done.

Most studies in the field have been done as masters' and doctoral dissertations, and frequently these studies are not published. Hence they have a tendency to go unnoticed. Further, most of the studies are highly parochial in that each of the three major religious groups tends to ignore what the other two are doing. This is especially unfortunate since many of the studies have used the same research design, the same measuring instruments, and in some cases have drawn similar conclusions.

An exploration of ways to open up channels of communication is badly needed at this time. Some way must be found to make masters' and doctoral researches more readily available so that new information can be assimilated into the field and so that unnecessary duplication of effort can be avoided. In a similar way, senior workers with different religious groups need some common vehicle for exchanging information. There probably will always be a certain amount of research and writing that belongs in parochial-type journals, but it would be helpful if some agreement could be reached on the types of research and other information relevant to assessment with clergymen that would be useful for all concerned to share. Perhaps this information might then be published in periodicals like the *Journal of Religion and Health* or the *Journal for the Scientific Study of Religion,* or various journals of the American Psychological Association.

REFERENCES

Arnold, M. B. A screening test for candidates for religious life. In Arnold, M. B., *et al. Screening candidates for the priesthood and religious life.* Chicago: Loyola University Press, 1962. Pp. 1–63.

American Psychological Association. Testing and public policy. *American Psychologist,* 1965, *20,* 857–992.

Barry, W. A. An MMPI scale for seminary candidates. Unpublished master's dissertation, Fordham University, 1960.

Bier, W. C. A comparative study of a seminary group and four other groups on the Minnesota Multiphasic Personality Inventory. *Studies in Psychology and Psychiatry,* 1948, *7,* No. 3. Washington: Catholic University of America Press.

Bier, W. C. A comparative study of five Catholic college groups on the MMPI. In Welsh, G. S., and Dahlstrom, W. D. (Eds.) *Basic readings on the MMPI in psychology and medicine.* Minneapolis: University of Minnesota Press, 1956. Pp. 586–609.

Bier, W. C. Psychological tests and psychic privacy. *Proceedings of the Catholic Theological Society of America,* 1962, *17,* 161–179.

Burke, H. R. *Personality traits of successful minor seminarians.* Washington: Catholic University of America Press, 1947.

Combs, W., and Soper, D. W. The perceptual organization of effective counselors. *Journal of Counseling Psychology,* 1963, *10,* 222–226.

Coville, W. J. Psychologists and the assessment of candidates for religious life: Part I. *ACPA Newsletter Supplement,* No. 59, Sept. 1962. (a)

Coville, W. J. Psychologists and the assessment of candidates for religious life: Part II. *ACPA Newsletter Supplement,* No. 60, Nov. 1962. (b)

D'Arcy, P. F. Constancy of interest factor patterns within a specific vocation of foreign missioner. *Studies in Psychology and Psychiatry,* 1954, *9,* No. 1. Washington: Catholic University of America Press.

D'Arcy, P. F. Review of research on the vocational interests of priests, brothers and sisters. In M. B. Arnold, *et al. Screening candidates for the priesthood and religious life.* Chicago: Loyola University Press, 1962. Pp. 149–203.

Davis, J. A. *Faculty perceptions of students*, II. *Faculty definition of desirable student traits*. Princeton: Educational Testing Service, 1964.

Dittes, J. E. Research on clergymen: factors influencing decisions for religious service and effectiveness in the vocation. In S. W. Cook (Ed.) *Review of recent research bearing on religious and character formation*. Research Supplement to *Religious Education*, 1962, *57*, No. 4. Pp. S-141–165.

Dunn, R. F. Personality patterns among religious personnel: a review. *Catholic Psychological Record*, 1965, *3*, 125–137.

Ford, J. C. *Religious superiors, subjects, and psychiatrists*. Westminster, Md.: Newman, 1964.

Friedl, L. P. Vocational interests of successful and unsuccessful seminarians in a foreign-mission society. Unpublished master's dissertation, Catholic University of America, 1952.

Kelley, Sr. Mary W. The incidence of hospitalized mental illness among religious sisters in the United States. *American Journal of Psychiatry*, 1958, *115*, 72–75.

Kennedy, E. C. A comparison of the psychological test scores of successful and unsuccessful major seminarians in a foreign mission seminary. Unpublished master's dissertation, Catholic University of America, 1958.

Kenney, C. E. Differential vocational interest patterns of successful and unsuccessful foreign mission seminarians. Unpublished doctoral dissertation, Loyola University (Chicago), 1959.

Kling, F. R. A study of testing as related to the ministry. *Religious Education*, 1958, *53*, 243–248.

Kobler, F. J. Screening applicants for religious life. *Journal of Religion and Health*, 1964, *3*, 161–170.

Lhota, B. Vocational interests of Catholic priests. *Studies in Psychology and Psychiatry*, 1948, *7*, No. 1. Washington: Catholic University of America Press.

McCarthy, T. J. Personality traits of seminarians. *Studies in Psychology and Psychiatry*, 1942, *7*, No. 4. Washington: Catholic University of America Press.

McCarthy, T. N. Personality trait consistency during the training period for a Roman Catholic congregation of teaching brothers. Unpublished doctoral dissertation, University of Ottawa, 1956.

McCarthy, T. N. Evaluation of the present scientific status of screening for religious vocation. In W. C. Bier and A. A. Schneiders (Eds.) *Selected papers from the ACPA meeting of 1957, 1958, 1959*. New York: American Catholic Psychological Association, 1960. Pp. 35–43.

McCarthy, T. N., and Dondero, E. A. Predictor variables and criteria of success in religious life: needed research. *Catholic Psychological Record*, 1963, *1*, 71–80.

Meissner, W. W. *Group dynamics in the religious life*. Notre Dame: University of Notre Dame Press, 1965.

Menges, R. J., and Dittes, J. E. *Psychological studies of clergymen: abstracts of research*. New York: Nelson, 1965.

Moore, T. V. Insanity in priests and religious: I. The rate of insanity in priests and religious. *American Ecclesiastical Review*, 1936, *95*, 485–498. (a)

Moore, T. V. Insanity in priests and religious: II. Detection of prepsychotics applying for admission to priesthood or religious communities. *American Ecclesiastical Review*, 1936, *95*, 601–613. (b)

Murray, J. B. Training for the priesthood, and personality and interest test manifestations. Unpublished doctoral dissertation, Fordham University, 1957.

O'Connor, J. P., and Stefic, E. C. Some patterns of hypochondriasis. *Educational and Psychological Measurement*, 1959, *19*, 363–371.

Pius XII. Applied Psychology. Address to a congress of the International Association of Applied Psychology, April 10, 1958. *The Pope Speaks*, 1958, *5*, 7–20.

Quinn, T. L. Differences in motivational patterns of college student brothers as revealed in the TAT, the ratings of their peers, and the ratings of their superiors: a comparison. Unpublished doctoral dissertation, Loyola University (Chicago), 1961.

Ristuccia, B. J. The psychologist's report and canon law. In A. A. Schneiders and P. J. Centi (Eds.) *Selected papers from the American Catholic Psychological Association meetings of 1960, 1961*. New York: American Catholic Psychological Association, 1962. Pp. 77–81.

Sacred Congregation of Religious. *The Apostolic Constitution Sedes Sapientiae and the General Statutes of the Sacred Congregation of Religious.* (2nd ed.) Washington: Catholic University of America Press, 1957.

Skrincosky, P. A comparative study of the standard form of the MMPI and a modified form of the same adapted for a seminary group. Unpublished master's dissertation, Fordham University, 1953.

Sweeney, R. H. Testing seminarians with the MMPI and Kuder: A report of ten years of testing. Unpublished master's dissertation, Loyola University (Chicago), 1964.

Wauck, L. A. An investigation of the usefulness of psychological tests in the selection of candidates for the diocesan priesthood. Unpublished doctoral dissertation, Loyola University (Chicago), 1956.

Weisgerber, C. A. Survey of a psychological screening program in a clerical order. In M. B. Arnold, *et al.* *Screening candidates for the priesthood and religious life.* Chicago: Loyola University Press, 1962. Pp. 107–148.

DISCUSSION

Frederick R. Kling: It has been both privilege and pleasure to review Dr. McCarthy's excellent paper on testing for the Catholic priesthood, and especially to note the many parallels with the situation in testing for the Protestant ministry, with which I am more familiar. My first thought as a discussant was to select some of these parallels—such as the concerns about vocational call and psychic privacy or the knotty research problems still defying unraveling—and to direct our attention and discussion towards one or two of these. But so succinct and convincing was Dr. McCarthy's treatment of each of these that I could find no suitable place to catch hold of his reasoning and attempt to stir up any controversy or debate.

Committed as I felt a discussant should be to developing some kind of altercation, I found myself forced to resort with misgiving and appropriate shame to what I at first thought was a very trivial matter of mislabeling a statistical table. Fortunately, my dearth of any other controversial material led me to forsake my habitual laziness and to track down the source of the information, whereupon I discovered that my quarrel was not just a trivial matter between Dr. McCarthy and me, but, on the contrary, a very substantial disagreement with Thomas Verner Moore, the "prime mover" who was instrumental in getting this whole business of testing for the priesthood started. As my indignation mounted, for good reasons which I shall shortly discuss, I learned that it is very difficult to vent one's anger toward the non-present author of a paper of thirty years ago. Thus I find myself in a third phase now, with very hostile attitudes towards Moore's many successors, both in Catholic and non-Catholic circles, who have so uncritically accepted as a basis for their own work his findings that priests are more prone to mental illness than are individuals drawn from the general population.

But let me begin with phase I—my trivial disagreement with Dr. McCarthy. He states that whereas the overall incidence of psychopathology among priests as found by Moore was lower than among the American population as a whole because of the total absence of syphilitic-type disorders among priests, the incidence of schizophrenia, paranoia, manic-depression, and alcoholism among priests was greater than for the American male population in general. These findings—regarding incidences—he says he summarizes in Table I, entitled "Rates of mental illness for priests and men-in-general." *

Now the meaning of incidences in this context is the likelihood that a certain thing is true—for example, that a priest is an alcoholic or a paranoiac. "Rates" can mean many things, but in this context should mean the same thing as "incidences." Now, it is a bit difficult to believe that 21 percent of all priests are hospitalized alcoholics, or that 29 percent are schizophrenics, even though this is the meaning that is necessary to the argument of Dr. McCarthy's paper. Consequently, the intended meaning must be the proportion of those hospitalized who have a particular diagnosis. If the overall hospitalization incidence for mental illnesses for priests and for men-in-general were given, it would be possible to recompute the

* See p. 49.

real incidence of each type of illness for priests and for men-in-general and to make a judgment about the truthfulness of the assertion that priests are more prone to certain illnesses. But it is not given, and one is left with the overall false impression of the table: that priests are in much worse shape than men-in-general. And it is this false impression which people have believed, sought to explain, and acted upon, and which I, too, would simply have accepted were it not for the excellence of Dr. McCarthy's paper in other respects.

Instead, I located Thomas Verner Moore's original paper, and I was appalled at what I found. Although Moore presents some ten elaborate tables, and does in fact draw the very type of conclusions —with their alarmist overtones—that Dr. McCarthy indicates were instrumental in initiating the interest in testing Catholic candidates for religious vocations, I could not find among the data he reported any adequate justification for the conclusions he reached. What I did find was the following:

1. That the percentages in question are not incidences, but are indeed proportions of those who are ill, and that they are drawn from more complete breakdowns containing 27 categories for the general population and only 14 categories for priests. Clearly, where there are fewer categories, the percentages for each category must in general be higher. In one case—alcoholism—there is a clear-cut division of the general population into patients with psychosis and patients without psychosis; but only the first of these is used as a comparison group for all hospitalized priests with alcoholism.

2. That the percentages are not comparable for a far more basic reason: those for priests and religious are based on all such hospitalized patients at a given moment in time, however long they may have been ill; however, those for the population in general are based exclusively on first admissions during the year 1933 in U.S. mental hospitals. It would be my expectation that long-term types of illnesses—not to mention diagnoses—would quite naturally be much more prevalent for the former base than for the latter. In any case, Moore's careful calculations of the degree to which the priests and religious percentages deviate significantly from the

general population percentages are completely meaningless, because of the different bases involved.

3. That where Moore does report truly comparable figures, they consistently indicate that the priestly population is much healthier than the general population. In terms of admission rates per 100,000, he reports 122 for priests, 124 for nuns, and 70 for brothers, to be compared with 214 for the State of Massachusetts, 357 for the U.S. Navy, and a deviously derived figure of 740 for the U.S. Army.* In terms of patients in hospitals per 100,000 population, he reports 446 for priests, 485 for nuns, and 418 for brothers, to be compared with 591 for Massachusetts and 600 for New York. So far as I can determine, these are the only comparable figures relevant to the point of the supposedly greater tendency of priests and religious toward mental illnesses in all the data Moore reported. To me, in the absence of any better statistics, they overwhelmingly indicate the diametrically opposite conclusion—a lesser tendency toward mental illnesses.

4. That Moore's conclusion "that the total incidence of insanity is so much lower [among priests and religious] than in the general population is due to the fact that the syphilitic types are absent" is unsupported by his data. In his only data dealing with diagnostic percentages for the general population, the "first admissions," only 1.9 percent of the male and 1.1 percent of the female diagnoses are clearly of a syphilitic etiology.† If Moore had any data indicating that some larger proportion of general-population cases were "syphilitic types," he fails to mention them. But discounting 2 percent, or even 5 or 10 percent, of the general-population cases would still result in a healthier prognosis for priests and religious than for the general population.

So much for Phase II of my quarrel. Let me move on to Phase III and inquire why it is that the unsubstantiated conclusions

---

* Dr. English has given us another figure for comparison—a rate of about 700 per 100,000 Peace Corps returns from foreign service for psychiatric reasons.

† Dr. Arnold is of the opinion that Moore might legitimately have regarded up to 11 percent of the male and 5 percent of the female diagnostic categories as syphilitic types because of the fact that in 1933 the term "general paralysis" did refer to syphilitic types. These proportions would still not justify his conclusions.

reached by Moore have stood so long unexposed and uncorrected. Indeed, how can it be that in 1966 in surveying the entire field of testing for the Catholic priesthood, Dr. McCarthy can write that interpretations of Moore's data up to now have "accepted the fact of the differences in rates as a valid comment on the incidence of psychological disorder among priests" and that "the major concern for the past thirty years has been to find reasons why priests as a group deviate from the general norm"? Has no one previously read Moore's paper with a critical eye? Has no one seen fit to replicate the study and to make sure that priests are in fact more prone to mental illness before encouraging the emergence of a new discipline to investigate reasons for the supposed proneness? Are self-reproach and abasement so fashionable among religious circles that we prefer to direct our scientific acumen towards finding out why we are in such sad shape before questioning whether we really are in sad shape in the first place? **

Dr. McCarthy's recounting of the history of testing for the Catholic priesthood places great importance on the influence of Moore's paper. He does, however, cite other factors which contributed to the movement to test and screen candidates for the priesthood. Even if Moore's conclusions are false—and all I can report is that I find them totally unsubstantiated and probably very misleading—

** The point raised by Rev. Kling with respect to Moore's work, although embarrassing to those who had uncritically accepted his findings, seemed to most of those present at the Conference to be a matter more of historical interest than of current significance. A replication of Moore's work with respect to Catholic sisterhoods was conducted for the hospital year January 1, 1956 to December 31, 1956 by Kelley (1958). She reported finding less hospitalization for mental illness among Sisters than among women-in-general. Other investigators (Kelley, 1961; McAllister & Vander Veldt, 1961, 1965; Vander Veldt & McAllister, 1962) have studied hospitalized mental illness among Roman Catholic clergy and religious without, however, the comparative references to other groups which was a prominent feature of Moore's initial work. Quite apart from these formal studies, the existence of psychological disorder among Catholic clergy and religious was evident enough to justify the introduction of psychological testing of applicants as a partial attempt to deal with it. Whether hospitalization for psychological disorder was more or less frequent among the clergy than among the general population seemed to be a matter of secondary importance. The problem was real enough. Actually, Moore's misinterpretation of his data, as pointed up by Rev. Kling, was something of a *felix culpa*, to the extent to which it contributed to an earlier interest on the part of Catholic groups in the psychological assessment of seminary candidates than would otherwise have been the case.—Ed.

they may nevertheless have initiated productive inquiry and a valuable service both to the Church and to the religious candidate himself. What I should like to see is that inquiry and that service carried forward, free from the atmosphere of morbidity and alarmism which I find to be one of the most striking but completely unnecessary parallels between Catholic and non-Catholic testing of religious candidates.

GENERAL DISCUSSION

Discussion of Moore's Study: At the opening of the discussion, Dr. McCarthy pointed out that the people at Catholic University who did the early studies prompted by Moore's research recognized from the beginning that there was a question about the extent to which Moore's findings could be generalized to all priests. That was one of the reasons for their studies. It is a fact, however, that the interest in this work among Catholics originated with Moore's paper, correctly or incorrectly interpreted.

Discussion turned for a time to interpretation of specific items in Moore's reported data as quoted by Dr. McCarthy and Rev. Kling. Fr. Bier directed attention toward some of the larger issues raised by this basic study. He considered one of the big problems to be the interpretation of the profiles emerging from studies of the characteristic groups that Dr. McCarthy had talked about. For example, in the finding that priests and seminarians are more submissive, introspective, passive, and perfectionistic than people in general, it should be noted that the criteria used in these evaluations are those set up for the general population. The evaluations should be reinterpreted to take into account the differences in goals to which this special group is committed from those of the general population.

In his work on this subject, Fr. Bier had developed a modified form of the MMPI. He proceeded on the assumption that with a large enough group of seminarians or applicants for the seminary the scores on any of the MMPI scales would distribute themselves roughly normally. He had found the assumption borne out in research on the basis of populations of 1,000 cases, which seemed to imply that members of this special group are as well adjusted for the kind of life they propose to enter as are people in the general population for the kind of life they intend to follow.

Broader issues involved: Out of the immediate context of discussion on Moore's paper, the following more general points were made:

A. Norms should be established not only for the clergy as separate from the general population, but for subgroups of the clergy—religious subgroups, such as the different Protestant denominations and the various orders within Roman Catholicism—and also for groups of different experience. Follow-up studies that Dr. Douglas and his colleagues had done relating scores on the MMPI and on the Edwards Personal Preference Schedule show that certain group shifts take place at different points, such as when the person enters the seminary, when he leaves it, and again when he is in the active ministry. It appears from these studies that the clergy are closer to the general norms than are seminarians. On other scales or indicators, however, the active clergy are more different from the general-population norms than are the seminarians.*

In addition to the criterion problems, another participant proposed that the mind-set of people as they approach their evaluation of the ministry is important. If there is a feeling among those who are served by the professional church as a whole that there is a certain brittleness about the ministry and that ministers cannot be evaluated objectively, what does this do to the studies of the role of the parish minister? How does it affect the responses of church people to questions about the minister's task, personality, and effectiveness? If, on the other hand, the people questioned are merely the professionals, the journalists who express their point of view in popular magazines, etc., this fact reveals something about the kind of problems we choose to look at when we evaluate the minister. Perhaps the studies of the ministry should contain a kind of inquiry that would bring out the basic feeling about the minister in terms of his level of emotional functioning. It would be helpful to know whether the people in a given church see the minister in

---

* This is part of an on-going career development study being conducted by Dr. Douglas. There are, as yet, no published results.—Ed.

a certain way, or whether the persons studying him see him that way: i.e., the outcome of the studies will be determined by this kind of mind-set.

B. The cultural ethos has an influence on the kind of research done and on its interpretation. There is often a resistance to data showing that widely held notions about the health and functioning of certain groups are not substantiated by investigation. There seems to be a great cultural investment in believing that there is morbidity, sickness, conflict, etc.

C. Though the need to move from the descriptive level to the interpretive level of research is valid, it is notable that description tends to become mixed up with interpretation and evaluation. One participant believed that there was need for more descriptive studies.

A psychologist added that good descriptions are hard to come by. He suggested that a valuable source would be to get descriptions from the analytic case histories of individual priests. Some of the work done by Dr. Bartemeier and his colleagues in Baltimore has shown that much of what is known about people and the guidelines used in the interpretation of projective techniques in depth derive from what Freud discovered in his analysis of individuals. Some profiles in depth would enable examiners to make better use of their tests, to analyze them in relation to some of the fundamental personality structures with defenses and adaptations.

D. Because of a possible vulnerability of psychiatrists and psychologists to the engagement of their professional skills in their concern about the mental health or the problems of a particular population, it may be that members of these disciplines have tended to foster the alarmist attitude that Rev. Kling had mentioned. Perhaps they have been too concerned with narrow data instead of interpreting the data in the light of the total system. For example, the prediction that fewer than half of the students entering college this year will complete the four years is remarkable. It has been suggested that half of that attrition rate will be the result of psychological factors.

The experience of the Peace Corps is that of the .7 percent of its volunteers who require termination of their services for psy-

chiatric reasons, only about .3 or .4 percent will require hopsital-
ization during the acute stage. The average length of hospitalization
is ten days. The morbidity beyond the acute episode is slight. The
Peace Corps interprets this as due to the basic health of the people
put under stress and the kind of treatment given in the acute phase.
These facts lead to the conclusion that psychiatrists and psychologists
may more readily pick up pathological manifestations, often missing
the parameters of health that may be even better if one knew
how to understand them within the total cultural framework.

E. It appears that the fragmentation that occurs when a person
has completed his training and enters upon his duties may decrease
the effectiveness of his functioning. The Peace Corps has found
that volunteers who did particularly well in the training period do
not always do equally well under the stress of the field situation.
Apparently they needed the group support of the training community. The person who is somewhat abrasive in the midst of
community support will often be more effective in the relative
isolation of the field, where he is left to his own resources. The
same kind of fragmentation may, it was suggested, operate in the
case of the seminarian when he is sent to an assignment in the
ministry.

A somewhat similar process of fragmentation has been observed
in the course of psychoanalysis, a psychologist noted. Patients who,
in the earlier period of analysis, appear to be on the verge of
a psychotic break do not actually become psychotic. As autistic
fantasy and much tension and anxiety come out, a process of disorganization and fragmentation occurs. But this period of disinte-
gration is preparatory to a reorganization of the personality. There
is self-confrontation as the person comes to grips with what he
has been repressing. Therefore, when persons in the process of
professional development appear to be disturbed, it is necessary to
distinguish between the one who is seriously psychopathological
and the one who has enough flexibility and resiliency to achieve a
resynthesis on a higher level as the result of having passed through
such turbulence.

F. A possible reason for some failures to spot candidates who
are going to encounter difficulties later, a priest-psychologist sug-

gested, is that the screening process, even if it extends over a period of several days, catches the candidate at a particular period, one of stress because he has just made a perhaps tentative decision about what he will do with his life, and in a temporary, probably depressed state. Even when supplemented by interviews and case histories and other biographical material, the short and anxiety-filled period is likely to give a somewhat inaccurate view of the candidate's real personality.

Another point concerned elevated MMPI profiles sometimes found in seminarians. The same psychologist suggested that, after some years in the seminary, men may become more introspective and self-critical; therefore in responding to the MMPI they admit many unfavorable things about themselves that they would not have admitted when they were candidates. Hence it may be that, in assessing people at various stages in their seminary training and later, examiners may have data that cannot be trusted because they are contaminated by a response set of this kind.

Dr. McCarthy's response to the discussion: Dr. Dittes raised questions about two parts of Dr. McCarthy's paper. First, Dr. Dittes reiterated his statement of the unresolved elementary research problems and how little, especially about prediction, he was willing to say could be done with confidence. Then there was Dr. McCarthy's description of a fairly elaborate testing program that he presumably endorses. From a research point of view, Dr. Dittes believed that the collection of data that psychologists and others concerned with selection like to use raises ethical questions about the possible good that such a testing program does to the candidate and to the institution that is paying for the program. He wondered how Dr. McCarthy justified this expenditure of effort.

Dr. McCarthy replied that he viewed this question in the light of the objectives of the assessment program. He believed that one of the genuine contributions the psychologist can make is to describe what *is* about a person—his typical ways of adjusting, his interests, his motivations, his abilities, and the like. This describing of the salient personality features is frequently confused with the actual decision about accepting or rejecting a candidate. It is important to remember that the psychologist does not normally have the final say with regard to the candidate's starting his career. His opinion may be the major determining one, but it is not final. His first task, therefore, is to provide relevant information to the person who is to make the judgment of the candidate's suitability, information that could not be obtained so easily and quickly in any other way. Having this information at the beginning of the training period enables the seminary director to eliminate the severely sick, the homosexual, the psychotic, and other unqualified persons.

The evaluation also has value for the seminaries that choose to use it in helping the seminarian's formation. The use of information obtained through the candidate-appraisal program for counseling those who are accepted rather than simply for the elimination of doubtful cases presents certain problems. Even recognizing these problems, however, Dr. McCarthy believed that the benefits outweigh the difficulties. The evaluation often reveals attitudes of a candidate that, if examined and clarified in a counseling relationship, may lead to a better understanding. Counseling based on such information may also help the seminarian to understand how his attitudes, viewpoints, and the like may influence his ministry and the relationships to the people with whom he will eventually be working.

Dr. McCarthy thought that being asked to make a judgment, in the absence of clear evidence of pathology, about the likelihood of a certain candidate's turning out to be an effective priest presented one of the greatest difficulties now, because there is not sufficient empirical evidence to warrant making such judgments. In exercising his authority to make these judgments, however, the seminary director has two basic pieces of information to aid him: his knowledge of the seminary situation and the psychological information on the individual candidate. Though the decision of how to put these two pieces of information together rests ultimately with the seminary authority, generally, Dr. McCarthy believed, it is more effectively done through collaboration with the psychologist.

In his summary to the discussion of his paper, Dr. McCarthy first addressed an answer to Dr. Steinberg's query about feedback by remarking that there is great difference of practice among the various religious groups he served, ranging from no feedback at all to very extensive feedback, both for those rejected and those accepted.

Several participants had expressed concern about testing at given periods and thus getting different pictures of the personality. Fortunately there is good literature on this subject. Although most of the studies are cross-sectional, a few are longitudinal. In both designs one finds the differences mentioned. Dr. McCarthy's doctoral dissertation dealt with this subject (McCarthy, 1956). During the formation of a Catholic teaching brother, one finds an increase in withdrawal and other psychological changes as he goes through his training. The changes seem to center on critical choice points in the training period, and they seem to be situationally appropriate.

Dr. McCarthy agreed with the statement that the only correct interpretation is the one made in relation to the situation in which the individual finds himself. It is important to keep this in mind.

Finally, it seemed to Dr. McCarthy that when many of the programs started there was a hope that accumulating this psychological information would eliminate some of the difficulties in decisions that have to be made about a prospective seminarian. Instead, he thought that the seminaries were finding the same thing that happens with greater education: increased information often multiplies decisions, rather than decreasing them. This fact has tended to create tensions rather than to reduce them.

REFERENCES

Kelley, M. W. The incidence of hospitalized mental illness among religious sisters in the U.S. *American Journal of Psychiatry*, 1958, *115*, 72–75.

Kelley, M. W. Depression in the psychoses of members of religious communities of women. *American Journal of Psychiatry*, 1961, *118*, 423–425.

McAllister, R. J., & Vander Veldt, A. J. Factors in mental illness among hospitalized clergy. *Journal of Nervous and Mental Disease*, 1961, *132*, 80–88.

McAllister, R. J., & Vander Veldt, A. J. Psychiatric illness in hospitalized Catholic religious. *American Journal of Psychiatry*, 1965, *121*, 881–884.

McCarthy, T. N. Personality trait consistency during the training period for a Roman Catholic congregation of teaching brothers. Unpublished doctoral dissertation, University of Ottawa, 1956.

Vander Veldt, A. J., & McAllister, R. J. Psychiatric illness in hospitalized clergy: alcoholism. *Quarterly Journal of Studies of Alcohol*, 1962, *28*, 124–130.

TESTING FOR THE PROTESTANT MINISTRY

JAMES B. ASHBROOK*

THE ISSUE OF PSYCHOLOGICAL TESTING for the screening and selection of Protestant ministers needs to be set within the larger context of psychological testing generally.

Nineteen-sixty-five turned out to be the year of public barrage. Previously, attacks had stressed *The tyranny of testing* (Hoffman, 1962), brain watching (Gross, 1962), and the naked society (Packard, 1964). An earlier polemic decried the mediocre, cookie-cut conformity of *The Organization Man* (Whyte, 1956). By 1965 public agitation culminated in two congressional committees investigating uses and abuses of "psychological tests." The personality inventories, especially the Minnesota Multiphasic Personality Inventory, bore the brunt of criticism over "invasion of privacy."

Appearing before the Senate Judiciary's subcommittee on con-

* The author is indebted to a number of people. His understanding of research for Protestant clergymen has been dependent upon contact and discussion with other members of the Research Council of the Ministry Studies Board: Kenneth H. Breimeier, Clifford E. Davis, Harry DeWire, James E. Dittes, Samuel Z. Klausner, Frederick R. Kling, Edgar W. Mills, and Donald E. Super. Others including Charles F. Kemp, James N. Lapsley, and Carroll A. Wise also shared their thinking with the author.

stitutional rights, Brayfield (1965) represented the consensus of the American Psychological Association. His testimony centered on the nature of testing. The intent is the humane use of human resources. The origins reside in the scientific study of human variability. Since assessment of human beings is always taking place, testing attempts to reduce errors of judgment based on the lack of objective data. Such procedure increases the accuracy of conventional methods of unaided human judgment from 5 to 15 percent (Brayfield, 1965). Appropriate use of tests, however, depends upon qualified administration and evaluation as well as the availability of a variety of data in decision-making.

Psychologists have long been cognizant of the limitations of testing. High-school and college grades constitute the most efficient predictions, yet these coefficients fall within the range from .40 to .60. At best, tests tend to be imprecise instruments which allow only broad, general statements with a wide range of error (Goldman, 1961, p. 175). The sphere of uncertainty increases as we look at the less objective criterion of occupational "success." Apparently, whatever "success" means, it can be reached by such a variety of abilities, behaviors, and characteristics that predictors are of "limited usefulness" (Goldman, 1961, p. 183).

The history of large-scale assessment procedures is sobering (O. S. S. Assessment Staff, 1948; Kelly & Fiske, 1951; Holt & Luborsky, 1958). Only the Peace Corps stands out as an exception* (Carp, 1965). Vernon spent a year at the Center for Advanced Study on the Behavioral Sciences critically surveying conflicting viewpoints regarding personality structure and methods for its measurement in assessment (Vernon, 1964). Taking as his major criterion whether a given instrument permits more accurate predictions about people, he found no evidence supporting the superiority of clinical methods over naïve approaches. Objective approaches proved equally unfruitful because of such variables as social desirability, acquiescence, and other test-taking attitudes. A review of the volume concluded:

* The selecting-"in" and selecting-"out" decisions were determined on the basis of a wide variety of information, observation, an intermediate selection-board decision, and a final selection-board decision. In addition, the criterion is not a projected long-term career prediction, but for a two-year period.

In spite of considerable effort by the author and occasional testimony
to the contrary, the complex and unsatisfactory state of the field proves
overwhelming, leaving the reader with a pessimistic feeling about the
value of personality assessment in practical situations [Holtzman, 1965,
pp. 509–510].

Our overview of testing suggests certain conclusions. Testing constitutes a responsible approach to human variability and task com-
plexity. At best, it tends to be imprecise in what it measures and
limited in what it predicts. It can neither be dismissed as worthless
nor embraced as panacea. Testing represents one approach that
holds out possibility, however slight, for reducing the extent to
which judgments are based on inaccurate data.

We now ask: what has been the picture of testing among Protestants? Are any procedures producing desired results?

WHAT HAS HAPPENED

During the 1920s and early 1930s, the scientific method in sociology and psychology was first employed in examining ministerial
functioning and church life (May, 1934; Douglass & Brunner,
1935). Missionary societies found the expense of sending out "misfits" too costly to treat casually. They pioneered in using psychological tools in their assessment procedures as auxiliary to theological considerations (Higdon, 1956; Masserman, 1955; Masserman &
Palmer, 1961; Saxe, 1959; Williams, 1958). The screening of missionary candidates will not be considered because of the special
focus of that task. By the end of World War II, increasing interest
among churchmen centered upon possibilities held out by psychological testing (Billinsky & Guilles, 1947, Davis, 1950; Froyd,
1956). Because so little research has been done with Negro seminarians and ministers, this paper will deal only with white seminarians and ministers.

Denominational Programs. Among denominations, the most extensive and intense use of testing for screening has been in the Protestant Episcopal Church. A church canon directs that an applicant
submit to an "examination that shall cover the man's mental and

nervous as well as his physical condition." Since 1949, the House of Bishops has interpreted that to include a "psychological examination and urged examiners to use, whenever possible, psychological and psychodynamic tests as part of their examinations" (Booth, 1960, p. 102). In light of the evidence such a blanket requirement appears open to question.

Booth has been the best known of the examiners for the Protestant Episcopal Church (Booth, 1963). Over a 24-year period he conducted 400 examinations of first-year students of General Theological Seminary in New York and postulants of the Diocese of Newark, New Jersey. From a detailed study in 1953 of the first 163 tested he concluded that the procedures used "yielded satisfactory results," though what "satisfactory" meant was not specified. He made no follow-up in terms of specific criteria.

Without going into detail about Booth's procedure certain conclusions stand out. In 1960 he suggested that:

only rarely are candidates to be eliminated on the basis of serious pathology;
undesirable traits appear among the satisfactory candidates as well as among the unsatisfactory candidates;
the strength of undesirable traits cannot be measured accurately;
eliminating candidates "on the basis of psychiatric classifications would deprive the church of some of its most valuable ministers."

In 1963, despite the laboriousness of the procedure, Booth still insisted on its practicality. However, questions persist. He pinpointed the precariousness of prediction in the unknown interaction of the individual with the attitudes and expectations of significant others. Consider his conclusion:

This task has always appeared to me extremely difficult, rather more so with the increasing amount of experience. Sometimes I have been assailed by doubts as to whether the results warranted the efforts; but again there were experiences that reassured me. Some of them were among the most rewarding experiences of my professional life [Booth, 1963, p. 272].

We sense here a sensitive, conscientious clinician looking back on almost a quarter-century of testing, and wondering whether the results justified the effort. The task grew in difficulty in direct ratio to his experience. What he refers to as reassuring and rewarding appears to be therapeutic relationships, not decisions about screening-"in" or screening-"out." For him, testing must be linked with therapy.

A careful follow-up of Episcopal procedures was conducted by Douglas (1957) for the Diocese of Massachusetts, as an extension of a smaller validation study by Allport & Fairbanks (1953). Douglas' sample consisted of 45 men who had been accepted and ordained since 1949. For the first time a systematic effort was made to include lay people in the appraisal, in addition to ecclesiastical authorities. While differential effectiveness in pastoral and administrative roles could be understood and predicted, "no adequate method of putting the pieces back together again into an estimate of total effectiveness" could be found (Douglas, 1957, p. 157). Because no single type of minister could be regarded as the norm, and because no single type of personality could be rejected automatically, the day seemed far off when computers would replace bishops (Douglas, 1957, p. 160).

The United Presbyterian Church U.S.A. developed two batteries of recruitment (Froyd, 1956). One was a simple battery for "preliminary counseling" on the local level. The other was more extensive, recommended for men taken under the care of presbytery and required of applicants to denominational seminaries. About five percent of those tested appeared to have personality and academic problems which made the ministry "inadvisable"; about 33 percent had minor personality difficulties (Davis, 1950). However, testing is used for counseling, not screening. The American Baptist Convention has contracted with the Presbyterians to use their services for Baptist applicants to the seminary.

The United Lutheran Church initially modeled its program on the Presbyterian pattern. Recently they have moved away from the "psychometric" approach to one in which the candidate is dealt with on several bases in addition to test scores. The testing is sequential. The Strong Vocational Interest Blank and the Minnesota Multiphasic Personality Inventory are administered to candidates, usually in the sophomore year of college. The MMPI is readministered in the senior year along with the Miller Analogies Test. About 35 percent of those tested required additional attention. The Wechsler Adult Intelligence Scale, Rorschach, and House-Tree-Person tests are administered and problems dealt with by a clinical psychologist.

From 1955 to 1958 Harrower (1963, 1964) tested 135 entering Unitarian-Universalist seminary students. She developed Scales of Mental Health Potential derived from performance scores on eight psychodiagnostic tests. These were correlated with lay and denominational evaluations of ministers still in the parish six to seven years later. All that can be said with confidence is that the battery indicated that "the most seriously disturbed" would be "poor risks." It failed to differentiate in any clear way among the successful (+), the basically successful (+?), and the questionable (?) ministers. She concluded:

. . . it would seem that psychological tests and our concepts of positive mental health potential give us no clue as to which students will voluntarily withdraw, decide on a teaching career in the religious field, enter a different denomination, or leave the ministerial field completely [Harrower, 1964, p. 58].

A summary of denominational programs suggests the following:

1. Most of the work has been done by those denominations with more clearly defined doctrines of church and ministry (Protestant Episcopal Church, United Lutheran Church, Lutheran Church Missouri Synod, United Presbyterian Church U.S.A.), or by those denominations with doctrines more culturally adapted (Unitarian-Universalist Churches). In the former instance we have conceptual clarity; in the latter cultural adequacy. The rest of the denominations, in the more doctrinally ambiguous middle ground, have done little as denominations.

2. A survey of structures and procedures for guiding ministerial candidates based on 129 replies from 10 denominations indicated "low priority given to the need for objective measures to assist in the process of assessment."

3. The results of predictions based on psychological screening for ministerial performance generally are discouraging.

4. Where psychometric instruments are used a great deal of descriptively normative data is accumulating, but the data are not linked with other criteria.

Seminary Activity. Even though testing in theological schools has been extensive, the picture appears confused. A survey conducted in 1961 by the Ministry Studies Board (Table 1) disclosed that in

TABLE 1. TESTS USED BY FIVE OR MORE THEOLOGICAL SCHOOLS*

Test	No. of Schools	Per-centage
Minnesota Multiphasic Personality Inventory	52	58
Strong Vocational Interest Blank	28	31
Structured-Objective Rorschach Test	17	19
Miller Analogies Test	15	17
Graduate Record Examination	14	17
Ohio State Psychological (all forms)	13	15
Guilford-Zimmerman Temperament Survey	9	10
California Test of Mental Maturity	7	8
Bernreuter Personality Inventory	7	8
Thematic Apperception Test	5	6
Allport-Vernon-Lindzey Study of Values	5	6
Wechsler Adult Intelligence Scale	5	6
Otis-Lennon Mental Ability Test	5	6

* Ministry Studies Board, *Newsletter*, April, 1962.

89 schools answering the questionnaire and using instruments (19 additional schools used no tests) 72 different instruments were being administered: 30 personality inventories, 25 achievement tests, 17 vocational and interest tests. Each school averaged 3.7 tests. Table 1 shows the most frequently used. Not only was there a conglomeration of instruments present, but changes were frequent. During the preceding five years, 32 schools had made changes, usually dropping one instrument in favor of another. The testing was used primarily for guidance and counseling rather than for screening.

A summary of available seminary studies and information indicates:

1. Value orientation based on the Allport-Vernon-Lindzey *Study of Values*. In contrast to college men in general, seminarians tend to be more religiously and socially oriented and less theoretically, economically, and politically oriented. Non-persisting seminarians scored slightly lower on the economic scales and significantly higher on aesthetic scale (Maehr & Stake, 1962).

2. Grade-point average and seminary academic performance. College grade-point average is generally the best predictor of seminary achievement, but exceptions are too numerous for individual prediction (Breimeier, 1948; Cockrum, 1952; Richards, 1957; Webb & Goodling, 1958). Reading skills of vocabulary and a speed of more than 240–300 words per minute are necessary (Cockrum, 1952; Webb & Goodling, 1958; Knowles, 1959). Those who deviate from MMPI norms tend not to perform in line with measured academic potential (Webb & Goodling, 1958; Ashbrook, 1962; Ingram, 1963).

Faculty ratings of personality effectiveness and potential correlate above .70 with grade-point average (Goodling & Webb, 1959; Ashbrook, 1962).

3. Intelligence, interest, personality, overall effectiveness. Personality, intelligence, overall effectiveness, and field-work ratings are highly intercorrelated (Goodling & Webb, 1959; Ashbrook, 1962). The Lawyer scale on the Strong Vocational Interest Blank showed highly significant correlations with intelligence, personality, and overall effectiveness (Goodling & Webb, 1959).

Stern, Stein, and Bloom (1956) conducted the most impressive assessment program of seminarians. They evaluated three desirable and three undesirable students as judged by a faculty. Since successful seminarians are not *ipso facto* successful ministers, the significance of the study lies in the methodology of the team. They extended the concept of job analysis to embrace the total situation: the person being assessed, the social and interpersonal demands of the setting, and the standards (expectation values) of those who evaluated the job performance.

The most significant research among Protestants has been the

Theological School Inventory.* The TSI was developed by Kling (1958) to determine the strength and type of motivation for the ministry characteristic of men entering theological schools. Three of the twelve scales estimate the strength and nature of the call to the ministry; one the concept of the call; one a personality measure; while the others assess "categories of motivation"—i.e., particular aspects of the ministry or conscious reasons of the individual which make it attractive. Additional data include biographical background and expressions of confidence in meeting ten characteristic roles of the parish ministry. The norms of the Inventory were based on a sample of 2,300 students in 53 theological schools (Dittes, 1964). Smaller samples were used in correlating TSI scores with selected items of biographical information (Kling, Pierson & Dittes, 1963),† student self-report of motivation and interviewer ratings (Dittes & DeWire, 1963), personal background, performance in seminary, and post-seminary vocational choice (Dittes, 1963a), and TSI score changes during seminary (Dittes, 1963b).

The TSI is not considered a predictive instrument. Rather it aims primarily at the guidance and counseling of students. Dittes states the fact unequivocally:

Generalization from any reported finding to a particular student needs to be done with great caution, and with the expectation that the generalization is more likely to be wrong than right, especially if it is applied to a particular decision in a non-reflective manner [Dittes, 1964, p. 6].

The face validity of the TSI, as assessed by the correspondence between the test profile and the self-ranking and faculty-rating of motivation for a student, was most discernible for Intellectual Concern (I) and Evangelistic Witness (E). All seven of the correlations, however, were statistically significant, indicative of substantial correspondence (Dittes & DeWire, 1963). The inventory appears able to assist the student in seeing his conscious or preconscious

* Appreciation is expressed to J. E. Dittes for reading the section on TSI for accuracy.
† This and the following three research bulletins referred to in the text are furnished with the TSI Manual *Vocational Guidance of Theological Students* by Dittes (1964).—Ed.

motivations more clearly. While the correlations between TSI scores and such criteria as dropout of school, placement index, grades, and rated effectiveness in ministerial demands tended to be significant, they proved to be low (Dittes, 1963a).

Some evidence suggested that individuals scoring low on Definiteness (D), Natural Leading (NL), or Special Leading (SL) scales are "less likely" to stay in school or enter the parish ministry than those who score high. An examination of the correlations in different schools discloses the need for caution in such generalization. Table 2 shows the correlations for seven schools with N of 497.

TABLE 2. CORRELATION IN DIFFERENT SCHOOLS BETWEEN TSI SCORES AND PLACEMENT INDEX (LARGE SAMPLE)*

	Brite	CRDS	Drew	Southern Baptist	Union	United	Yale	Total Sample
N =	41	39	81	105	83	49	99	497
D (Definiteness)	−.26	−.20	.20	.08	.16	.29	.22	.15
NL (Natural Leading)	−.11	.00	.15	−.03	.10	.07	.15	.08
SL (Special Leading)	−.43	−.18	.09	.40	.02	.04	.20	.12
CC (Concept of Call)	−.15	−.16	.04	.10	.11	.21	−.05	.10
for p = .05 r =	.30	.31	.22	.19	.22	.28	.20	.09

* Dittes, 1963a, Table 2. The placement index assumed that post-seminary choice ranges along a single scale with dropouts scored as 1, non-religious work as 2, non-pastoral religious work as 3, non-parish pastoral work as 4, parish work as 5.

Only five of the 21 correlations were significant at the .05 level. Three of the seven schools had no significant correlations. Special Leading (SL) correlated −.33 at Brite, .40 at Southern Baptist, .20 at Yale, and .12 for the total sample with parish placement index. Students scoring high on SL at Brite are interpreted as being less likely to go into the parish ministry, while students scoring high on SL at Southern Baptist are interpreted as being more likely to go into the parish ministry. Even though the r of .12 for the total sample was significant at the .05 level, it can hardly be considered substantial.

A tentative interpretation of Social Reform (R) suggested that higher scores tend "to show greater interest in other ministries than the parish" (Dittes, 1964, p. 65). An examination of the evidence for the inference discloses a correlation of −.14 for preference for the parish and away from teaching, just barely significant at the .05 level (Kling, Pierson, & Dittes, 1963, table 1). Interest in the following types of ministry showed nonsignificant correlations with Social Reform (R) of −.11 for the parish, .10 for missions, −.07 for minister of religious education, .02 for chaplaincy, and .11 for teaching ministry (Dittes, 1963a, table 12). When R is combined with D, NL, and SL, patterns of prediction may be mutually supportive even though correlations be low. Prediction, however, must be very cautious.

Other examples could be cited to underscore the point that the relationship between TSI scores and such objective criteria as entering the parish ministry or some other type of religious work is rather tenuous. While a significance level of .05 may be useful research, it is certainly questionable in prediction when the size of the correlation ranges from .09 to .13 for the total sample. Dittes is right: "generalization is more likely to be wrong than right"!

Differences among theological schools are highlighted by the mean TSI scores for each school. Similarities are also apparent. Consider the mean scores for the two schools shown in Table 3. Concordia Lutheran scores were slightly higher on Definiteness (D), Natural Leading (NL), Special Leading (SL), and Concept

TABLE 3. MEAN TSI SCORES FOR COLGATE–ROCHESTER DIVINITY SCHOOL AND CONCORDIA LUTHERAN SEMINARY*

	N	D	NL	SL	CC	FL	A	I	F	L	E	R	P
CRDS	36	52.6	47.2	47.5	46.3	59.6	8.0	14.7	11.3	11.3	9.6	11.9	16.3
CLS	125	55.4	49.2	48.9	47.6	46.9	10.8	10.9	9.9	11.4	18.4	8.6	13.4

* Dittes, 1964, adapted from Appendix II, Table 2.

of Call (CC); considerably higher on Acceptance by Others (A) and Evangelistic Witness (E); and considerably lower on Flexibility (FL), Intellectual concern (I), Social Reform (R), and Service to Persons (P). From that combination we may infer that students at Colgate–Rochester tend to find the seminary atmosphere congenial to their rebelliousness and their more scholarly interest in ideas, social action, and the well-being of individuals; they tend to be wary of the parish and traditional forms of ministry. In contrast, students at Concordia tend to be oriented toward traditional patterns of church and ministry. Such patterns enable us to understand interseminary variations more easily and clearly.

The question now arises whether the mean score profile of the TSI constitutes a descriptive or an evaluative norm. Suppose a student showed scores that implied he would "fit in" more easily at Colgate–Rochester than at Concordia? What decision would an administrator or counselor make? Dean Breimeier of Concordia† reports such a case. He indicates that "the test can't tell us whether it is better for him (and us) to be somewhat uncomfortable here and enter our ministry or leave for some other school. I personally hope," he concludes, "he stays because we need his point of view. If he does, the test will have helped us and him understand the point of tension. Not by any means an unimportant value."

The use of the TSI and other tests in counseling deserves more attention than the scope of this paper affords. Dittes presents characteristic uses of the TSI (Dittes, 1964, pp. 9–11) and strategies in using it in guidance (Dittes, 1964, pp. 41–44). Goldman (1961) offers an extended and helpful discussion of the subject.

Because of the tremendous ferment within theological education and among theological students, the TSI may not have as much face validity as the research indicates. Validity may also decline increasingly with time. Dittes (1964, pp. 4–5) has warned of the possibility of irrelevancy in pointing to "certain systematic differences between the original sample of ministers and contemporary theological students," "the greater maturity of the ministers whose statements were sampled to produce the TSI," and changing conceptions of ministry and motivation.

† Personal communication, December 17, 1965.

In spite of the limitations touched on above, the TSI provides the counselor of seminary students and the researcher on the ministry with an invaluable instrument. Local data need to accumulate. Post-seminary data need to be discovered. No other instrument has been so carefully developed for the Protestant ministry.

We have examined the TSI in some detail because validity studies have been completed only recently. It is unequivocally a counseling instrument. It aids in clarifying both differences and similarities among students and schools. It must not be used for decisions about screening, selection, or prediction.

In 1962 a conference was held on psychological research for clergy. At that time Dr. Fred Brown concluded:

The main point to be emphasized at this time is that we possess imperfect tests with which to evaluate complex individuals against criterion settings about which we know too little [Brown, 1962].

What has emerged in the intervening period—including the TSI—only serves to reinforce that judgment. We paint a dark picture to discourage any naïve enthusiast who magically believes in the possibilities lurking within psychological testing for candidates or successful effective ministers.

WHAT IS HAPPENING

What can we say of the current situation after 20 years of increasing interest in psychological testing and ten years of mounting research?

There is a pragmatic pessimism that cannot be discounted. Billinsky made the point more than a decade ago (1956) at the 20th Biennial Meeting of the American Association of Theological Schools:

As long as our seminaries are short of students, as long as our churches are asking for more ministers, as long as anyone who is interested in entering the Christian ministry can find a theological school that will admit him, as long as we ourselves are unable to define the image of the Christian ministry we can rest assured that no tests will ever be devised to solve our problems [Billinsky, 1956].

Testing cannot solve recruitment difficulties. Testing cannot reduce seminary dropouts. Testing cannot eliminate parish-ministry deficit. Testing is not likely to prevent ministerial misfits.

We might hazard the suggestion that much of the naïve hope invested in testing reflects loss of spiritual power. Denominational officials and seminary personnel are painfully aware of the complications surrounding mental and emotional breakdown among ministers, although evidence indicates that the difficulties are not greater than the general population and may be even less (Oates, 1961). Perhaps a parable of our Lord applies to those who would use tests for purposes of separating the weeds from the wheat (Mt. 13:24–30). He urges men not to pull up the weeds because of the danger of pulling up the wheat as well. Only at harvest time can the two be separated without loss. Apparently, the argument of the parable is a caution against premature judgment, and even though Christ's men have been manifest as those who love Him and love others because they have been loved, the ultimate dividing line has not yet been drawn and cannot be drawn. From a theological viewpoint anxious overinvestment in testing possibilities reflects a theology of works and not of faith.

Quite honestly, are we being swept up in a torrent of change? The 1950s saw a loosening of our understandings of church and ministry from those of pre-World War II. In spite of the loosening, the patterns of society persisted without great surface disruption. The 1960s, however, witness to rapid and radical disruption of traditional patterns. Protestant turmoil displays an increasing polarization between those who press for a flexible involvement in culture and society and those who insist upon a firmness of identity and traditional purpose. Little agreement can be found on such basic issues as the nature of faith, church, and ministry. If test predictions proved poor in a relatively stable period, what can they possibly do in a fluid period?

A summary of cumulative studies and the current situation suggests the following conclusions:

1. Testing is highly questionable when used for such global criteria as successful seminarian or effective professional performance.

2. Testing may be used very cautiously for such differential criteria as academic achievement or administrative ministerial responsibility.

3. Testing can be helpful in vocational guidance as far as providing a student with a profile of how his interests, values, and motivations correspond with those of theological students and/or ministers.

4. The use of testing may be desirable if it is: (*a*) minimal and restricted to non-overlapping essential information unavailable from other sources; (*b*) sequential and specialized as need arises from warning signs in a student's actual performance in the classroom or in the field, or from warning signs in paper-and-pencil tests. When specialized testing involving personality dynamics is called for, it ought to be combined with a therapeutic exploration with the person.

5. Testing is essential in two instances: (*a*) for comparisons across populations such as seminarian/non-seminarian or minister/non-minister; and (*b*) for consensually validated indicators for understanding the minister and ministerial functioning.

WHAT NEEDS TO HAPPEN

Having rejected testing as contributing in any widespread and significant way to the screening and selection of seminarians or ministers, I would immediately press for the place of testing in understanding the contours of our concern with church and ministry today. For that purpose, testing must cease to be a rather conventional gathering of already obvious data. We require a more systematic conceptualization of what we are about. Working models or descriptive diagrams are needed to develop an overall strategy. Crucial to model-building is systematic conceptualization and definition of salient variables and the specification of indicators for variable measurement. Such procedures make possible the consolidation and accumulation of information and insight. With empirical and experimental data we can then test and refine our working models—thus, we hope, resulting in clearer understanding.

There are three such working models that may be fruitful for a major research campaign. They sharpen career pattern, career setting, and career output.

A Working Description of Career Pattern. A working model for career pattern exhibits persistency through time by holding space constant. Such a model keeps before us an individual's development from the viewpoint of career pattern. It provides crucial transition points which enable us to draw together the cumulative experience of the individual and to relate that to the *next* phase of his career. Each period represents a bridge in a sequence of bridges. It reminds us of the difficulty of skipping over periods in long-term projections that fail to take account of intermediate experience.

A number of theoretical models have been advanced to understand vocational development: trait-and-factor theory, cultural-psychodynamic theory, psychoanalytically derived theory, identity and self-concept theory, interpersonal relationships and need-satisfaction theory, and social-system-interaction theory (Bachrach, 1957). Regardless of the particular theoretical structure, the proposed working model may be divided into five major periods with subperiods within the divisions. The model proposed is adapted from ideas supplied by the following authors: Ginzberg, Ginsburg, Axelrod, and Herman (1951), and Super (1957).*

Period 1: randomness in infancy and childhood. The focus includes family background and structure (siblings, parents, interactions) as well as salient experience. The period would end in the seventh and eighth grades.

Period 2: anticipation in adolescence. The focus includes experiences from early high school through college. Exploration of the world of work would tend to be (*a*) random in early high school, and (*b*) directed in late high school and early college as the individual more actively seeks alternatives (Felton, 1949; Bittinger, 1964). Tentative commitment would appear in later college as

---

* Additional ideas were contributed by D. V. Tiedeman in a lecture on "Vocational Development: Issues in the Study of Work and Identity," given at Ohio State University, Summer Quarter, 1961.

interests, abilities, and values become clearer. If positive indicators of effective ministry are uncertain, at least we can say on the basis of accumulating descriptive norms that certain patterns of interests, abilities, and values are less likely to be congruent with existing ministerial populations than other patterns (Bridston & Culver, 1965).

Period 3: transition in young adulthood. Here the student finds himself in seminary. During this period there comes both a crystalization of direction and a meeting of specifications demanded for ministry. (*a*) The crystalization process includes: interests, motivation (conscious considerations and unconscious personality dynamics), values, modes of response such as typologies, needs, and, to a lesser degree, abilities (Dodson, 1957; Morse, 1963; Dittes, 1964). (*b*) Specifications are made up of graduation, ordination, and placement or the context in which one works initially (Dittes, 1963a).

Period 4: implementation in early adulthood. Having specified his vocational choice, the individual begins implementing his self-image through professional activity. The first five years may be regarded as the period of perfecting his vocational commitment. The second five years may be seen as the period in which he establishes growing confidence in his vocational identity, his ability to meet the job demands, and his discovering satisfaction with the direction chosen.

Period 5: maintenance in middle and later adulthood. With the implementation of vocational choice successfully carried through, the individual enters the longer period that usually covers the rest of his career development. It includes a stabilization period between about 35 and 55 years of age. There follows a period of simplification of vocational extension and involvement that supports career identity into retirement. In a more restricted form the simplification continues that identity in the phasing-out process until death.

Each period represents a career development task that must be worked through if the individual is to move into the next period.

Criteria for successfully working through are explicit between the periods of anticipation and transition in terms of graduation from college and matriculation in seminary, and between the periods of transition and implementation in terms of graduation from seminary, ordination, and placement. Either an individual accomplishes these tasks or he does not. Within these periods and in the other periods criteria are less decisive.

A Working Description of Career Setting. As we need a model that moves through time, so we need a model that exhibits consistency across space by holding time constant. As there are focal points in time, so there are focal points in space. An individual cannot be appraised by any single pattern of personality, interests, values, motivations, needs, or abilities. Those variables are always situationally relevant both for their actualization and for their effectiveness (Gibb, 1954)

FIGURE 1. A WORKING MODEL FOR MINISTERIAL
CAREER SETTING*

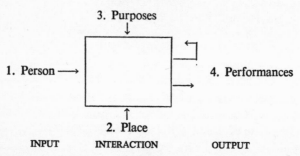

* Adapted from Gibb (1954), Stogdill (1959), Etzioni (1961), and Shartle (1961).

A model for career setting, as shown in Figure 1, based upon the work of Gibb (1954), Stogdill (1959), Etzioni (1961), and Shartle (1961), suggests four major variables:

1. The person who constitutes the input in the interactional system, whether as student, seminarian, candidate, or minister.

2. The place in which the interaction takes place, whether school, church, or community.

3. The purpose(s) of the salient reference groups in the place of interaction.

4. The performance or output. Since the interaction of person, place, and purpose(s) of the reference groups is transactional in that it affects and modifies the person, place, and purpose(s), output goals include those for the person and for the organization.

In card games the value of a card is not inherent in the card but determined by the nature of the game played. In "hearts" the queen of spades has a negative value of 13 unless a player takes all the heart cards in addition to the queen of spades. In "crazy eight" a deuce of any suit has a value of 20 as a wild card, while a joker, which is not used in most games, has a value of 50. Similarly, the value ascribed to the performance output depends upon the "set" or defining value system of the salient reference groups within a particular setting at a particular time.

Illustrative of the importance of "set" is the observation of Stern, Stein, and Bloom that "there seem to be significant differences between those characteristics which make for success in theological school and those which make for success in the ministry . . . ; when the environment changes in critical details a new assessment is necessary" (Stern, Stein, & Bloom, 1956, pp. 248–249).

Each of the four career setting variables have subvariables which constitute their defining attributes.

1. The person includes: (a) background—biographical data, environmental influences, and family configuration; (b) motivational patterns—unconscious personality dynamics and conscious or preconscious motives and concerns; (c) abilities and intelligence; (d) interests; (e) values—social, economic, political, religious, theoretical, and aesthetic; (f) beliefs—theological and socioeconomic; (g) needs;* (h) modes of response—typologies such as Gustafson's seminary students (Gustafson, 1957), ways in which people become aware of the world and come to conclusions about

* As measured, for example, by the Edwards Personal Preference Schedule (Edwards, 1953).

the world,† or MacKinnon's differentiation of the creative, the conflicted, and the civilized individual (MacKinnon, 1965).

2. The place includes: (a) geographical location in terms of part of the country and kind of community; (b) institutional setting, whether school, parish, or hospital; (c) group structures and tasks.

3. The purpose includes: (a) concept of church and ministry, such as Episcopal, Congregational, Presbyterial, or Connectional; (b) salient reference groups and their norms, aspirations, expectations as perceived and prescribed. Such reference groups would include higher participants or leaders, lower participants or regulars, peripheral participants or those with few institutional connections, denominational official, peers, and self. The reference groups' expectancy patterns represent phenomenological evaluations symptomatic of their attitudes and needs.

4. The performance output or criterion is dependent upon the "set" of place and purpose(s). Because of the transactional character of person-place-purpose interaction in which each is affected and modified, output may distinguish between criteria specifically related to the individual and/or the organization. Such a differentiation enables the researcher to separate, say, ministerial effectiveness from church success.

A Working Description of Career Output. By holding time (career pattern) and space (career setting) constant we may examine career output. To do so the following two models are suggested as ways by which we may analytically approach the decisive issue of "criterion." The models are adapted from the following authors: Parsons, Bales, & Shils (1953); Etzioni (1961); and Klausner (1962, 1964).

The first model, as shown in Figure 2, represents an approach to the goals of career output. The horizontal-vertical and the left-right divisions produce four dichotomous dimensions. The upper left goal may be designated as purely instrumental: the lower right goal purely expressive. The upper right goal may be regarded as

† As measured, for example, by the Myers-Briggs Type Indicator (Myers, 1962).

primarily instrumental with expressive modifications; the lower left goal primarily expressive with instrumental modifications.

Instrumental goals are defined as those performances that create and sustain the organization or person in adapting to or functioning better in the setting. That would include such goal indicators as graduation, size of church membership, perceived group success, or minister's salary. Instrumental means adapt the organization or person to the environment in order to achieve general purposes through specific activities.

FIGURE 2. A WORKING MODEL FOR MINISTERIAL
CAREER OUTPUT GOALS*

	Instrumental	Expressive
Instrumental	Instrumentally Instrumental	Expressively Instrumental
Expressive	Instrumentally Expressive	Expressively Expressive

* Adapted from Etzioni (1961).

Expressive goals are defined as those performances that establish and enhance the manifest purpose(s) of the organization or person. These provide meaning, a life orientation, a sense of direction. That would include such goal indicators as members' taking a personal interest in the organization, perceived group effectiveness, or the minister's being a "man of God." Expressive meanings have no utilitarian intent beyond that of giving expression to what constitutes the purpose(s) of the organization or person.

Admittedly, these are abstract dimensions, both of which may be present in any specific performance output. The means of adaptation are used to express the meaning(s) of existence. A church organization or minister may be regarded as instrumentally oriented in going out into all the world to proclaim the Gospel; yet the communication of the gospel may be the expressive goal. A church organization or minister may be regarded as expressively oriented in terms of a supporting relational community of responsible love of God, neighbor, and self; yet the specific goal outputs may be instrumental. While careful definition has been sought, the distinction between expressive and instrumental goals, especially in the ambiguous middle, cannot be thought of as exclusive and absolute. Expressive and instrumental foci of intent, however, are construed as usually being in tension. Instrumental goals may swallow up expressive meanings. Expressive goals may reject instrumental means.

A church organization is one in which caring concern for all people represents its manifest purpose, recognized and reported as such by most participants. As with other social institutions (Merton, 1957), a church organization also reveals to the observer latent purposes, unrecognized by most participants. Latent purposes in church organization might include such unrecognized motives as a participant's wanting prestige associated with belonging to an organization with which certain "elite" individuals are associated, or his wanting an opportunity to exercise leadership.

Church organization requires of the minister both expressive and instrumental goals. An exclusive attention upon expressive goals would indicate a virtual break with the cultural setting and its evaluations. An exclusive attention upon instrumental goals would indicate a virtual disregard of the inner purposes that uniquely constitute the organization's existence.

A manifestly functional situation results when the organization and the minister are found by an investigator to be high in both expressive and instrumental attributes. Unexpected consequences follow when the organization and minister are found to be low in both expressive and instrumental attributes. An intermediate functional situation results when organization and minister are found to be instrumentally involved in activities with the manifest purpose of increasing love of God and neighbor. In such a situation there would be the unexpected consequences of maintaining the organization or gaining personal advantage. Because of the success-achievement orientation of American society, an intermediate functional situation results when the minister is instrumentally involved in both expressive and instrumental goal output.

The working model of career output goals needs to be refined to designate norm indicators of the goals. Figure 3 presents a working model for career output norms. There are four phases in the process of action analysis. Within each of the four quadrants are norms indicative of instrumental or expressive goals. Those norms are determined by four dimensions: two define attitude orientation and two define object orientation. Each quadrant, defined by its four dimensions, represents a phase-in-action space.

FIGURE 3. A WORKING MODEL FOR MINISTERIAL
CAREER OUTPUT NORMS*

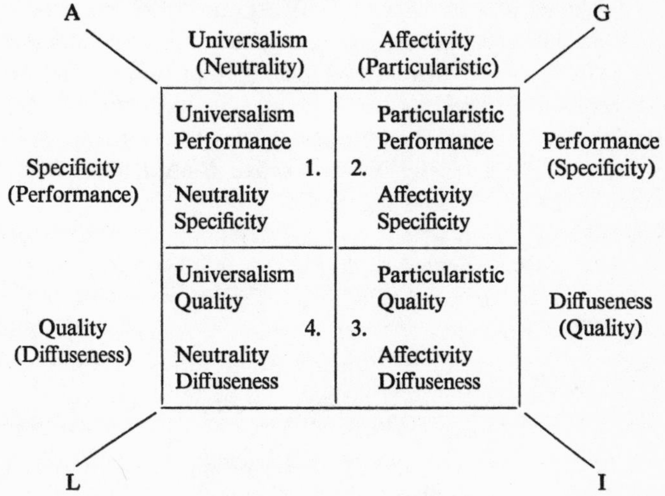

A			G
	Universalism (Neutrality)	Affectivity (Particularistic)	
Specificity (Performance)	Universalism Performance 1.	2. Particularistic Performance	Performance (Specificity)
	Neutrality Specificity	Affectivity Specificity	
Quality (Diffuseness)	Universalism Quality 4.	3. Particularistic Quality	Diffuseness (Quality)
	Neutrality Diffuseness	Affectivity Diffuseness	
L			I

A–Adaptive   G–Goal gratification   I–Integration   L–Latency

* Adapted from Parsons, Bales, & Shils (1953); Etzioni (1961); and Klausner (1964).

The diffuseness-specificity dimension designates an attitudinal orientation. Is the output oriented to multiple and broad or single and narrow characteristics and relationships? Diffuseness represents "wholeness" in the organization or person. Specificity represents "segments" in the organization or person. Diffuseness would include such norms as the person's enacting a role more than a particular role-enactment in itself, an inclusive range of interactions more than a single and segmented interaction, or a global-effectiveness criterion. Specificity would include such norms as restricted and precise role-enactments, an exclusive range of interactional concerns, or a differential effectiveness criterion.

The affectivity-affective neutrality dimension designates an attitudinal orientation. Is the output an end in itself in terms of personal involvement or is it seen in the context of other and ongoing relationships? Affectivity represents personal, emotional involvement expressing immediate and direct gratification; affective neutrality represents less personal, more detached involvement directed toward delayed and less direct gratification. Affectivity would include such norms as expressing unqualified care for another ("I have a personal stake in what's happening") or uncalculated moral commitment. Affective neutrality would include such norms as evaluating another's ability to do a job, acknowledgment of limits irrespective of personal feelings, or active control, discipline, and calculation of individual involvement.

The quality-performance dimension designates an object orientation. Is the output oriented to that which is inherent in the organization or person or to what is done? Quality represents what an organization or person "is"; performance represents what an organization or person "does." Quality would include such norms as salvation, *agape,* community, justification by faith, man of God, or the "good" dimension postulated by McCann (1954) and used by Douglas (1957) in his study of effectiveness. Performance would include such norms as increases in membership, current expenses, and attendance at worship or the "able" dimensions (McCann, 1954; Douglas, 1957).

The universalistic-particularistic dimension designates an object orientation. Is the output an instance of a general nomothetic lawful relationship or an instance of a specific idiosyncratic special relationship? Universalistic represents the rightness or wrongness of a procedure; particularistic represents loyalty or faithlessness to a relationship. Universalistic would include such norms as obeying the letter of the law, completing a project, or being a Christian. Particularistic would include such norms as fulfilling the spirit of the law, participating in ongoing process, or becoming more truly human. A quasi-particularistic pattern is found whenever there is an individualizing of the universal or a maintaining of the universal in a particularistic context (Klausner, 1964, p. 101).

Each dimensional cluster is made up of two attitudinal descriptions and two object descriptions representing norms of the two goal descriptions. There are the two attitude orientations of diffuseness-specificity and affectivity-affective neutrality and the two object orientations of quality-performance and universalism-particularistic. A shift from one quadrant to the next means a shift in attitude and object orientations (Parsons, Bales, & Shils, 1953, pp. 179–190).

In cluster phase 1, for example, are located instrumentally instrumental goals. These goals are constituted by specificity and neutrality attitudes and universalistic and performance objects. In cluster phase 3, as another example, expressively expressive goals are constituted by particularistic and affectivity attitudes and diffuseness and quality objects.

The phase process or action space proceeds clockwise from cluster 1 through cluster 4. Each phase constitutes overt activity in the changing state of the social system. Such an analysis enables the investigator to see more clearly both the independent and the interrelated "functional significance" of an act.

The Adaptive-instrumental phase requires the organization or minister to accommodate to external "reality demands" in the setting. The instrumentally oriented attitudes marked by specificity and affective neutrality are combined with instrumental orientation to objects marked by universalism and performance.

The instrumentally expressive phase of Goal-gratification requires the organization or minister to take into account internal "reality" needs. The instrumentally oriented attitude of specificity is linked with the expressive attitude of affectivity. Those attitudes are directed toward objects marked by expressive particularity and instrumental performance.

The Integrative-expressive phase requires the organization or minister to loosen attention from instrumental considerations. Instead, expressive attitudes of diffuseness and affectivity are directed toward expressive objects of particularity and quality.

The Latency-maintenance phase requires the organization or

minister to maintain the system when it is in a state of inactivity or when one of the phases in action space is dominant. The expressive attitude of diffuseness is combined with the instrumental attitude of neutrality. Both are directed toward objects marked by expressive quality and instrumental universalism. In effect, cluster phase 4 constitutes the "ideal" that undergirds, embraces, and is reflected through the other three phase clusters. Consequently, we would anticipate some overlap among norm indicators.

Application of the Career Output Description. The application of the career output model enables us to examine criteria systematically. Such application requires that we choose, define, indicate, and measure output variables. We may look at either general or specific criteria or both; at either single or multiple criteria or both; at short-run or long-term criteria or both (Dittes, 1962).

From the career pattern transition period of seminary and the implementation and maintenance periods of professional activity we select two norms each to illustrate the fruitfulness of the model.

Consider the young adult in the transition period when he is enrolled in seminary. We may take a criterion such as "intellectual ability." Stated as a hypothetical ideal it belongs in phase 4 of action space. Intellectual ability may be defined as consisting of (*a*) the ability to meet academic requirements, and (*b*) the capacity to meet scholarly demands. Indicators of academic ability would be such norms as grades for specific courses, grade-point average, or graduation. Indicators of scholarly capacity would be such perceptual and conceptual discrimination as scores on personality and intelligence tests, or faculty and peer appraisals of intellectual performance and potential. Academic ability is only indirectly related to scholarly capacity. The directional movement of the norm indicators of the goal concept "intellectual ability" would be as follows:

Adaptation to the "reality demands" of the seminary period requires intellectual ability. The ability represents a certain minimum of intelligence within a narrow range of variability as measured by a standard instrument. The ability requires achieving a certain minimum grade-point average that cumulates in the successful completion of course requirements. The ability means meeting explicit and implicit expectations of faculty and administration in order to graduate.

Goal-gratification of the seminary period requires passing specific courses in specific subject areas and achieving competence in a major field of concentration. Various subtest scores or the verbal-performance ratio on standard instruments would be indicators measuring specific and single criteria.

The Integrative-expressive phase of the seminary period consists of appraisals of the student's ability to utilize perceptual and conceptual discrimination in his task as seminarian. The appraisals would include both his actual performances and his potential possibilities as seminarian and eventual minister.

The Latency-maintenance phase of the seminary period maintains the intellectual ability of the seminarian integrating both its academic and its scholarly expressions. When specific academic ability is dominant, general scholarly capacity is not lost. When general scholarly capacity is dominant, specific academic ability is not ignored.

An unpublished study entitled "An exploratory study of some relationships between personality variables and achievement in seminary" conducted at Texas Christian University by R. A. Hunt in 1963, employing 45 students from Brite Divinity School and 36 students from Perkins School of Theology, illustrates a use of the output criterion of intellectual ability. The criterion norms were: (1) an achievement index of over- and under-achievement made up of a test of academic ability and the use of grade-point average; (2) faculty ratings of success in seminary; (3) faculty rating of predicted success as a pastor; and (4) an ability test.

Independent variables were construed as being interested in and making a decision for the ministry as measured by the Theological School Inventory; personality variables as measured by Taylor's Manifest Anxiety Scale (Taylor, 1953), scales K and L of the MMPI, and Jones's Pensacola Z Survey (Jones, 1957); philosophies of human nature as measured by Wrightsman's Philosophies of Human Nature Survey (Wrightsman, 1963); self-concepts related to significant persons and tasks of the ministry as measured by Osgood's Semantic Differential (Osgood, *et al.,* 1957) and Worchel's Self-Activity Inventory (Worchel, 1957); and over- and under-achievers as measured by faculty ratings.

The criterion indicators of intellectual ability would be grouped in the phases of action space as follows:

> Adaptive-instrumental phase 1—Ability Test; Grade-
> Point Average;
> Achievement Index

> Integrative-expressive phase 3—Faculty Rating Seminary
> Success; Faculty Rating
> Potential Success as a
> Pastor

As anticipated because of the Latency-maintenance phase 4, we would expect to find considerable overlap among the indicator norms. Intercorrelations of criteria are shown in Table 4. Grades, faculty ratings, and Achievement Index show correlations above .70, which appears to be a common pattern (Ashbrook, 1962). Tests of academic ability correlated in the .30s with grades and in the .20s with faculty ratings. Such a pattern tends to support the postulate of intellectual ability's being constituted by academic ability and scholarly capacity, with the two only indirectly related. The correlations of faculty rating for seminary success and pastoral promise are high but show more discrepancy at Perkins than at Brite.

Another example of a norm construct from the seminary period would be the hypothetical model developed by Stern, Stein, and Bloom (1956, pp. 77–89) of the "ideal" student at a liberal Protestant seminary (McCormick) in the Midwest. The model included the student's potentiality for effective ministry in that denomination (Presbyterian) as well as his ability to meet academic demands. The functional student model used as a criterion was as follows:

1. *Interpersonal Relations.* Includes capacity for involvement with others, the ability to interact skillfully with peers, superiors, and subordinates, without arousing hostility or rejection. Such rapport will involve social sensitivity, tact, and confidence in social contact.

TABLE 4. INTERCORRELATIONS OF MEASURES
OF ACHIEVEMENT[a]

Variable	Grade-Point Average	Faculty Rating Seminary	Faculty Rating Future	Achieve-ment Index
Perkins				
Ability Test[b]	.38	.20	.29	.01[c]
Grade-point Average		.74	.85	.93[c]
Faculty Rating Seminary Performance			.79	.71
Faculty Rating Future Effectiveness				.80
Brite				
Ability Test[b]	.31	.24	.26	.01[c]
Grade-point Average		.75	.74	.95[c]
Faculty Rating Seminary Performance			.95	.72
Faculty Rating Future Effectiveness				.70

[a] R. A. Hunt. An exploratory study of some relationships between personality variables and achievement in seminary. Unpub. mimeo. paper. Fort Worth, Texas: Texas Christian University, 1963; Table 1.

[b] Perkins: Miller Analogies Test; Brite: Otis Mental Ability Test.

[c] These correlations are expected as a function of the statistical procedures for regressed scores. The groups were dichotomized which fixed the mean at 1.00.

Aggressive impulses should be well socialized, and the individual should appear as autonomous rather than dependent or dominant.

2. *Inner State.* Characterized by high energy, consistently purposively directed.

3. *Goal Orientation.* Will be persistent in attacking problems, although not inflexible. When confronted with possible failure, the individual will counteract, restriving in order to overcome obstacles, rather than withdrawing or otherwise avoiding the issue. Although primarily intraceptive, the student will focus on people and personal relations. The structure under consideration here . . . involves dramatic, idealistic social action, active modification of reality to conform to a private value-system, and the expression of ideals in concrete action. The content of this structure should be socio-political as well as ethnical-religious.

Indicators of the criterion output would be grouped in the phases of action space as follows:

Adaptive-instrumental phase 1—Wechsler-Bellevue
Test of Adult Intelligence
(Wechsler, 1955, 1958).

Goal-gratification phase 2—an Autobiographical
Questionnaire (probably).

Integrative-expressive phase 3—Rorschach Ink-Blot
Test (Rorschach, 1942), Thematic
Apperception Test (Murray, 1943).

Neither Wechsler-Bellevue data nor arbitrary clinical judgments provided sure clues to the assessors in discriminating between the three desirable students and the three undesirable ones. However, there was unanimity of assessment concerning three students' being congruent with the hypothetical model and three students' being markedly different from it *and* from each other. The decisions represented a "complete replication of the faculty's judgment."

While such criteria as intellectual ability or the model of the potentially effective pastor as a seminarian provide useful clues for assessing the seminary transition period of a minister's career pattern, these are not necessarily predictive of criteria applicable to later periods. As Stern, Stein, and Bloom discovered, subsequent research uncovered "rather striking differences" between effective ministers and potentially effective ministers. Their report stated:

The successful minister (selected by this same faculty) may, for example, lack the personal charm and tact considered so important in the student. Such findings make it quite clear that the prediction of ultimate professional performance cannot, without further inquiry, be based on criteria related to success as a student. Furthermore, it is also evident that scholastic and academic performance are not always related to factors which are important for success as a professional in this field [Stern, Stein, & Bloom, 1956, pp. 87–88].

In the implementation and maintenance periods of adulthood we consider the criteria of "religiousness" (Klausner, 1964) and "member involvement" (Ashbrook, 1966) as illustrative of the use of the career output model.

Stated as a hypothetical ideal, "religiousness" belongs in phase 4 of action space. The ideal may be defined as consisting of (a) intensity of "participation in religious institutions," and (b) "commitment to a set of beliefs." Indicators of participation would be frequency of attendance at worship or other designated church activities. Indicators of commitment are only indirectly related to participation and would be "responses to a set of items of belief." Movement in the cluster phases of action space would be something like the following:

Adaptation to the "reality demands" of the adult period requires "religiousness." Religiousness involves a certain frequency of general attendance in the organization and a certain general acknowledgment of a belief system. Without these an individual would not be classified as part of the output of the organization or minister.

Goal-gratification requires frequency of attendance and participation in specific activities of the organization and a certain personal acknowledgment of specific aspects of the belief system.

The Integrative-expressive phase consists of appraisal of the individual's vital integration of participation and belief both as a person and as a member of the organization. There is participation of high intensity without calculation, resulting in a vital religious life.

The Latency-maintenance phase maintains the religiousness of the person integrating both activity involvement and conceptual affirmation. When specific participation is dominant, general affirmation is not lost. When general affirmation is dominant, specific participation is not ignored.

An example of the beginnings of an analytical development of the criterion of religiousness has been cited by Moberg:

Most of a church's objectives may be subsumed under the headings of faith ("to cause people to accept a system of related values and beliefs —an ideology, or creed, or faith"), attitudes ("to cause people to adopt certain attitudes toward the divine, however defined, and toward their fellow men—attitudes derived from the ideology or faith"), and action ("to cause people to engage in certain behavior consonant with those attitudes") [Moberg, 1962, p. 220].

Stated as a hypothetical ideal, "member involvement" belongs in phase 4 of action space. The ideal may be defined as consisting of (a) "the kind of individual motivation members report for their involvement in the organization" whether of low intensity (calculative) or of high intensity (moral commitment), and (b) "the kind of activity in which members engage as functions of the organization," whether it be expressive activity enhancing the communal relationships and communicating meanings or instrumental activity maintaining the organizational means of adaptation. Indicators would be responses to items about the intensity of involvement in expressive and instrumental activities. Movement in the cluster phases of action space would be something like the following:

Adaptation to the "reality demands" of the adult period requires "member involvement." Member involvement necessitates participation of at least moderate intensity in instrumental activity related to organizational encouragement, responsibility climate, financial participation, and property responsibility as dimensions of church activity emerging from a factor analysis of responses to items about member involvement.

Goal-gratification requires participation of at least moderate intensity in the instrumental activity of phase 1 and participation of at least moderate intensity in expressive activity related to interest in church life, involvement satisfaction, fellowship life, and self-involvement as dimensions of church activity emerging from a factor analysis of responses to items about member involvement.

The Integrative-expressive phase consists of participation of high intensity (moral commitment) in both the instrumental and expressive activity dimensions mentioned above.

The Latency-maintenance phase maintains member involvement integrating moral commitment of high intensity in both expressive and instrumental activity. When instrumental means are dominant, they are engaged in as ways of achieving expressive purposes. When expressive purposes are dominant, instrumental means are the ways of adaptation to express the meanings of the organization's or minister's existence.

The difficulty of choosing criteria, systematically defining them, and measuring them cannot be overemphasized. Despite the most rigorous of efforts there remains "a recalcitrant oddness at the heart of things" (Barron, 1963, p. 270). Even so, the task must be pursued with rigor if psychological testing is to aid the church in its ministry.

SUMMARY

In spite of a great deal of activity by denominations and seminaries, testing for seminarians, candidates, or effective ministers does not appear powerful enough to be used as a basis for screening and selection. It may aid in situations requiring specific objectives. It may help in vocational guidance and counseling. It is essential for comparative purposes among different populations and for consensually validated meanings of concepts like minister and ministerial functioning. It is not a magical tool. It takes its place alongside a variety of sources of information for understanding.

In planning "the strategy of major campaigns" in psychological testing for clergymen, three possible working models or descriptive diagrams have been suggested. There is a model for career development; a model for career setting; and a model for criterion output analysis. We hope that, with some consensus about the major contours of the territory we seek to map, we can accumulate substantive knowledge, consolidate it into more adequate theory, and formulate more empirically testable hypotheses. Only in some such process as this will testing make its most fruitful contribution to understanding clergymen.

REFERENCES

Allport, G. W., & Fairbanks, R. J. (Eds.) *An evaluation of present methods for selecting postulates in the Episcopal Diocese of Massachusetts.* Boston: Episcopal Diocese of Massachusetts, 1953.

Ashbrook, J. B. Evaluating seminary students as potential ministers. Unpublished master's dissertation, Ohio State University, 1962.

Ashbrook, J. B. The relationship of church members to church organization. *Journal for the Scientific Study of Religion,* 1966, 5, 397–419.

Bachrach, P. B. A progress report on the scientific careers project. *Journal of Counseling Psychology,* 1957, 4, 71–74.

Barron, F. *Creativity and psychological health.* Princeton, N.J.: Van Nostrand, 1963.

Billinsky, J. M. A panel discussion: Using the results of testing. *Twentieth Biennial Meeting.* Dayton, Ohio: American Association of Theological Schools, 1956. Pp. 135–137.

Billinsky, J. M., & Guiles, A. F. *A.N.T.S. Psychological Test.* Newton Centre, Mass.: Andover Newton Theological School, 1947.

Bittinger, E. F. Realism and vocational expectations: a study of the changes in the patterns of vocational expectations and other characteristics of 32,056 seventh through twelfth grade boys and a sample of 1,729 boys who selected the ministry in the Washington, D.C. metropolitan area with respect to the hypothesis of increasing realism with advancing age. *Dissertation Abstracts,* 1964, 25, 3155.

Booth, G. The psychological examination of candidates for the ministry. In H. Hofmann (Ed.) *The ministry and mental health.* New York: Association Press, 1960. Pp. 101–124.

Booth, G. Tests and therapy applied to the clergy. *Journal of Religion and Health,* 1963, 2, 267–276.

Brayfield, A. H. Testimony before the Senate Subcommittee on Constitutional Rights of the Committee on the Judiciary, June 8, 1965. *American Psychologist,* 1965, 20, 888–894.

Breimeier, K. H. The prediction of success at a theological seminary. Unpublished master's dissertation, Washington University, 1948.

Bridston, K. R., & Culver, D. W. *Pre-seminary education.* Minneapolis: Augsburg Publishing House, 1965.

Brown, F. Some observations upon the use of psychological tests in the selection and assessment of candidates for ministerial training. Paper read to Conference on Psychological Research, November 20, 1962, sponsored by Board of Theological Education, Lutheran Church of America, 231 Madison Avenue, New York, N.Y.

Carp, A. Testimony before the Senate Subcommittee on Constitutional Rights of the Committee on the Judiciary, June 9, 1965. *American Psychologist,* 1965, 20, 916–922.

Cockrum, L. V. Predicting success in training for the ministry. *Religious Education,* 1952, 47, 198–202.

Davis, C. E. Psychological techniques in the enlistment work of the church. *American Association of Theological Schools Bulletin,* 1950, 19, 122–130.

Dittes, J. E. Research on clergymen: factors influencing decisions for religious service and effectiveness in the vocation. In S. W. Cook (Ed.) *Review of recent research bearing on religious and character formation.* Research Supplement to *Religious Education,* 1962, 57, No. 4, Pp. S-141-165.

Dittes, J. E. TSI scores in relation to personal background, performance in seminary, and post-seminary vocational choice. *TSI Research Bulletin,* No. 3. Washington: Ministry Studies Board, 1963. (a)

Dittes, J. E. Changes in TSI scores during seminary. *TSI Research Bulletin,* No. 4. Washington: Ministry Studies Board, 1963. (b)

Dittes, J. E. *Vocational guidance of theological students: A manual for the use of the Theological School Inventory.* Washington: Ministry Studies Board, 1964.

Dittes, J. E., & DeWire, H. Face impression study: correlations of TSI scores with student self-report of motivation and with interviewer ratings.

TSI Research Bulletin, No. 2. Washington: Ministry Studies Board, 1963.

Dodson, F. J. Personality factors in the choice of the Protestant ministry as a vocation. Unpublished doctoral dissertation, University of Southern California, 1957.

Douglas, W. G. T. Predicting ministerial effectiveness. Unpublished doctoral dissertation, Harvard University, 1957.

Douglass, H. P., & Brunner, E. *The Protestant Church as a social institution.* New York: Harper, 1935.

Edwards, A. L. *Edwards Personal Preference Schedule.* New York: Psychological Corporation, 1953.

Etzioni, A. *A comparative analysis of complex organizations.* New York: Free Press, 1961.

Felton, R. A. *New ministers: a study of 1,978 ministerial students to determine the factors which influence men to enter the ministry.* Madison, N.J.: Drew Theological Seminary, 1949.

Froyd, M. D. Pre-testing for the ministry. *Christian Century*, 1956, *73*, 769–770.

Gibb, C. A. Leadership. In G. Lindzey (Ed.) *Handbook of social psychology.* Cambridge, Mass.: Addison-Wesley, 1954, Vol. 2, pp. 877–920.

Ginzberg, E., Ginsburg, S. W., Axelrod, S., & Herman, J. L. *Occupational choice.* New York: Columbia University Press, 1951.

Goldman, L. *Using tests in counseling.* New York: Appleton-Century-Crofts, 1961.

Goodling, R. A., & Webb, S. C. An analysis of faculty ratings of theology students. *Religious Education*, 1959, *54*, 228–233.

Gross, M. *The brain watchers.* New York: Random House, 1962.

Gustafson, J. M. Theological students: varieties of types and experience. In H. R. Niebuhr, D. D. Williams, & J. M. Gustafson. (Eds.) *The advancement of theological education.* New York: Harper, 1957. Pp. 145–173.

Harrower, M. Psychological tests in the Unitarian-Universalist ministry. *Journal of Religion and Health*, 1963, *2*, 129–142.

Harrower, M. Mental health potential and success in the ministry. *Journal of Religion and Health*, 1964. *4*, 30–58.

Higdon, E. K. *New missionaries for new days.* St. Louis: Bethan Press, 1956.

Hoffman, B. *The tyranny of testing.* New York: Crowell-Collier, 1962.

Holt, R. R., & Luborsky, L. *Personality patterns of psychiatrists.* New York: Basic Books, 1958.

Holtzman, W. E. Does it work?: Review of *Personality assessment: A critical survey*, by P. E. Vernon. *Contemporary Psychology*, 1965, *10*, 509–510.

Ingram, O. K. Student recruitment. *Duke Divinity School Bulletin*, 1963, *28*, 188–198.

Jones, M. B. The Pensacola Z survey: A study in the measurement of authoritarian tendency. *Psychological Monographs*, 1957, *71* (23, Whole No. 452).

Kelly, E. L., & Fiske, D. W. *The prediction of performance in clinical psychology.* Ann Arbor: University of Michigan Press, 1951.

Klausner, S. K. Research methodology in religion and psychiatry. *Journal of Religion and Health*, 1962, *1*, 387–404.

Klausner, S. K. *Psychiatry and religion.* New York: Free Press, 1964.

Kling, F. R. A study of testing as related to the ministry. *Religious Education*, 1958, *53*, 243–248.

Kling, F. R., Pierson, E., & Dittes, J. E. Relation of TSI scores and selected items of biographical information. *TSI Research Bulletin*, No. 1. Washington: Ministry Studies Board, 1963.

Knowles, R. H. Differential characteristics of successful and unsuccessful seminary students. *Dissertation Abstracts*, 1959, *19*, 1655–1656.

MacKinnon, D. W. Personality and the realization of creative potential. *American Psychologist*, 1965, *20*, 273–281.

Maehr, M. L., & Stake, R. E. The value patterns of men who voluntarily quit seminary training. *Personnel and Guidance Journal*, 1962, *15*, 537–540.

Masserman, J. H. *The practice of dynamic psychiatry*. Philadelphia: Saunders, 1955.

Masserman, J. H., & Palmer, R. T. Psychiatric and psychological tests for ministerial personnel. *Pastoral Psychology*, 1961, *12* (112), 24–33.

May, M. A. *The education of American ministers*: Vol. III. *The institutions that train ministers*. New York: Institute of Social and Religious Research, 1934.

McCann, R. V. The Nature and varieties of religious change. Unpublished doctoral dissertation, Harvard University, 1954.

Merton, R. K. *Social theory and social structure*. (rev. ed.) New York: Free Press, 1957.

Moberg, D. O. *The Church as a social institution*. Englewood Cliffs, N.J.: Prentice-Hall, 1962.

Morse, P. K. The Strong Vocational Interest Blank and Minnesota Multiphasic Personality Inventory as measures of persistence toward the ministry as a vocational goal. *Dissertation Abstracts*, 1963, *23*, 3239–3240.

Murray, H. A. *Thematic Apperception Test*. Cambridge, Mass.: Harvard University Press, 1943.

Myers, I. B. *The Myers-Briggs Type Indicator: Manual*. Princeton, N.J.: Educational Testing Service, 1962.

Oates, W. E. (Ed.) *The minister's own mental health*. Great Neck, N.Y.: Channel Press, 1961.

Osgood, C. E., et al. *The measurement of meaning*. Urbana, Ill.: University of Illinois Press, 1957.

O.S.S. Assessment Staff. *Assessment of men: Selection of personnel for the Office of Strategic Services*. New York: Rinehart, 1948.

Packard, V. *The naked society*. New York: McKay, 1964.

Parsons, T., Bales, R. F., & Shils, E. A. *Working papers in the theory of action*. New York: Free Press, 1953.

Richards, J. M., Jr. The prediction of academic achievement in a Protestant Theological Seminary. *Educational and Psychological Measurement*, 1957, *17*, 628–630.

Rorschach, H. *Psychodiagnostics: A diagnostic test based on perception*. (Transl. by P. Lemkau & B. Kronenburg.) Berne: Huber, 1942 (1st German ed., 1921).

Saxe, R. H. Psychometric testing and missionary selection. *Bibliotheca Sacra*, 1959, *116*, 249–258.

Shartle, C. L. Leadership and organizational behavior. In L. Petrullo & B. M. Bass (Eds.) *Leadership and interpersonal relations*. New York: Holt, Rinehart & Winston, 1961. Pp. 310–325.

Stern, G. G., Stein, M. I., & Bloom, B. S. *Methods in personality assessment*. New York: Free Press, 1956.

Stogdill, R. M. *Individual behavior and group achievement*. New York: Oxford University Press, 1959.

Super, D. E. *The psychology of careers*. New York: Harper, 1957.

Taylor, J. A. A personality scale of manifest anxiety. *Journal of Abnormal and Social Psychology*, 1953, *48*, 285–290.

Vernon, P. E. *Personality assessment: A critical survey*. New York: Wiley, 1964.

Webb, S. C., & Goodling, R. A. Test validity in a Methodist theological school. *Educational and Psychological Measurement*, 1958, *18*, 859–866.
Wechsler, D. *Manual for the Wechsler Adult Intelligence Scale.* New York: Psychological Corporation, 1955.
Wechsler, D. *The measurement and appraisal of adult intelligence.* (4th ed.) Baltimore: Williams & Wilkins, 1958.
Whyte, W. H. *The organization man.* New York: Simon & Schuster, 1956.
Williams, M. O., Jr. The psychological-psychiatric appraisal of candidates for missionary service. *Pastoral Psychology*, 1958, *9* (89), 41–44.
Worchel, P. W. Ability screening of flying personnel. *School of Aviation Medicine*, Randolph AFB, Texas. March, 1957.
Wrightsman, L. S. The measurement of philosophies of human nature. Paper read at the meeting of the Midwestern Psychological Association, Chicago, May, 1963.

DISCUSSION

E. Austin Dondero: I think that there are some questions raised or implied by the approach that Dr. Ashbrook has taken. Putting it in less elegant style than he did, the questions could be phrased somewhat like this: Should we let history decide what the work of the minister is going to be? In other words, are we simply going to test people all along the line after they have had some training and experience within the scope of ministerial preparation and work, find out what has happened to them, and thereby frame our concept of what they should be? Or, as Dr. Ashbrook has suggested, should we attempt to decide the course of history in the sense of having some models (after serious consideration of the role of the minister) by which we can evaluate and judge, and by which we can phrase and shape our training program?

Implied, I think, in this approach, is the fact that the author feels that there is an interactive effect here—in other words, that we have to do both. We have to look at what history is telling us, and also take some courageous steps to try to shape the history.

There is, I feel, a "world view" of the ministry that is needed— an "outside" view, a sort of detached view as to what this vocation in life is supposed to be and what its practitioners are supposed to be doing. At the same time a view from the "inside" is needed in terms of the men and women who are actually engaged in the work of the ministry.

But if we decide that we want an inside view of what the work of the minister is going to be, I think that again there are some questions raised. Will this view of the ministry that we get from the inside in looking at the people engaged in the work be strongly determined by the individuating personality characteristics of the people in it, or will the view that we have from inside be in part determined by the particular developmental experience and phase through which the minister is passing and thus be evaluated in a somewhat global fashion almost as apart from this particular individual?

The concept of the ministry that those of us who are in it have now may not be quite the same as the concept that the beginning student has, or, as Dr. Ashbrook implied, as we might have at the later stages of development.

And so the question is: What is the proper view of the work of the minister? Must we adjust our views according to the particular developmental phase or experiential phase of the person? Is the view of the ministry resistive to any modification except that we wait for the person to pass on to the next developmental phase?

I think these are some of the questions that are implied in the model that Dr. Ashbrook has suggested. I personally feel that models in this work have high value, and I think that they reflect some of the positions taken in the discussions so far.

One of the problems which I see in the use of models is that often, to make the model completely understandable, we have to live in the hope that we can come upon or set up a study of a person or several persons who go through the development, that we can follow them all the way through, constantly assessing what is happening to them, and so forth. But as you well recognize, that has built-in hazards in the sense that a person might be so completely evaluated, so well-tested, so sensitized to the fact that he is being studied, that his maturation might be biased, and that his unusual history of being the object of all this kind of research may obfuscate, actually, some of the things that are really happening to him.

I was a little bit uneasy with the model that Dr. Ashbrook presented, wherein he held time constant, because I think it may too easily lend itself to a view that personality is somewhat static. However, he nicely sidestepped this problem by hinting that the particular view of the ministry which is needed must be in a constantly refined perceptual framework, that indeed there is a transactional phenomenon which is needed if we are going to understand the ministry. This is one of the strengths I see in his call for models—that there is this transaction going on.

In support of Dr. Ashbrook's uneasiness about the fruits of ministerial testing as expressed in the first part of the paper, and perhaps to give a platform for launching some discussion about this problem and for tying in some of the comments of the earlier presentations, I think it is quite possible, if we turn to testing, to gather what someone has called "meaningless data." I would like, very briefly, to show you some of the problems that can come up if we resort to testing without a model.

I have been doing testing for about six or eight years now, and I just recently completed an analysis of some test data over the past six years. I am going to refer to two test instruments, to show what can happen, and to show what care is needed in interpretation and to suggest where models can be of great help.

In our program I used the Sixteen Personality Factor Questionnaire (Cattell, *et al.,* 1957). For three years I accumulated data and analyzed these data. In the fourth year of the testing program there was a dramatic change in the mean values achieved by the people who were applying, and the same persisted during the fifth and sixth years. There were significant differences on every scale between every comparison for every scale except one. I could not help wondering what was happening.

I kept insisting to my assistants that they were scoring incorrectly. They refused to go along with me, and so I undertook to spot-check their scoring. I found out that they were correct. I could not figure out what happened until I recalled that there was a change of significant personnel in the recruiting program, and that the people who were charged with recruiting were different. All of a sudden we were getting different norms.

The problem that worries me is this: Suppose I had established norms for the vocation in terms of the first three years, or suppose, not having those first three years, I established them on the basis of the norms for the second three years. Which are right?

Further, I made a similar analysis during the same six years for the Minnesota Multiphasic Personality Inventory (MMPI) (Hathaway & McKinley, 1967). There were very few, if any, significant changes in the test scores. Again, this posed some questions about testing. It may suggest, for example, in terms of models, that perhaps these two tests are truly testing quite different things. That, of course, is a statement of no great importance. But that one of them is a more stable measure of the things we are looking for than the other may well be so.

Why is it that one test will persist over the years in giving stable and consistent results and another one will not? Maybe we have, as Dr. Fred Brown suggested earlier, to hope that we can go much deeper into getting criteria for our evaluation of the ministry rather than simply employing—if I dare use the term—the superficial level of so many instruments—test instruments—that we are using. I think Dr. Ashbrook's call for models is a movement in this direction. For that reason I think it is a very significant contribution.

GENERAL DISCUSSION

Clarification from Dr. Ashbrook: In reply to a question about the sense in which he used the term "movement" when he spoke of "movement through action space" to describe a progression from cells 1 through 4 in his Figure 3, Dr. Ashbrook said: "If we take the matter of graduation from a seminary, the norm indicated would be in the adaptive phase. It is a specific, universal, neutral performance. Underlying graduation is the capacity to receive some kind of gratification in relation to a major field of concentration, the ability to master a field, the kind of relation between verbal / performance scores, which is a more particularistic and personal investment in the process. There is a specificity in the performance operation. In 'integration' we are dealing with diffusion and quality as well as affectivity and the particularistic in terms of perceived and rated potential or performance as a seminarian, which we could even say meant perceived potential as a minister.

"Intellectual ability can be broken into capacity to be graduated, scholarly capacity to perform competently in a particular discipline as well as to function generally, regardless of what the matter happens to be.

"The movement in action space is a movement from a generalized and yet specific neutral performance to a differential kind of thing. We say we cannot predict total effectiveness in the minister; we can say something about differential effectiveness. I am more cautious about what we can say of the effective person who is utilizing the role pattern of minister to project his person. We have here, in a sense, the undergirding organization of the person according to that particular construct that is present in the various phases." As for what has moved, Dr. Ashbrook said that it was "simply the focus of attention; what we have pulled out of the background into the foreground."

Dr. Douglas observed that he had found it extremely difficult to relate analysis of the kind Dr. Ashbrook had outlined with actual people and situations. He thought of it as an interesting chess game, but not helpful in the construction of criteria and in making these criteria usable indicators for use in making decisions with regard to particular persons and situations. He hoped that somehow, sometime, Samuel Blizzard (1955) could share some of his findings with regard to reference groups in a project he had conducted some years ago in connection with lay ratings of ministerial performance. Dr. Douglas thought that Dr. Ashbrook had made an important point about varying expectations in relation to different frameworks.

Another bibliographic reference that was pertinent to Dr. Ashbrook's first diagram, Dr. Kildahl said, was the work of Abraham Maslow (1954, 1964), which would add some more flesh and blood to the skeleton of that diagram.

Asked whether, if someone developed and followed a model such as he had worked up, he would then amend his statement about having no faith in the predictive value of tests by orienting tests toward these stages and movements, Dr. Ashbrook replied that he was not sure. He thought that he would probably hold in abeyance the movement from mapping the parameters for the sake of understanding whether one should move from that level to decision-making. Recalling the investigations made within an

Episcopal diocese that he had mentioned in the first part of his paper, Dr. Ashbrook said that the report had been clear in saying that to screen in or out on the basis of tests would deprive the ministry of some of its most valuable characters. He related this to Jesus' parable of the wheat and the chaff: "Let it grow up until harvest time, and God in His good judgment will determine what are the weeds and what are the wheat."

Peace Corps Parallels: Experience in the Peace Corps, Dr. English said, bore out the importance of Dr. Ashbrook's view of the life of a minister as a continuum, with different phases in the long period in which he is involved at various levels. Even in the two-year period of service in the Corps it is found difficult to make decisions about the kinds of people who should be put in certain situations unless one looks at the whole process as a continuum. Looking at the twenty-one months of overseas service, the Corps staff had identified certain patterns that are characteristic of total populations despite occupational and cultural differences in their work settings. Without knowing those patterns it would be impossible to make recommendations about various kinds of system intervention. With 5,000 volunteers now returned to their own society, the Corps has identified three phases: that prior to entering the Corps, training, and the overseas situation. Upon return, there is a kind of recapitulation of these phases. Some of the people who undergo this process tend to grow in almost direct proportion to the difficulties they encounter in the process; others do not change much. A third group decompensate and break down, resulting in either selection out during training or premature termination overseas.

"Are there psychological tests," Dr. English asked, "that would help the more or less intuitive clinical judgment by showing how a person is coping with a particular phase of the process? After four months in the field, say, the volunteer is disturbed. The Corps needs to know in what direction the process is moving—in the direction of growth, or toward a kind of chronic syndrome, or toward a kind of decompensation that could lead to a premature return."

Dr. Douglas said that he did not think any one test would provide the longitudinal process kind of information. Though at some point one can look for consistency among evidence from different sources, he had found, particularly with seminary students, a great deal of inconsistency among sources, even though each would be a valid indicator of some part of the total picture. Because of the time process dimension, it is possible to get an almost archeological study of a personality.

Dr. Brown thought that, though it is difficult and expensive to do so, one can get this understanding of the so-called archeological layers in a test battery, just as it is possible to tell where a person is going in therapy as one becomes acquainted with the various patterns he reveals. One must have a clear picture of a particular model. One has to come to grips with the problem of inconsistency and the reconciliation of inconsistencies.

Granted that it would be interesting to find out what the various phases are, Dr. Arnold referred to the kind of test she had discussed earlier, the Story Sequence Analysis Test (Arnold, 1962) —one that would reveal the motivation and basic attitudes of the candidate or minister to various goals, to right and wrong action, to other people, and his ways of reacting to adversity. She thought that such a test, regardless of the existence of different phases, would help by giving a prediction of what a person would be likely to do in different kinds of situations.

Dr. Kildahl suggested that projective testing can help in the guidance process on the basis of Dr. Ashbrook's four variables of person, place, performance, and purpose. He added that in defining those four variables Dr. Ashbrook had done a service to all testers.

The Appropriateness of Models for Testing: An expression of concern about the present tendency toward model-making came from Dr. Arnold, speaking from her interest in brain models. She thought that the models project a picture of what reality would be like if it were organized in the way the model is organized, whereas actually reality does not work that way. One must find out how reality works and then figure out how one can explain its working so. Model-making jumps over this first step.

Though sharing Dr. Arnold's concern, Dr. Dittes said that he considered it necessary to set her objection beside the parallel dilemma Dr. Ashbrook had been dealing with. Unfortunately, looking at reality involves looking through certain kinds of lenses or instruments. One of the purposes of the model is to provide a set of ways of looking at reality. One is hopelessly lost in the purely modelless situation, Dr. Dittes believed. It is self-deceiving to think that there is anything as simple as just looking at reality.

Dr. Arnold mentioned the distinction between theory and model. One starts from the way reality looks to him, and then makes tests. In the process of using many tests, one works out a theory. The difference between a theory and a model is that a theory is based upon evidences, whereas a model is based upon reflection.

Dr. McCarthy, having understood Dr. Ashbrook to say that, because of having not yet related his model to practical realities, he would refrain from making a decision based on it, said he thought that in making judgments about selection people do have some kind of model in mind on which they base their decisions; in fact, he thought it impossible to avoid doing so. He thought that the advantage of having a model is that it helps one to recognize the tentativeness with which he may apply it.

Returning to the importance of keeping in mind the continuum of the service period, Dr. English remarked that if a test like the one described by Dr. Arnold were given to a Peace Corps volunteer in the first week of training, even though it gave an accurate picture of the person's motivation and perception of his way of coping at that period, the predictive value of that picture would lose its significance at, say, four months of service, when the volunteers are close to clinical depression. It would be still another picture after a year of service. The influence of the coping devices of other volunteers with whom one comes into contact in the field also enters the picture. There is great difficulty in trying to evaluate people who are still growing and changing through the situations they are exposed to. Therefore, he thought that to extend a model into a continuum is extremely valuable.

Dr. Arnold said that she had not meant to suggest that one would ask people how they would react to adversity, but that the readiness that people develop in the course of their lives to do something constructive in a tight spot shows up in the Story Sequence Analysis Test. Probably it also shows up in the selection tests given by the Peace Corps.

Some Practical Features of Testing: Father Bier called attention to the fact that there are practical decisions with respect to admission and ordination that have to be made. They have been made on very tenuous grounds—grounds that, even allowing for misgivings about available psychological instruments, would be made more substantial with the additional information that the psychologist can supply.

He suggested that the greater vocational commitment made by the Catholic priest as compared with that of the Protestant minister or the rabbi makes the limitation on the value of screening by tests mentioned by Dr. Ashbrook less applicable to the priesthood. One of the factors confronting those who select for the priesthood is the irrevocability of the choice made by those who enter it. This finality makes the antecedent decisions a great deal more pressing than they are with the Protestant minister or the rabbi, who may move to another profession after ordination without any opprobrium. The psychologist's contributions to the decision concerning the acceptance or rejection of a candidate for the Catholic seminary are perhaps even more needed than they are in the cases of the other faiths.

Referring to the points Father Bier had made, Dr. Ashbrook said he thought that the more explicitly examiners understand the demands of a situation the easier it becomes to predict. "The most explicit demand we know of in any situation is in relation to the grade-point average. The correlations for predicting grade-point averages run between .40 and .60, which improves our estimates to better than chance, maybe 13 to 15 percent. This is important, depending upon the kind of supply-and-demand relationship and of investment resources, training, and irrevocability of commitment, etc."

Dr. Ashbrook also reinforced Dr. Dittes's suggestion that among lay people a sort of aura of magic surrounds testing. Actually, testing is only one part of a vast range of available data necessary for decision-making, helping in the more efficient ordering of the data. As pointed out by Dr. English, there are at least two selection decision boards along the way, involving a great mass of data, a small part of which is related to testing. Dr. Ashbrook did not mean to reject testing and decision-making, but only to ask what the economic justification is for the blanket use of a highly refined instrument across the board. He thought that what the Lutherans are doing is significant. They have a sequential program, with a couple of tests in the freshman year in college and another set of tests and retests of MMPI in the senior year. Out of these, approximately 35 percent call for a closer look; another battery of tests is given these people. This is related to what Gotthard Booth (1963) has said about working therapeutically with testing.

In short, Dr. Ashbrook is in favor of tests' being regarded as increasing the probability of doing better than chance alone in decision-making and also of their use as an intervention therapeutic process.

As for the aura of black magic surrounding testing, Dr. Douglas said that this is not just a matter of the lay image; he thought that the practitioners of testing, trying to justify their work in areas where they are not quite certain of the validity of what they are doing, sometimes reinforce or even create the aura.

Interpretation of Test Results: Dr. Douglas wished to see more discussion of the process of interpretation of test results, both to the decision-makers and to the people being appraised. He thought that what Dr. McCarthy had said about the psychologist's responsibility being only to describe, and not to say yea or nay, was part of the psychologist's rationalization. The way he reports does influence decisions. And percentiles, Dr. Douglas said, are used magically—particularly the 50th percentile. The applicant is often made to feel that he should get closer to the mean for his group, if he is far below or above it. Seldom does anyone question what the scale is getting at. Nor does anyone raise the question whether the applicant wants to be like the standardization group, or whether he would prefer to be different.

Supplementing some of his earlier remarks, Dr. McCarthy noted that the matter of picking up 5 to 15 percent of the variance should be seen in relation to how much selection has gone on, before the prediction equation has been worked out. Psychologists often neglect to point out that they are generally dealing with extremely attenuated samples in their studies of clergymen. If the full range of possible scores were represented in the sample, the correlation coefficients with criteria of effectiveness could be appreciably higher. Tests do have a value in setting minimum levels at which one is going to cut.

The use of test information, he continued, is put into a helpful perspective by recalling what Harold Seashore* used to say: the psychologist's job is basically to reconcile discrepant information. Test scores derive their meaning from being fitted together into a meaningful pattern for an individual.

As had been noted in the discussion, because of developmental changes, one may get a different picture of a personality depending upon the time and circumstances under which the evaluation is done. Discrepant information can be reconciled by the adoption of a developmental viewpoint. Dr. McCarthy thought the discussion had led to an extreme position: participants seemed to have underestimated the continuity in life styles and to be suggesting that one finds greater inconsistency than there actually is.

Responding to Dr. Douglas's comment, Dr. McCarthy said that he had not intended to make the dichotomy so sharp in what the psychologist does. Actually, he thought that the psychologist has to do a certain amount of fabricating to fit things together for a particular person, which he thought defensible and useful so long as it is checked against reality.

Dr. Brown cautioned about the possibility of a person who has not had intensive experience with adolescents making serious errors in psychodiagnosis in cases in which there seems to be overwhelming pathology, because these young people are examined at various stress periods in their development. An encouraging fact is that

---

* Harold C. Seashore (1906–1965). From 1945 until his death, Dr. Seashore was Director of the Test Division of the Psychological Corporation. —Ed.

Dr. Zygmunt Piotrowski (1964) at Temple University is developing a computerized program for the Rorschach. It seems possible that within ten years or so the computer can, within a few minutes during which a person replies to the Rorschach cards before a screen and a microphone, produce a complete diagnosis and prognosis of that person. Dr. Piotrowski had also said that sometimes the computer brings out material so subtle that he had not picked it up. Some future developments, Dr. Brown thought, may cut expenses and provide new data differently acquired with which to work.

Dr. English noted that Peace Corps experience has confirmed Dr. Brown's remarks about the diagnostic problem. People who had not worked enough with adolescents have diagnosed adolescent turmoil as schizophrenia. He also agreed with Dr. Douglas's opinion about the great importance of interpretation of the data. Less than 20 percent of the Peace Corps volunteers who go overseas have been individually interviewed by a psychiatrist because the staff does not think that the involvement of a psychiatrist will help in the total population. It does help, of course, when the person is disturbed. The greatest value of the psychiatrist's judgment appears at the preclinical meeting before the selection board when he sits down with the assessment officers—psychologists—and goes over the data with them. Also appearing at the board are the training people and the country director, who comes back to give field information. As all the data are presented, the psychiatrists and psychologists are impressed with the great validity of the opinions of the lay people on the board. The combined work of the professional and lay people with their field experience brings forth something that is helpful.

REFERENCES

Arnold, M. B. *Story Sequence Analysis: A new method of measuring motivation and predicting achievement.* New York: Columbia University Press, 1962.

Blizzard, S. W. The layman's understanding of the ministry. In S. Southard (Ed.) *Conference on motivation for the ministry.* Louisville, Ky.: Southern Baptist Seminary, 1955. Pp. 50–65.

Booth, G. Tests and therapy applied to the clergy. *Journal of Religion and Health,* 1963, 2, 267–276.

Cattell, R. B., *et al. Sixteen Personality Factor Questionnaire.* (Rev. ed.) Champaign, Ill.: Institute for Personality and Ability Testing, 1957.

Hathaway, S. R., & McKinley, J. C. *Minnesota Multiphasic Personality Inventory: Manual for administration and scoring.* New York: Psychological Corporation, 1967.

Maslow, A. *Motivation and personality.* New York: Harper, 1954.

Maslow, A. *Religions, values, and peak experiences.* Columbus, Ohio: Ohio State University Press, 1964.

Piotrowski, Z. A. Digital-computer interpretation of inkblot test data. *Psychiatric Quarterly,* 1964, *38,* 1–26.

TESTING FOR THE RABBINATE*

FRED BROWN

THE PROBLEMS INVOLVED in the selection of the rabbinical students with particular reference to Orthodox, Conservative, and Reform groupings in Jewish communal life are somewhat different from those encountered among other denominations. These problems have their roots in the history of the rabbinate and in both divergent and changing conceptions of the rabbi's role and functions in congregation and community. This immediately becomes apparent when one considers the term "clergyman," for, prior to 1840, this term would have been meaningless to members of the Jewish community and had no historical or traditional sanction. Even today, and in the strict sense of the word, "rabbi" and "clergyman" are very far from synonymous, regardless of the fact that ordination implies consecration to the service of God.

*I am completely indebted to Dr. Paul Steinberg, Dean of Hebrew Union College, for the historical summary in this paper, and to Mr. Victor Geller, Field Director of Yeshiva University, for information on the current situation in the Orthodox rabbinate.

HISTORY OF THE RABBINATE

To obtain a clearer understanding of this distinction it is necessary
to review the history of the rabbinate from its inception to the
present time. The word *rabbi* was borne for the first time by
Gamaliel, the Patriarch and President of the Sanhedrin, signifying
his superior learning and authority to teach the Torah and to act
as judge. The literal meaning of the word is "master" or "expert."
It was to Gamaliel and to his son Simeon, and to Jochanan ben
Zakkai that the title *Rabban* (a higher rank than *rabbi*) was ac-
corded by their disciples because of their prominent scholarship
and learning. The title rabbi was officially first conferred by
Rabban Jochanan ben Zakkai on his disciples. It was in the period
of the Tannaim (A.D. 70–317) that the title came to mean "my
teacher" to everyone who had proved himself to be a qualified
teacher and interpreter of the Torah. The measure of his authority
depended largely upon the respect he had earned for himself as
scholar and interpreter. During this period the term *rabbi* was used
in a non-professional sense. He was not a paid official of the
community, nor did he receive any public support. The sages of
the Talmudic period were artisans and craftsmen and laborers in
every field. The sage Akiba was a shepherd, the great Hillel a
wood-chopper, and Joshua ben Hananiah a blacksmith. This was
in accordance with the counsel: "Make not of the Torah a crown
to aggrandize thyself, nor a spade wherewith to dig." Until the
middle of the fourth century, in Talmudic times, there was another
type of rabbi whose primary function was that of judge. Based
upon his character and knowledge of the law, he was appointed
by three Palestinian authorities with the approval of the Hasi (head
of the community) and was empowered to enforce the law and
impose fines.

The rabbinate was essentially an avocation until the late Middle
Ages. Political conditions and exigencies within and without the
Jewish community at the time made it increasingly apparent that
a kind of spiritual leadership was needed to direct and influence
Jewish life. The title of *rabbi* in the modern sense—namely, a

scholar appointed to judge and teach, and to lead in a community's spiritual life—is first found in the twelfth century. However, the relationship between the rabbi and the community was not official. The members of the community turned to him for advice and counsel. He taught the Torah and pointed the way, but his decisions had no binding power. The rabbi of the twelfth century then began to resemble, in part, the modern rabbi: a man who has proved his competence in Jewish scholarship and who has been appointed by the community to be available for religious guidance, to teach Jewish law and lore, and to act as a judge in civil matters. He accepted no compensation for his teaching, although he would accept fees for granting divorces, writing marriage contracts, and for serving at times as a marriage broker. Many of the rabbis of medieval Spain continued to earn their livelihood as physicians, while others supported themselves in trades and investments. But as the massacres of the Middle Ages increased and persecution intensified, it became increasingly difficult for rabbis to support themselves by some other livelihood, and salaries, from the fifteenth century onward, became quite usual. The tradition and law were circumvented by defining the rabbi's salary as "compensation for being prevented from engaging in a useful occupation." The principal function of the rabbi was to be an exemplar of the Torah, a student of the Law, and a respondent to questions of law asked by his congregation. In addition, he was responsible for the system of elementary education, the maintenance of synagogue ritual, and the supervision of the ritual slaughter in the community. Many rabbis of this period were interested in philosophy, philology, Biblical research, Arabic, and Latin.

After the explusion of the Jews from England (1290), France (1394), and Spain (1492), the Jews concentrated in Eastern Europe and were cut off intellectually from non-Jewish disciplines. The role of the rabbi also changed and there now emerged the *Rav,* the essence of piety and learning whose major concern was the Torah. He was revered and respected as the highest religious and legal authority, but despite his status and prestige his income was small.

In the eighteenth and nineteenth centuries Hasidism, a popular mystical movement, swept East-European Jewry. Its founder was Rabbi Israel ben Eliezer (1700–1760) who is also known as the Ball Shem Tov, the Master of the Good Name of God. The *Tsaddik* or saint was the leader, and, within the context of the movement's emphasis upon the emotional core of religion, its adherents stressed the guidance and inspiration one could gain from association with him. These religious leaders were essentially counselors who empathized with their people. This is exemplified in the statement of one Hasid: "Supposing someone comes to you and asks your help, you shall not turn him off with pious words, saying, 'Have faith, and take your troubles to God.' You shall act as though there were only one person in the world who could help this man—only yourself." The movement gradually degenerated. Superstition and obscurantism replaced faith and religious fervor, and the true charismatic was overcome by dynasties of *tsadikkim* who exploited the credulity of the people.

The period following the French Revolution and the nineteenth century saw the rabbi lose his function and status as teacher, judge, civil official, and even priest. It was natural that a new rabbinate, suited for a new era and influenced by the Revolution, was needed. Modern seminaries had their inception in 1829 in France and another was opened during the same year in Padua. In Florence a Collegio Rabbinico Italiano was opened in 1899. Other seminaries included those of Breslau (1854), Berlin (1827), Budapest (1877), London (1879), and Vienna (1893). The general orientation in this period was toward the broadening of rabbinic training to include the study of the sciences and metaphysics. The Jewish community in the United States established its own schools to prepare young men for the rabbinate. The first of these was the Hebrew Union College, founded by Isaac Mayer Wise in Cincinnati in 1875, and the second the Jewish Theological Seminary of America, opened in New York in 1886.

There was one very significant function that the European rabbi performed and which was vital to the survival of the Jewish community. He served as a liaison between the government (especially in Eastern Europe) and the community, communicating government edicts and regulations to members of the community and representing the latter in his contacts with government. In this respect the existence and welfare of the community depended upon his wisdom and judgment. In all other respects it should be emphasized that there is no function in all of Jewish life, from birth to death, that requires the presence of a rabbi. This stands in striking contrast to the priest who celebrates the Mass and listens to confession, or to the minister who performs baptism. Whereas Christian clergymen are essential to a wide variety of religious functions, the rabbi's presence as officiator is a matter of either courtesy or custom but is not a religious obligation.

TRAINING FOR THE ORTHODOX RABBINATE

While the conception of the rabbi changed in the nineteenth century, this was not true of the Orthodox group, which continued to follow the traditional pattern. There was no clearly defined conception of the rabbinate as a vocation, nor was there anything comparable to the Christian belief in a "call" to the ministry. If a child in the Hebrew school exhibited an outstanding aptitude for learning and manifested this in the speed with which he mastered talmudic subtleties, he was encouraged by parents and teachers to forge ahead with the hope that he would ultimately obtain his ordination and bring honor to parents and community by devoting his life to the Torah. There was no formal curriculum in the Yeshiva and no formalized and regulated examinations. When the aspirant believed he was ready for a thorough test of his ability to pursue his studies independently for the rest of his life and to assume the responsibilities of teaching and arbitrating, he presented himself to the head of the Yeshiva, and if the latter was convinced that he was ready for examination, he underwent a process comparable in some ways to an oral examination for a doctorate. Upon "passing" this he in no sense became a "practitioner" but continued to immerse himself deeper and deeper in Hebraic learning.

In the Orthodox community the notion of the rabbinate as a career area distinct from commitment to the life of a scholar is a relatively new and slowly emerging concept that is not eagerly accepted by the head of a Yeshiva but regarded as a regrettable aspect of mundane demands for a livelihood. This transition is reflected in resistance to and ambivalence toward the establishment of a formal curriculum in the Yeshiva, a resistance motivated by distaste for the drift toward professionalization.

The clash between the traditional concept of the rabbi, which is communicated in various subtle ways to the Yeshiva student, and the demands of an Orthodox congregation which is basically illiterate so far as scholarship is concerned and has begun to conceptualize the rabbi in terms of a more modern image, leads to frustration on the part of those who elect to "professionalize," and has resulted in an interesting phenomenon. An increasing number of these young men carry on their Hebrew studies and obtain their ordination while simultaneously taking a major (at Yeshiva University) in mathematics, chemistry, psychology, sociology, physics, and other fields. They then continue to live in accordance with Jewish tradition and beliefs, but enter fields that were formerly closed to them and thus escape the frustrations of an area that is relatively unstructured and vocationally unsatisfying. These young men may be found working in secular universities and in the laboratories of huge corporations where their professional skills bring them a sense of fulfillment and income without interfering with their devotion to religion.

For these reasons, among others, Yeshiva University does not have a selection program for prospective rabbinical students. As the demand for scientists and technologists increases it is very likely that the number of applicants for rabbinical training will dwindle. This can be attributed to the fact that apart from medicine and law, there were until the recent past very few professional fields that were open to the bright Jewish young man.

TRAINING AND SELECTION FOR THE CONSERVATIVE RABBINATE

The Jewish Theological Seminary of America (JTS) trains rabbis for the Conservative wing of the Jewish community which holds a position somewhat midway between Orthodox and Reform Judaism. From a large number of senior-high-school and college students who are interviewed, a final pool of from 25 to 35 rabbinical students constitutes the entering class. Most of these students are well known to the school by the time they have reached the second year of college, as they have been observed at affiliated Hebrew schools and Hebrew summer camps. Selections are made upon the basis of entrance examinations comparable to those utilized for the selection of Ph.D. candidates; a comprehensive qualifying self-administered examination at home and dealing with personal attitudes toward the vocation (e.g., "why do you want to be a rabbi?") and the applicant's conception of Jewish, world, and ethical problems; college transcripts; letters of recommendation; and an interview by three members of the Admissions Committee. In doubtful cases the applicant is interviewed by a psychiatrist who is a member of the teaching staff. Approximately 23 out of 25 applicants selected by these methods are graduated and seem to function effectively in their congregations, although this opinion is only an impressionistic one.

The JTS does not utilize any type of psychological test for the evaluation of applicants for rabbinical training. One reason for this has already been stated: namely, the fact that the majority of applicants are known to the school and have undergone an unobtrusive screening over a period of several years. The second reason lies in the attitude of the psychiatrists on the teaching staff who are skeptical of tests and have advised against their use as screening devices. From time to time when a student is suspected of being a "problem" he is referred to a member of the psychiatric staff, who may initiate any testing which he thinks is necessary.

ONE SELECTION PROGRAM FOR THE REFORM RABBINATE

The Hebrew Union College (HUC), Jewish Institute of Religion, trains men for the Reform rabbinate and conducts this training in New York City, Cincinnati, and Los Angeles. Prospective students in New York are referred to psychologists who have no connection with the institution for individual psychological examinations and are also interviewed by a psychiatrist. From 25 to 30 applicants are tested each year, but this procedure and the psychiatric impression are used to *screen out* applicants whose psychopathology appears to be too great to warrant a successful adaptation to the scholastic demands of the school. The psychological reports are sent to the Dean at his home, are not put into the applicant's record, and are not made available to the Admissions Committee. The nature of this testing program is such that no data are accumulated and no predictions are involved.

A long-range research project was established at Hebrew Union College in 1950 and continued up to 1959. This study was guided by a recognition of the fact that, although projective techniques provided a magnificent instrumentality for the evaluation of personality in depth, no one actually knows whether there is any correlation between what the tests reveal and the qualities that make for successful performance in the profession or vocation for which it is expected to screen candidates. Consequently, when projective tests are used to rule candidates in or out, there is the danger of ruling out good prospects and admitting poor ones.

In this project we had no intention of making selections upon the basis of psychological test reports. A battery of psychological tests was administered to each candidate which included the Wechsler-Bellevue Scale (Wechsler, 1955, 1958), Bender Gestalt (Bender, 1938), Human Figure Drawings,* Rorschach (1942), selected TAT cards (Murray, 1943), Sentence Completion Test,† and the Word-Association Test.** The comprehensive psychological reports were submitted to the then Dean of the college, Dr. Abraham Franzblau, were seen by the psychiatrist *after* he had made his decision, and were then filed away until sufficient data could be accumulated on each man to warrant correlative studies of the relationship between the multidimensions of the psychological material and the similarly multidimensioned factors that compose the full spectrum of success or failure criteria. It was felt that this would require a twenty-year period of study. After two years of "pilot study" to test out procedures and to accustom the

---

* A well-known example is the Draw-a-Person Test developed by Machover (1949).—Ed.

† A typical example is the Rotter Incomplete Sentences Blank (Rotter & Rafferty, 1950).—Ed.

** Examples are the Free Association Tests developed by Rapaport, Gill, & Schafer (1946, Ch. 2), and by Kent & Rosanoff (1910).—Ed.

Admissions Committee to this unusual operation, the actual study was begun in 1950 and all candidates were tested in ten-years' entering groups. It was decided to wait ten years for each group until they completed their education and had at least five years in the ministry, the period to terminate in June, 1969. At that time all material relevant to an assessment in depth of the rabbi and the job became available, ranging from his years as a student to the current status of his vocational effectiveness.

The Admissions Committee was given a psychiatric judgment by the psychiatrist who served as the consultant to the Institution throughout the ten-year testing period, and by Dr. Franzblau, who also served as Professor of Pastoral Psychiatry. For each applicant one of the following was submitted: "No psychiatric contraindications" or "Admission contraindicated on psychiatric grounds." While the latter judgments were arbitrary, Dr. Franzblau's 25 years of association with the Institution and its admission committees had led to the conclusion that overt homosexuals and frank psychotics had little or no chance of success in the ministry. Of the 240 candidates screened in twelve years (two years "pilot" and ten years study), only nine were refused psychiatric clearance on this basis and two were accepted despite refusal to grant psychiatric clearance. The latter are now serving in the ministry. The project has complete psychological reports on 120 men; 76 have graduated and have been in the ministry for five years or more, and the last of the group will have completed at least five years in their vocation by 1970.

FOLLOW-UP PLANS

The formulation of relevant criteria is a formidable task that must be accomplished if the testing approach is to be a realistically oriented one, and particularly in the light of changes that have taken place in the role and functions of the rabbi. In the Conservative and Reform congregations, and to some extent in the larger Orthodox ones, the rabbi has become the administrator of an institution. Unless there is a fulltime executive director, the rabbi carries burdensome responsibilities that include the Men's Club, Sisterhood, Youth Groups, Young Couples Group, Educational activities, Board and Committee memberships, fund-raising, inter-denominational contacts, and a host of others that were never dreamed of by the rabbi–scholar of the older tradition. In addition to this he is expected to deliver interesting sermons, to conduct services, and to officiate at weddings, funerals, and other occasions.

The first and easiest step in the evaluation procedure will be to ascertain the degree of relationship between the psychological assessment and the psychiatrist's clinical formulation. The second will determine the number of candidates who completed their training or failed to do so, and the third will focus upon the rabbi's subsequent career. In all cases an attempt will be made to test certain hypotheses concerning ego strength and personality integration, versatility of coping resources, stability of reality testing processes, empathic resources and their availability to the individual, level of affective differentiation, approach to new situations in terms of originality-stereotype polarities, self-concept, ability to profit from experience, degree of sensitivity and tactfulness, nature of the defensive structure in terms of flexibility and rigidity, diagnostic formulation, and other personality variables relevant to the adaptive process and matched wherever possible with definable components of the "job" situation.

What might turn out to be unfortunate is the fact that these psychological evaluations were made by clinical psychologists who thought in terms of psychopathology and its presence or absence. Consequently, such appraisals would be very useful in screening psychiatric patients with reference to disposition (in-patient or out-patient treatment), diagnostic classification, and accessibility to one of several types of treatment by psychiatrists in private practice. Whether the personality dimensions under consideration have long-range significance for the operational efficiency of the rabbi remains to be determined.

In conclusion, apart from the "screening out" procedures currently employed at the HUC, there are no testing programs at the present time for the selection of prospective rabbis. It is to be hoped that the proceedings of this meeting will encourage rabbinical seminaries to consider the utilization of psychological tests both for screening and for long-range prediction purposes.

REFERENCES

Bender, L. A visual motor Gestalt test and its clinical use. *American Orthopsychiatric Association, Research Monographs*, 1938, No. 3.

Kent, G. H., & Rosanoff, A. J. A study of association in insanity. *American Journal of Insanity*, 1910, *67*, 37–96; 317–390.

Machover, K. *Personality projection in the drawing of the human figure: A method of personality investigation.* Springfield, Ill.: Thomas, 1949.

Murray, H. A. *Thematic Apperception Test.* Cambridge, Mass.: Harvard University Press, 1943.

Rapaport, D., Gill, M., & Schafer, R. *Diagnostic psychological testing.* Vol. II. Chicago: Year Book Publishers, 1946.

Rorschach, H. *Psychodiagnostics: A diagnostic test based on perception.* (Transl. by P. Lemkau & B. Kronenburg). Berne: Huber, 1942 (1st German ed., 1921).

Rotter, J. B., & Rafferty, J. E. *The Rotter Incomplete Sentences Blank.* New York: Psychological Corporation, 1950.

Wechsler, D. *Manual for the Wechsler Adult Intelligence Scale.* New York: Psychological Corporation, 1955.

Wechsler, D. *The measurement and appraisal of adult intelligence.* (4th ed.) Baltimore: Williams & Wilkins, 1958.

DISCUSSION

John P. Kildahl: In response to Dr. Brown's paper, I have three comments and a recommendation.

1. First, I want to tell a story in reference to those three comments: I vividly recall visiting a new parish pastor who had just received his Doctor of Theology degree from a certain theological seminary, and who had now been in his first parish for about six months.

In his handsome church office he had framed his new diploma, and hung it on the wall. The degrees from this particular seminary are written in Latin. Consequently, my friend said that he had translated his diploma and written the English words in exactly the corresponding place on the cardboard on the back of the diploma and then hung it on the wall.

I can still recall the pathos in his voice as he pointed to his diploma and he said, "In six months not only has no parishioner asked me to translate it; no one has even asked me what it was!"

This is my first point: That satisfaction and success in the seminary are not necessarily correlated with satisfaction and success in the parish. In response, then, to Dr. Brown's implicit impression that twenty-three out of twenty-five of these young men had done well in seminary, and were doing well in the rabbinate: I think this is the kind of thing that should be followed up very carefully. In the seminary, *books* are the raw material. However, in a parish, *people* tend to be the raw material. Many new clergymen are thus rather disappointed in the disparity between what constituted having a good life in seminary, and what constitutes having a good life in the parish.

ii. This relates to my second point, namely, that there can scarcely be an entity called "testing for the rabbinate" or "the ministry."

Dr. Brown properly mentioned that one hardly knows what it is to be a rabbi because of the varied and burdensome responsibilities. Here I have a positive suggestion. I submit to you that testing for the rabbinate or the ministry should consist of a general personality assessment, more on the nature of aptitude testing than on the nature of a screening process.

In my own practice of psychotherapy, I have had very little difficulty referring somebody to the New York University Testing and Advisement Center, where he expects he will be tested for aptitudes. Rather than undergoing a screening procedure, the person is comforted in the conviction that the testing will help him uncover goals, and set directions for his life.

I would like to suggest that our testing should be designed to help a candidate or a seminarian or a clergyman toward the *style* of religious work where he may be fulfilled personally and do fruitful work.

Let me cite some examples from my own experience in the individual testing of missionary candidates over the last ten years, using a battery similar to Dr. Brown's, although I do add the MMPI.

In these missionary candidates, the psychological evaluation simply describes the candidate's assets and liabilities.

The report speaks in almost anecdotal form of how this person might react to administrative details, or to the lack of observable rewards or status. Can he be expected to have a fair number of original ideas, or is he too far out? Will he tolerate supervision? Can he work independently, and so on? The report, of course, is based on psychodynamics and character structure, but does not speak this language. This report is then combined with that of a psychiatrist. Certain selected missionary officials read the report, and together with all the other data at hand, make a judgment regarding the type of missionary service that will be suitable.

In general, I oppose the testing for the purpose of saying *yes* or *no,* with the exception of those same three pathological categories that Dr. Brown mentioned.

In this connection, may I cite other examples, to indicate what constitutes suitability? We test candidates for career missionary service—that is, the missionary who will go out for a five-year term and return for a furlough, and then another five-year term, and so on. There is also another category, that of short-term missionary, someone who is usually single, who goes out for three years, who is not expected to learn the language of the country, and who at the end of the three years will return permanently to the United States. It comes the closest to the Peace Corps.

Other testing programs involve deaconess candidates, and, finally, also stewardship personnel—that is, people who conduct capital-fund-raising campaigns for congregations throughout the United States.

My point is this: We have found clearly observable differences among these groups. That is, the career missionary is not very much like a three-year missionary, who is certainly not like a deaconess, who is certainly not like a capital-fund-raiser.

But the profession of the rabbinate or the ministry, I am suggesting to you, is as varied as the difference between a fund-raiser and a deaconess. To predict that one will make a good rabbi or a good minister is just as difficult as to say that one will be a good missionary *and* a good deaconess *and* a good fund-raiser.

III. A third response that I have concerns the society, or the environment, or the culture, in which one is to be a clergyman.

One rabbi told me that he had forty ordained rabbis in his congregation. I ask you, what must he be like to survive in that milieu? To be a minister in Hayfield, Nebraska, is a far cry from Central Park West. Psychological testing, combined with a certain cultural sophistication, enables one to describe more accurately how one will adapt himself.

To cite another example, we have learned not to recommend an acting-out type of passive-aggressive person for missionary service in Japan. We would have a bull in a china shop in that culture, where a slight inflection of the voice may mean the difference between empathy and insult. Such behavioral nuance may be beyond many characters. On the other hand, a neat obsessive may revel in it. We try to send that kind of a person to that kind of a culture.

So, also, I recall a girl who went to Central Africa, where she was an immense success. She loved the principal native dish, which is variously described as a soup-porridge-stew and hash combination. This was a girl whose character structure was such that she was most at home on the business end of a broom. She was a doer and not a thinker. But she would have been most unhappy in many sophisticated urban cultures.

Therefore, my third response to Dr. Brown's paper concerns the very crucial necessity of knowing what character structure can best fulfill itself in what kinds of environments. In general, again, there are no "yes" or "no" answers. But, there can be psychological testing to aid in a prudent counseling process, to steer a person in a direction where he may find himself the most fruitful.

In summary, these three things: We should be alerted to the differences between seminary success and parish success. We should be alerted to the style of religious service that is best suited to a person. We should scrutinize the environment in which certain kinds of persons can do their best work.

Finally, keeping in mind these factors, I have this recommendation: We can use our tests most prudently in the counseling and supporting process, and I hope that some day we might have an Arden House Conference on the pastoral care of pastors; that is, the follow-up use of testing for the purpose of nurturing, supporting, and focussing a man in his religious vocation.

GENERAL DISCUSSION

The participants found that they were not well informed about the rabbinate. As a consequence, the major portion of the discussion period was devoted to responses on the part of Dr. Fred Brown, the author of the paper, and Dr. Paul M. Steinberg, Dean of Hebrew Union College, to the questions put to them by the participants relative to the training of the modern rabbi and his role in the community. In summary form, the discussion went as follows:

Paul M. Steinberg: Dr. Steinberg said that at Hebrew Union College in New York, Cincinnati, and Los Angeles those concerned with the testing program for the rabbinate are not particularly interested in securing the commitment of the persons whose needs they are trying to meet; rather they are trying to understand the people who come to the college's three centers. "We want to understand their personality structure, their capabilities, their intelligence, their verbal ability, their capacity for conceptualizing. The tests serve as tools for this.

"We note that when our students begin to work as student rabbis in their third year they actually begin to function as rabbis. From Monday through Friday they are students, sitting at the feet of masters of subject matter. From Friday night to Monday morning they are the authorities in their congregations. They really switch roles from Friday night to Monday morning."

Students who have two critical needs, Dr. Steinberg said, seem to do quite well as student rabbis: one is the need to help people, to be really interested in them; the other is the need to be liked. "We are using our tests to help these students complete their program of studies, to guide and assist the faculty counselors in their work with the students, and to guide and assist the field-work supervisors."

Fred Brown: In answer to the question whether the various Old Testament priestly roles, such as that of prophet, head of the synagogue, etc., were extant today, or whether they have been melded into the role of the rabbi, Dr. Brown said: "Both the Levites and the priests (*Kohēnim*) derived from Aaron of the tribe of Levi. Prior to the building of the Temple by Solomon, laymen participated with the priests in religious functions, but with the building of the Temple Zadok founded the Jerusalem priesthood. The priests offered sacrifices, officiated at all sacred functions, and served as teachers. The Levites, in the period of the Second Commonwealth, were singers who chanted the chorus while the priests were offering the sacrifices and blessing the people. During the era of the Second Commonwealth, the authority went into the lay hands of the Pharisees. With the destruction of the Temple in A.D. 70, the priests lost virtually all their prerogatives and the rabbis took over the former basic function of the priests—teaching and interpreting the law." Today, Dr. Brown continued, the priestly blessings in the Orthodox and Conservative congregations on the High Holy Days are performed by a man who may be a peddler or may work at a sewing machine in a dress shop, if he is a member of the priestly cast. In a Reform congregation the rabbi or the assistant rabbi may bless the congregation. Actually, a member of the congregation may be equally empowered. He does not need any special charisma to bless the congregation if he wishes to do so and if the congregation wishes him to. If any ten men form a prayer group, any one of them may go up to the pulpit and conduct the service. This is true in the Orthodox, Conservative, and Reform groups who hold morning and evening prayer. There is no such thing as a function of this kind that is carried over from ancient times.

Paul M. Steinberg: "What makes a person a rabbi—just finishing the course of studies?" asked one of the participants.

Dr. Steinberg replied: "A rabbi is a Jew who has achieved a certain degree of excellence in Jewish studies. He is otherwise no different from any other person in the Jewish congregation. As Dr. Brown has said, any Jew may officiate at a service; he need not be ordained. Ordination is a rite—the laying on of hands—administered by a rabbi to a disciple. The first act of ordination took place in the time of Jochanan ben Zakkai, about A.D. 70.

"There has been a change in the role and status of the rabbi. In the past, his status depended upon his mastery of his subject matter and his knowledge of the law. Today it is often dependent upon personality. Personality has really supplanted knowledge. Administration has supplanted ministration. In short, a man's ability to do many tasks really well has given him the status of a Jewish community leader."

It was only in the fifteenth century, Dr. Steinberg added, that the rabbi began to receive a salary from the community. Rabbis always had some other vocation. The saintly rabbis of the talmudic period were wood-choppers, blacksmiths, and the like. One was forbidden to earn money for being a rabbi, for having superior knowledge. One should study the Torah for its own sake.

Asked whether the goal of the Hebrew Union College testing program was to select persons who would function as full-time rabbis, Dr. Steinberg said that it was. "Today the rabbi is a professional person. The requirement for admission to our seminary is a B.A. degree; therefore our graduates have had a four-year college education in the liberal arts before entering their five-year seminary training period."

To an inquiry about who ordains, Dr. Steinberg replied that it was the president of the college.

"Immediately upon ordination, the graduate is placed in one of the services, for all of our men must be available for service in one of the military branches. They may also serve in the Peace Corps or on a college campus. They will devote themselves to full-time ministering to the Jewish community.

"We test for the total personality of the applicant. We want to see what kind of person he is. We want to know all we can about him from the tests in addition to his academic record and his letters of reference.

"We do not test for a belief in God, for we do not feel that it is possible to test for a 'commitment.' There is a wide range of belief about God, especially within the Reform ministry. No one would be so presumptuous as to say, 'You must believe this way about God.' We do, however, ask that you believe in God. People who may have been quite orthodox in their observance have undoubtedly entered our rabbinical school. No one is forbidden to observe the dietary laws or to put on the phylacteries. Some of our people have done these things."

Answering a question about how much the person who ordains has access to the data gained from testing and observing, Dr. Steinberg said: "There is continuous feedback." The current testing program, he noted, is a change from the early program, which was one of research, as Dr. Brown had reported. When he came to the college he felt that he did not want to wait ten years. He wondered what was going to happen to all the people who had gone through the program. The college considered themselves responsible for giving these people feedback so as to be of assistance to them. It also seemed to be a good way of encouraging them to go into therapy. A number of the college's students have been in therapy, not because they needed it, but because the college authorities thought it would help them gain a better understanding of themselves.

Fred Brown: A question addressed to Dr. Brown about the importance of pastoral counseling as a function of the rabbi in the Orthodox, Conservative, and Reform congregations—and if it is important, how does that fact fit in with the relative lack of attention paid to psychological and psychiatric screening in the assembling of candidates?—brought this answer:

"The rabbi in the Orthodox community in the Middle Ages and up until the destruction of the Jewish community in Europe always played an important role as a counselor, although he was not called a pastoral counselor. He was the person who dealt with the problems of separation and divorce, after first trying to bring about a reconciliation. He handled business disputes. With his wide knowledge of the talmudic law, he dealt with torts, damages, and many other legal problems. The people of the Jewish community and of the Ghetto and the Pale went to him, therefore, instead of to the local courts

"The rabbi was also a man with perspective; he was not involved in the hard, grinding job of earning a livelihood. He was a leader and an exemplar. He had wisdom, mellowness, objectivity. He had to be oriented to his task and to be extremely humane because of the talmudic injunctions emphasizing repeatedly that no human being's sense of self-esteem must be threatened. The rabbi was respected for his fairness. So there was pastoral counseling, but not as we know it today.

"The Yeshiva University Mental Health Project embodies pastoral counseling in the modern sense. It attempts to teach rabbis something about psychodynamics, psychotherapy, and the meaning of certain test findings. All this is done, not to swerve the students away from the rabbinate, but to help them use their religious resources to salvage something from the past, from the traditional concept of the rabbi, bringing it into a new context. This is difficult to do, because there is always a danger of trying to create a paperback psychiatrist. The rabbi frequently becomes confused about what his resources are. These are matters that have to be clarified.

"As we know, today more people turn to the clergyman than to the psychiatrist, the psychologist, or the physician for help with their troubling situations. Therefore, it is part of the responsibility of the rabbi to know when to refer a congregant to a member of the mental-health professions and when to deal with the situation himself. In the Chassidic community today as portrayed in the little Yeshivas in Williamsburg, the rabbi fulfills precisely the function of the medieval rabbi. A kind of empathizing human experience enables him to deal with complex problems. He has an unverbalized, inarticulate knowledge of psychodynamics. In fact, looking at the Talmud carefully today one is impressed with the many insights sprinkled through it, insights based upon observation of people's behavior and motivation."

Paul M. Steinberg: Dr. Steinberg noted that Maurice Friedman's book, *Martin Buber: The life of dialogue* (Friedman, 1955), which, as its title implies, centers on the writings of Martin Buber, particularly *Between man and man* (Buber, 1955), provides many in-

sights into the role of the rabbi and the Chassidic tradition. The
director of the Lubovitchah Yeshiva schools in this country, Dr.
Steinberg observed, is a very modern man, who advises people
on every kind of situation that confronts them. He mentioned also
Rabbi Joseph B. Soloveitchik, an Orthodox rabbi and probably
the world's foremost talmudic scholar, who has participated in the
Yeshiva University Mental Health Project. The people concerned
with that project are in fact very modern.

Brother Dondero asked whether it would be accurate to say
that the great thrust of encouragement for men who want to become rabbis must come from the people in authority who decide
that a certain person would make a good rabbi. Or could one put
it another way by saying that the status of rabbi is open to a man
of intelligence? Could a boy aspire to it if he worked on the upper
echelon?

Dr. Steinberg replied that this is so. There have been some
interesting developments, he said. "There was a time when one
could say that Orthodox rabbis came from the lower economic
group, the Conservative rabbi from the middle class, and the
Reform rabbi from the upper-income group. A number of years
ago, however, men with Orthodox backgrounds began to come
into Reform. In the past fifteen years we find that Reform is repro-
ducing itself.

"I should add that we are finding the best recruiters to be the
men in the field—the rabbis. This brings us to the role of the
rabbi as an exemplar. The Chassidic rabbi, as Dr. Brown said,
was an exemplar. The famous rabbi Leo Beck, when asked what
the message of the minister should be, replied, 'The message of
the minister must be himself.' In other words, a man must deliver
himself. The rabbi who delivers himself as the message is the
recruiter."

William G. T. Douglas: Dr. Douglas voiced his strong approval of
Dr. Kildahl's comments about the need for aptitude testing to get
a sense of the candidate's style of religious life, where he may
operate most effectively, and what may be done to give him support and guidance in the fulfillment of his potential. It is not just

a question of screening out, of nursing along the sick, but of determining the strengths, the potentials of the man, and finding into what setting he can most appropriately be directed.

"It is interesting," Dr. Douglas continued, "to note that within at least some Protestant circles there are stirrings of interest in the Orthodox rabbinate pattern of having a secular vocation at the same time as one is training oneself to think theologically. It is what I would call a multiple-competence ministry. At the same time there is the ability to reflect with theological wisdom on meeting the issues. A number of Protestant theologians are pointing in this direction."

Fred Brown: Asked for further comment on how he was going to proceed with his research, how he intended to check the psychological test reports against the man's functioning in the rabbinate, Dr. Brown said: "We will have to find out as much as we can about the various areas of functioning within the congregation and within the community. We shall have to get together with the rabbis, with the board of directors. Perhaps we shall do a survey study of members of the congregation, using a kind of polling technique, a scaling, rating technique. These will be some of the objective criteria that we shall use in the evaluation of a man's efficiency, the level of his functioning and its spread in the community. We shall try to establish and evaluate operational factors rather than deal with the concepts of success and non-success. This will take in levels of operational efficiency and extent of involvement."

REFERENCES

Buber, M. *Between man and man.* Boston: Beacon, 1955.
Friedman, M. S. *Martin Buber: The life of dialogue.* Chicago: University of Chicago Press, 1955.

III
Testing Outcomes

A FOLLOW-UP STUDY OF PSYCHOLOGICAL ASSESSMENT

DAVID W. CARROLL, S.J.

THE RECENT AND WELCOME VOLUME prepared by Robert Menges and James Dittes (1965), their *Psychological Studies of Clergymen,* in which they abstract for us some 700 books, articles, and dissertations, pointedly illustrates the amount of study that has been done during the past decade in this area. When they come to group titles under main categories or headings, it is apparent that the greater number of these psychological studies of clergymen have attempted to search out information necessary to answer two key questions. Dittes (1962, p. S-142) puts them this way: 1.) who is the clergyman as distinguished from the non-clergyman? and 2.) who is the *effective* clergyman as distinguished from the *ineffective* clergyman? Most research to date has been an attempt to answer the first question, to search out those traits, characteristics, dispositions, attitudes, interests and motivations which help to distinguish the clergyman from the non-clergyman. Until recently, for the good reason of greater difficulty, there has been much less effort to answer the second question concerning the *effective* clergyman and how judgment is to be made about potential that promises future success and effectiveness in the ministry.

I see little need to spend many of my words trying to convince this gathering of a need to evaluate the effectiveness of psychological testing programs in their effort to predict at the time of a candidate's application who will be the future effective clergyman. Many of you are actively engaged in screening applicants for the ministry and almost as many have made and reported your attempts to evaluate the effectiveness of your screening procedures. Your research has been trying to isolate predictive variables of success in the ministry, to find those hard-to-come-by performance criteria that can be shown to correlate with the predictive variables. It is likely that there is no one here who would not admit the need for a full-scale study of a psychological testing program screening applicants for the ministry, once it has been in operation for a certain number of years. To date, as far as I know, there has been no systematic evaluation of an entire testing program. Some of the information needed to improve the effectiveness of screening programs for the ministry can only be gotten at in a follow-up study which would take a new, current, controlled look at 1.) those who are tested in a screening program, accepted for ministry training, and are still persevering in their vocation; 2.) those who were tested in the same program and were admitted to training, but who have not persevered and are now classified as the "dropouts"; 3.) those who were tested in the program but never admitted.

GENERAL PLAN OF THE RESEARCH

I would like to serve as a primer of the group's discussion of follow-up studies of assessment by telling you briefly about some work I have been doing during the past several years (Carroll, 1968). It has been in the nature of a follow-up study. Its principal aim was to determine how successfully the clinical judgments based upon the results of a battery of psychological tests (ACE,* Ohio

* American Council on Education, Psychological Examination for College Freshmen. After 1954, the ACE, which had been prepared by the Cooperative Test Division of the Educational Testing Service, was discontinued. The

State [Toops, 1958], Bier's version of the MMPI,† Sentence Completion and Figure Drawing) and a brief record of personal history have predicted degrees of effectiveness in applicants who were accepted into a Catholic religious order of men to be trained for the ministry.

The subjects of the research were persons who had been screened at the time of their application for admission to the religious life in one of the oldest of the psychological screening programs conducted under Roman Catholic auspices. When the research was begun in 1963, the screening program had been in operation for 14 years. The first applicants tested in the program were in the last year of their course of studies before beginning their ministry in the priesthood. Other individuals who were tested before admission were at every stage of training distributed over a 15-year span. It seemed a reasonable assumption to make, that, of those who entered the religious life and persevered, some would have made a very good adjustment and would have been considered quite effective religious-in-training, others would have made an adequately good adjustment and would be called religious-in-training of average effectiveness, and, finally, some who entered the religious life and had persevered would have been less successful in making adjustments to the life and would be considered less effective religious-in-training. Since at the time of their application for admission to the religious life a judgment about their future promise had been made on the basis of psychological test data, there was an opportunity to investigate whether the original predictions about these individuals agreed with estimates of performance determined by current faculty and peer evaluations.

During the 14 years that the testing program, which provided subjects for this research, had been screening applicants for the

---

testing program here described continued to employ the test, however, because of the cumulative norms which had been developed on it for the sample of seminary candidates being tested.—Ed.

† This modification, which consists basically in the elimination of 33 items (mostly of religious content) from the front portion of the test and the substitution of a similar number from the back portion (beyond item 366), has been developed for use with seminary applicants. It cannot be released for more general use until work is complete on the normative samples needed for the interpretation of test results.—Ed.

religious life and subsequent ministry, a total of 1155 applicants had been tested. Of this total number, 830 applicants were admitted to the training program of the religious order. Of these 830, 528 were persevering when this research was begun, and could be classified as religious- or clergymen-in-training. The study was designed to follow-up these 528 individuals. Of these 528 potential subjects, 428 could be reached. The remaining 100 were scattered literally around the world. Of these 428 who were invited to participate in the study, 386 accepted the invitation, and these made up the research sample. This meant that 90 percent of those actually invited to participate in the study agreed to cooperate. The fear that the 10 percent who refused the invitation would for the most part have come from the group of the originally least promising proved to be groundless. The individuals who declined to take part in the research were found to be distributed, as was the experimental sample, on an almost 1–2–1 ratio into the high, average, and low categories of original promise.

The purpose and aim of this research was to determine whether the original prediction, made on the basis of psychological tests and a brief personal history, about the future effectiveness of these 386 individuals bore any relation to outcome. Outcome, for this study, was performance of the individuals in their training program. The criterion of performance was evaluation by their superiors and peers made on a rating scale that investigated the presence in an individual of characteristics considered important to the effectiveness of the religious—the clergyman-in-training.

One of the more difficult questions to respond to in developing psychological screening procedures as an aid to personnel selection and in evaluating the effectiveness of the procedures is the troublesome issue of performance criteria. How does one judge when a person is doing an *effective* job? How, for example, does one judge who is the effective religious-in-training, the religious-in-training of average effectiveness, and the religious-in-training of below-average effectiveness? Effectiveness means different concrete manifestations in different vocations, professions, trades.

What are the characteristics of the effective religious-in-training? The successful approach of Stern, Stein, and Bloom (1956) in developing performance criteria for Protestant theological students was followed. More than forty experienced administrators, teachers, and counselors, veteran religious of the same order as the subjects of the research sample, were asked to list the characteristics that each believed were always found in the effective, above-average religious-in-training. Thirty-eight of those polled did submit lists of characteristics they considered important. Some of these lists were long, some short, some quite full in explaining the meaning of the characteristics set down, others less specific. In all, 231 separate items were suggested. These went into a pool of items. It was from this pool that the characteristics of the effective religious-in-training and the subsequent Faculty Rating Scale were drawn and constructed. The procedure employed was something like a sorting technique. The 231 items were given to three different psychologists. They were asked to sort the items into categories and then to name the category: that is, to set down the personality characteristic which all the items in the category seemed to be describing. The plan called for the three to do the sorting independently at first and then to come together to compare sortings. It was agreed beforehand that an item would finally be placed in a category whenever at least two of the psychologists agreed on its location by having independently placed it in an identical or similar category. In the case of items that had not been placed by the independent sortings of at least two of the sorters into categories that seemed to be alike, the three sorters came together after their independent sortings and by discussion agreed upon the proper classification. The sorters finally settled on nineteen categories into which they judged all 231 items could be placed. In other words, the psychologist-sorters made the judgment that in the view of those who pass judgment upon the effectiveness of the religious-in-training there are nineteen characteristics which need to be evaluated in any adequate assessment of performance.

Before constructing the Faculty Rating Scale which was to be used to obtain current evaluations of the individuals in the research sample, all items that fell under each characteristic were arranged logically to form a criterion model for that characteristic. In this way, an attempt was made to use all the items to describe in a coherent way the meaning of the characteristic in the language of those who contributed to the pool of items. To understand the Faculty Rating Scale used in the research, one needs to be familiar with the characteristics deemed necessary in the effective religious-in-training.

Following is a listing and description of the characteristics considered important for the effective religious-in-training. The characteristics are presented here in an order of prominence, going from the characteristics listed most frequently by the persons polled to those less emphasized. After giving the characteristic a name, an explanation of what is meant follows. This description or explanation is listed as the criterion model. Under this heading, an attempt is made to include all the elements that were suggested as encompassed by the characteristic in question. Finally, the number or numbers of the questions on the Faculty Rating Scale* which investigate each of the characteristics are given. The most frequently mentioned characteristics were represented on the Faculty Rating Scale by three questions, others by two, and the remainder by one. In three instances—namely, characteristics 11, 12, and 19—it was necessary to ask more questions on the Faculty Rating Scale than the relative number of items in the pool would have required. The additional questions were needed in these three instances in order to reflect the meaning which these characteristics had for those who contributed to the pool of items. The characteristics investigated were the following:

1. *Industriousness–Perseverance*

The criterion model: The effective person wishes and is able to work hard with diligent persistence at tasks assigned to him. He can keep a goal clearly in sight as he carries through a long-range project to completion. This means that he is able to stand up under pressure of routine, does not give up as soon as the task has lost its initial interest or when the going gets rough, and can continue to work quietly on difficult tasks without seeing immediate results or getting rewards. He is energetic in making effective use of time: i.e., he is not excessively devoted to recreation, gripe-sessions, light reading, exercise, outings, etc. He has the good work habits of efficiency: thoroughness or a knack of

* The Faculty Rating Scale is given on pages 171–173.—Ed.

tying "all loose strings" in contrast to the careless or rushed approach; promptness, i.e., beginning and getting projects done on time; accuracy or concern for exactness and correctness.

Questions on Faculty Rating Scale: 21, 22, 23

2. *Concern for others*

The criterion model: The effective person is a man who has genuine concern for others. This love for people manifests itself in various ways. He is interested in people in the flesh and for their own sake, sensitive to their needs, understands them in their problems and their successes and can accept them under both conditions. He is outgoing and warm in his dealing with all classes of people so that they know he likes to be with them. As a result, people find him amiable and are able to approach him. He realizes that more is done by graciousness than by harshness. He is a force for unity in his community life because he tries positively to improve relations between people.

Questions on Faculty Rating Scale: 1, 2, 3

3. *Emotional balance and maturity*

The criterion model: The effective person possesses a reasonable degree of emotional balance. This implies a personality in which reason and emotions are well developed and wisely blended. He manages himself well—his emotions, his moods, his passions. He is not carried away by feelings but is self-disciplined, self-controlled. He has the emotional strength to face the monotony of study and the pressure of college-level examinations without extreme tension and periods of stress exhaustion. In all circumstances he has a certain serenity, in contrast to the moody individual who reacts unpredictably and excessively to various events and occurrences. He has an emotional "toughness" (so that he feels self-secure and free from an excessive need for the attentions of others which invites exaggerated demonstrations of affection, effeminate quarrelling, sulking, etc.) needed to face the human loneliness of the priesthood but not an emotional "hardness" which would make him insensitive to people.

Questions on Faculty Rating Scale: 4, 5, 6

4. *Docility*

The criterion model: The effective person is one who possesses that great medieval virtue, *docilitas,* a dynamic disposition to be educated by others. He is willing to be guided by those over him, to do his best in a program determined by someone else because he is free from false individualism and libertarianism. However, his is not passive acceptance, without penetration, of ascetical or intellectual principles but the open-mindedness of proportioned receptivity which admits there may be something that can be learned from others. This docility is a respect for, not a servile fear of, authority and tradition which enables one to follow directions without losing initiative and accept correction without losing generosity.

Questions on Faculty Rating Scale: 15, 16, 17

5. *Commitment or involvement*

The criterion model: The effective person is one able to engage himself totally in the life he has chosen. He has made an irrevocable commitment to the religious order so that no price of sacrifice and generosity will be too high for him to pay in order to become a full member. He is completely loyal to his religious order, to its spirit, its aims, its methods of training, and its program of apostolate. Should doubts occur to him about phases of the life in the order, he readily solves them because of his great confidence in the order on the basis of an implicit trust in the order and its training. Almost as if born to it, he has a great filial love for the order, for his fellow-religious, for the order's works, so that he lives, breathes, works for the order in any capacity, with all his talents and with no reservations. He is conscious of himself as a part of the religious order as its representative. He has an accurate and well-defined self-image as a member of the order because from among the various ways that a man can live out his love of God, he freely selected the way of life of his religious order which becomes not only the divine will for him but his own fullest expression of love for God.

Questions on Faculty Rating Scale: 7, 8, 9

6. *Good judgment*

The criterion model: The effective person is able to give a balanced assessment of a human situation in contrast to the gauche, odd, awkward. He can apply general principles to individual situations with confidence and correctness, and in the proper hierarchy of values. He combines the ability (a kind of brains-and-common sense) to size up men and situations with the stability needed not to be led astray by emotional pressures. He is able to evaluate in modern movements, interests, modes of thought, and expression what is solid and based upon permanent values, as opposed to the ephemeral, the superficial. He is not automatically swept into acceptance of everything new or blindly against tradition. He possesses that sound judgment and tact, a sense of practicality and reality, that knows how to get people to heaven.

Questions on Faculty Rating Scale: 10, 11

7. *Responsibility*

The criterion model: The effective person lives with an awareness of obligations to be filled, in contrast to empty-headedness. He accepts the responsibility that springs out of his situation, especially for his own spiritual development and intellectual formation, without seeking undue autonomy. When asked to undertake a project or an assignment, he accepts it even though it may not be of primary interest to him. He can be trusted to perform the task promptly, expeditiously, efficiently, completely. In the event that he finds a task beyond his competence, he will report back.

Questions on Faculty Rating Scale: 19, 20

8. *Generosity*

The criterion model: The effective person is generous and magnanimous. He gives himself generously to the religious order and is always on the look-out for what more he can do for God and the Church. He is ready to help in common enterprises, to work for and with the group. Quite different from the "operator" who is minded to push only his own personal projects, he is not self-seeking but eager to commit himself wholeheartedly to assigned tasks and to discover ways of advancing the common cause even at the sacrifice of his own time, entertainment, relaxation. He is able to make a gift of himself, his time, his work, his kindness without expecting a return.

Questions on Faculty Rating Scale: 32, 33

9. *Self-reliance*

The criterion model: The effective person is one who does not need to have his mind made up for him by another whenever a practical choice is possible. He can get along without mothering. He stands back from the detailed circumstances of a situation, lets its voices be heard, reflects upon them, criticizes them, and finally comes up with a personal stand in confrontation. Once taken, he is able to hold onto this personal stand even in the face of non-acceptance on the part of others. His independence of judgment enables him to lead rather than to be led by the crowd. And so, he shows substantial independence of personal attachments and especially of crowd pressures, without being a lone wolf or closed to genuine friendship.

Questions on Faculty Rating Scale: 26, 27

10. *Initiative*

The criterion model: The effective person is not passive. He does not wait for decisions being made for him to fit each contingency but has the ability and the urge to seize upon situations and, if possible, to master them to his (or others') advantage. Willing to submit to direction, his talent for creative initiative, an idea-generating ability, keeps him alert to see needs, to figure out remedies, to originate courses of action that get things done and done better. He has the ever present spirit of moving forward rather than of being held back or waiting for a push, and with it all a courageous, self-reliant willingness to stick one's neck out.

Questions on Faculty Rating Scale: 24, 25

11. *Intelligence*

The criterion model: The effective person is able to form judgments on the basis of evidence. Put another way, he is able to think independently. This means that he need not necessarily be a scholar or an intellectual but he should have a progressive mind, up-to-date without necessarily being "modern." His intellectual life should not be repetitious. Specifically he should be possessed of an intelligence and memory at least equal to that of the average graduate of a good college so that he may enjoy at least moderate success in studies. He should never find studies a torment.

Questions on Faculty Rating Scale: 12, 13, 14

12. *Sociability*

The criterion model: The effective person is a man who is able to get along with others, with superiors–peers–inferiors, with people of widely differing temperaments, personalities, "philosophies." He is outgoing and warm in his dealing with all classes of people in and out of the religious order so that people know he likes to be with them. He can communicate his feelings and thoughts to others and is able to empathize with them. He is polite and sensitive to the demands of social grace that call for neatness of appearance and carefulness of speech in contrast to slovenliness in his person and rowdiness in his talk.

Questions on Faculty Rating Scale, 34, 35, 36

13. *Self-acceptance*

The criterion model: The effective person has arrived at a substantially honest and accurate estimate of his assets and liabilities (intellectual, spiritual, social, emotional, physical). He is able to distinguish between what he must accept and what he can and should seek to change in himself. He can accept himself as he is and not equate differences from others as, by that very fact, inferiorities or deviations from the norm. This personal and objective self-appreciation enables him to work at maximum efficiency, all else being equal, with a minimum of negative comparison of self against the achievements of others. In brief, he has the courage to face up either to the fact of his own mediocrity or to the demands of his superior ability without flinching.

Questions on Faculty Rating Scale: 28, 29

14. *Intellectual humility*

The criterion model: The effective person is open to the efforts of his teachers and superiors to direct and educate him because he realizes his need for knowledge, need for filling out his intellectual self. He has a respectful attitude toward ideas which have appealed to many in the past, though, because of his healthy critical attitude, he does not necessarily agree with the conclusions, nor is he sympathetic to the arguments. He has a tendency to receive ideas from teachers and books as true and realizes that it is best to follow programs outlined by teachers even though he does not see how they promote his best interests at this time.

Questions on Faculty Rating Scale: 18

15. *Genuine and broad interests*

The criterion model: The effective person is one who is sensitive to a wide spectrum of values so that he is not narrow or closed-in. He has broad interests, can enjoy the cultural and intellectual aspects of life, is up on current events, finds relaxation in sports and athletics. He has the intellectual interest and curiosity of the "professional" and so cannot tolerate half-knowledge, inaccuracy, shoddiness in his work but is always seeking improvement and perfection of himself in his goals, field, and role.

Questions on Faculty Rating Scale: 40

16. *Cheerfulness–Optimism*

The criterion model: There is a basic cheerfulness of personality about the effective person. Like others he feels the hardships of life, the dullness of routine but is not overcome, depressed by them. Leaning preferably to the optimistic rather than to the pessimistic view of things, he maintains a readiness to see the better side in contrast to the tendency to complain and worry. He does not permit himself the luxury of cynicism but sees the world and man as they are, good and bad, and never gives up.

Questions on Faculty Rating Scale: 38

17. *Sense of humor*

The criterion model: The effective person has an ability to face the gap between the ideal and the real with equanimity. He has the ability at once to cherish and to laugh at the human predicament or incongruity, particularly his own. His sense of humor gives him the ability to rebound quickly from setbacks because he does not take himself over-seriously.

Questions on Faculty Rating Scale: 39

18. *Obedience*

The criterion model: The effective person is an obedient man who knows that every group must have a leader. He sees in the ordinary government of his superior the will of God for him and strives to obey in act and in will, even when the use of authority has not yet been tempered to the relative maturity of the subject, when obsolescent laws have not yet been taken off the books. He values obedience of judgment as an ideal.

Questions on Faculty Rating Scale: 37

19. *Flexibility–Adaptability*

The criterion model: The effective person is one who is in a continual process of decision, choice, election. This means that he loses no time in regrets about previous decisions or in worries about future possible problems. He does not allow past options to become so petrified that this solidification prevents his constant reassessment of the means of service he is using, the price of continuing effectiveness in a constantly changing world. Though he is entirely committed to the task at hand because he believes he is doing it for God, he is for the same reason able to let go at a moment's notice, change residence, associates, assignments to cooperate in the program of another or in something called for by superiors. He has the psychic mobility associated with open-mindedness which enables him to adapt to new people and new situations.

Questions on Faculty Rating Scale: 30, 31

In constructing the Faculty Rating Scale, an effort was made to draw up a set of questions which would provide a means of rating in the case of each individual all the characteristics considered important for the effective religious-in-training. What resulted was a 40-item scale. It was possible to give seven different scores in answering each question of the Faculty Rating Scale about an individual. This seven-point scale provides these evaluations: 1.) Considerably above average in this regard; 2.) Somewhat above average in this regard; 3.) Slightly above average in this regard; 4.) Average in this regard; 5.) Slightly below average in this regard; 6.) Somewhat below average in this regard; 7.) Considerably below average in this regard. To rate an individual's performance, it was necessary to give him a score of one to seven on each of the 40 questions that investigated the 19 characteristics of effectiveness. In order to provide a feel for the criteria against which individuals were measured, the questions on the Faculty Rating Scale are produced here:

1. Is he a person who has genuine concern for others? This involves being interested in people for their own sakes, sensitive to their needs, able to accept them in both their failures and successes.
2. Is he a force for unity in his community life? That is, does he try positively to improve relations between people?
3. Does he have true friends and not merely acquaintances, i.e., people who as individuals mean something to him as an individual?
4. Does he possess emotional balance, a personality in which reason and emotion are well developed and wisely blended so that he is not carried away by feelings but is self-disciplined, self-controlled?
5. Has he serenity of disposition in contrast to the moody individual who reacts unpredictably and excessively to various events and occurrences?
6. Does he have the emotional "toughness" needed to face the human loneliness of the priesthood (free, i.e., from an excessive need for the attentions and sympathy of others) but not an emotional "hardness" which would make him insensitive to people?

7. Is he a man who is able to commit himself totally to his order so that he would not consider any sacrifice required by the order too great?

8. Is he a person who is loyal to his order, to its spirit, its aim, its method of training?

9. Has he a lively interest in and deep concern for the works of his order?

10. Does he use good judgment and common sense in practical matters, in contrast to the gauche, odd, awkward?

11. Is he able to evaluate in modern movements what is solid and of permanent value as opposed to the ephemeral, the superficial?

12. Can he think independently, i.e., form judgments on the basis of evidence so that his intellectual life is not merely a repetition of what he has heard from others?

13. Is he a man of intellectual promise?

14. Has he been successful in his studies?

15. Does he possess docility, i.e., a dynamic disposition to be educated by others and a willingness to be guided by those over him?

16. Is he one who can question traditions and customs without losing his basic willingness to learn from the past?

17. Is he a man who can follow direction and accept correction without losing initiative?

18. Does he have a respectful attitude toward ideas which have appealed to many in the past?

19. Is he a man with a sense of responsibility and awareness of obligations to be filled?

20. Can he be depended upon to accept an assignment even though it may not be of primary interest to him, and carry it through to a satisfactory conclusion?

21. Does this man have the ability to stick at a given job or assignment "over the long haul," not giving up as soon as the task has lost its initial interest?

22. Does he have enough physical stamina to do serious, prolonged work?

23. Does he use his time effectively and efficiently? Does he have good study-habits and does he avoid wasting time?

24. Is he one who can initiate action, who leads rather than is led by the crowd?

25. Does he have talent for creative initiative, an idea-generating ability, that enables him to originate courses of action?

26. Is he a man who can make his own decisions whenever a practical choice is required?

27. Once he has taken a personal stand on some question or issue, is he able to maintain it even in the face of non-acceptance on the part of others?

28. Has he arrived at a substantially honest and accurate estimate of his assets and liabilities (physical, emotional, social, intellectual)?
29. Does he have the courage to face, without flinching, the fact of his own mediocrity or the demands of his superior ability?
30. Does he have flexibility which enables him to adapt to new people, new ideas, new situations?
31. Is he capable of constant reassessment of his own means of service in order better to adapt to a constantly changing world?
32. Is he able to make a gift of himself, his time, his work, his kindness without expecting a return?
33. Is he ready to help in common enterprises, to discover ways of advancing the common cause even at the sacrifice of his own interests?
34. Is he amiable and approachable and consequently liked by people?
35. Is he a person who is able to get along with many different types of people (with superiors–peers–inferiors, with people of widely differing temperaments, personalities, "philosophies")?
36. Is he sensitive to a requirement of social grace by manifesting care in his personal appearance?
37. Is he an obedient man?
38. Is he optimistic rather than pessimistic, able to see the favorable rather than the dark side of things?
39. Does he have a sense of humor which enables him to laugh at human predicament and incongruity, including his own?
40. Does he have broad interests, able to enjoy the cultural, intellectual, and recreational aspects of life?

Let me return now to the basic procedures followed in the research. It was possible on the basis of original test data to sort the 386 subjects into three groups of *original* promise so that 97 of these individuals could be called the group of original high promise, 193 could be called the group of original average promise and 96 could be called the group of those originally least promising. On the basis of current faculty ratings using the Faculty Rating Scale, the sample of 386 was divided likewise into three groups, so that again the top 25 percent became the group of better-than-average effectiveness, the middle 50 percent became the group of average effectiveness and the remaining 25 percent became the group currently rated by the faculty as below-average in effectiveness. Three criterion groups of effectiveness were also separated according to the same proportions on the basis of peer ratings derived from the Faculty Rating Scale.

A word should be said about the reliability of the current faculty and peer ratings given to the same individuals by different faculty raters and different peer raters. The main purpose of the research was to compare the original prediction made about a man with a current evaluation of his performance in the religious life. A crucial issue that had to be faced in this matter was whether evaluations of performance obtained from faculty and peers could be accepted as reliable assessments of performance. It seemed reasonable enough to maintain that if agreement between the two faculty raters of an individual and agreement among the three peer raters was close, the ratings could be considered reliable. There had been 26 sets of faculty raters and 26 groups of peer raters. To obtain reliability coefficients for raters in each of these sets and groups, Winer's (1962) Analysis of Variance technique was used. The average coefficient of reliability for the peer ratings was found to be .79, while that for the faculty ratings was .74. The range of coefficients for the peer raters was .96 to .64, with a median of .78, and a standard deviation of .08. For the faculty raters, the range of coefficients for the 26 sets of raters was .92 to .39, with a median of .77, and a standard deviation of .15. Since the faculty and peer raters were found to be in substantial agreement, the ratings were accepted as reliable current evaluations.

All 386 subjects who agreed to take part in the research were asked to retake the MMPI and the Sentence Completion Test that had been originally taken at the time of their application to the order. The purpose of this retesting was to provide a means of determining whether faculty and peer criterion groups differed significantly in their original and current MMPI and SCT scores.

The research sought to answer four questions: 1.) Does outcome in terms of effectiveness as judged on the Faculty Rating Scale agree with prediction about promise as judged on the basis of a battery of psychological tests? 2.) Are the faculty criterion groups and peer criterion groups, those judged on performance as above-average or average or below-average, really different in the scores they obtained originally and currently on the MMPI and the Sentence Completion Test? 3.) Are there some individuals among the 386 who would be selected by all the ratings, faculty and peer, and by test scores as belonging to the same category of effectiveness? If there are any such individuals would they differ in their original and current MMPI and Sentence Completion Test scores even though the larger faculty and peer criterion groups might not differ? 4.) Finally, is there a change in personality test scores? Since this was in some ways a longitudinal study it was possible to determine whether individuals' scores changed for the better or the worse and to look for patterns that might suggest whether length of time in training or critical periods in the religious life affected scores on the personality tests.

THE RESULTS

To answer the first question proposed for research, simple Chi-square procedures were followed. It was a matter of seeing the relationship that existed between the original high-promise, average-promise and least promising groups with the currently evaluated better-than-average, average, and below-average groups in effectiveness. When the currently evaluated faculty criterion groups were compared with original predictions, as seen in Table 1, it was found that 162 individuals had been placed by original predictions about promise in categories identical with those assigned by current faculty evaluations of these same men. The Chi-square

TABLE 1
ORIGINAL PREDICTIONS COMPARED WITH
CURRENT FACULTY EVALUATIONS

| | *Faculty Evaluation* | | |
	above-average	average	below-average
Original high promise	35	48	14
Original average promise	40	99	54
Original low promise	22	46	28
Chi-square 12.15	P is between .02 and .01		

value showed that the relationship of prediction to outcome was significant beyond the .02 level. The Contingency coefficient was found to be .16.

The picture that emerged from comparison between original prediction about promise and current peer evaluations of effectiveness was different. The comparison is seen in Table 2. It can be seen from the Chi-square value that the relationship of prediction to peer evaluation was not clearly better than chance. The Contingency coefficient in this case was .14. For reasons given below, it seemed that peer ratings were not as valid as faculty ratings. These reasons helped to explain why there was not a closer relationship between prediction of promise and peer evaluation of performance.

TABLE 2
ORIGINAL PREDICTIONS COMPARED WITH
CURRENT PEER EVALUATIONS

	Peer Evaluation		
	above-average	average	below-average
Original high promise	22	55	20
Original average promise	45	89	59
Original low promise	30	49	17
Chi-square 7.75	P is between .20 and .10		

The second question that the research sought to answer concerned itself with the criterion groups set up by faculty and peer ratings. It asked whether the criterion groups that could be formed on the basis of faculty and peer ratings were really different in the original and current test results. To answer the question, a one-way analysis of variance was applied to the scores obtained by the criterion groups on the clinical scales of the MMPI and the four subscales and the Total Adjustment scale of the Sentence Completion Test. The results of these analyses can be summarized briefly by pointing out that the criterion groups formed by current faculty ratings showed no significant differences in their original MMPI scores or in their Sentence Completion Test scores. However, when the current MMPI clinical scale scores of the faculty-evaluated criterion groups were analyzed, several real differences were found. On six scales (D, Pd, Sc, Ma, Si and a special Re scale), the difference between the faculty-rated above-average group and the below-average group was found to be statistically significant. While original SCT scores of the faculty and peer-rated criterion groups showed no differences at all, current SCT scores on all the subscales (i.e., scales measuring family adjustment, sexual adjustment, interpersonal adjustment, and self-concept adjustment) and the total adjustment scales showed differences that were statistically significant between the faculty criterion groups. The current SCT scores of the peer-rated criterion groups showed no differences between the groups. It seemed evident from these analyses that faculty evaluations of effectiveness bore rather close relationship to the criteria of adjustment used in MMPI and SCT interpretation. Peer evaluations did not bear this same relationship. This finding provided evidence for a conclusion that faculty evaluators were better, more objective raters than peer evaluators.

It was expected, when the research was begun, that there would be certain individuals about whom all the indices—i.e., faculty ratings, peer ratings, and test results from the MMPI and the SCT —would agree. This expectation was not realized. In only four cases did all the indices agree in assigning an individual to the exact-same category. In these four cases, the individuals were all placed in the average group. Examining the MMPI profiles and the pattern of adjustment presented on the SCT by these four persons, the best that can be said is that they offer a picture of average overall adjustment judged by norms for the population from which they come.

The final question of the research centered on changes in personality test scores that do occur. What is the factor responsible for these changes? Is it age?—is it simply a matter, that is, of length of training so that those longer in the religious life would tend on the average to have higher and therefore poorer scores on personality tests? Or, can certain specific periods in the person's training be pointed to as critical periods, whether early or late in the training, when personality test scores register evidence of greater anxiety, poorer adjustment?

The procedure followed in an attempt to find evidence to answer whether length of time in training or critical periods of training affect test scores was uncomplicated. Original and current MMPI clinical scale scores and the SCT scores of the individuals at each of six levels of training were tested for differences. The clearest fact that emerged from the analysis was that on almost every scale of the MMPI and the SCT there had been a mean *increase* in scores for individuals at every level of training. Beyond that, no simple answer suggested itself to support the length-of-training hypothesis or the critical-period hypothesis. If, however, one had to go further and search for less certain but somewhat probable indications, it could be said that individuals at the third level, the philosophers, consistently registered mean scores on the MMPI scales and the SCT that were higher and significantly different at the .01 level from the scores they had obtained when they took the tests at the time of their application for admission to the religious life. This partial evidence may give some support to the "critical-period" hypothesis. Individuals at the third level of training had been in the order for from five to seven years, had been studying most of this time, and were still six years from ordination. This could be a low period in their lives. It could be a critical period in their religious training, and their personality test scores could be registering the fact of greater pressure, higher levels of anxiety, and deeper feelings of frustration at this time of their religious life than they had experienced or would later experience.

CONCLUSION

The results of the research bore out three of the original four hypotheses. It has served to underline that the psychologist who sets up a screening program for the religious life does have a measure of success in predicting about the future promise of applicants. If the correlation between prediction and outcome was not highly positive, it must be remembered that the sample used was a highly attenuated one since neither "dropouts" nor those rejected were considered. And so, while the research underlines that there is still a margin of error in selecting out who will be the effective religious-in-training, the screening psychologist on the basis of his psychological test data did manage to achieve some relationship between his predictions and faculty evaluation of actual performance even for this attenuated sample. If his predictions did not agree as closely with peer evaluations of performance, there were several reasons detected in the course of the research to explain this disagreement. Fundamentally, it seems that peer evaluators, since they felt obliged to criticize many aspects of the Faculty Rating Scale and, no doubt, would have preferred different emphases on the scale, really could not use the Faculty Rating Scale that had been given them. While evidence from the present study did not confirm the hypothesis which said that faculty and peer criterion groups would differ in their original MMPI and SCT scores, there was incontrovertible evidence that faculty evaluators distinguished groups that proved to be significantly different on several MMPI scales and on all SCT scales in current testing. Individuals may have changed. Faculty were evaluating persons as currently known. The faculty evaluation distinguished the better-adjusted from the more-poorly-adjusted. Finally, the research evidence did show that personality test scores increase on the average over original test scores. There is no evidence to conclude that personality test scores worsen the longer a person spends in the religious life, but there may be critical periods when adjustment does become poorer.

REFERENCES

Block, J. *The Q-sort method in personality assessment and psychiatric research*. Springfield, Ill.: Thomas, 1961.

Carroll, D. W. *Initial psychological prediction as related to subsequent seminary performance*. (Doctoral dissertation, Fordham University) Ann Arbor, Mich.: University Microfilms, 1968, No. 68-3682.

Dittes, J. E. Research on clergymen: Factors influencing decisions for religious service and effectiveness in the vocation. In S. W. Cook (Ed.) *Review of recent research bearing on religious and character formation*. Research Supplement to *Religious Education*, 1962, *57*, No. 4. Pp. S-141–165.

Menges, R. P., & Dittes, J. E. *Psychological studies of clergymen: Abstracts of research.* New York: Nelson, 1965.
Stern, G. G., Stein, M. I., and Bloom, B. S. *Methods in personality assessment.* New York: Free Press, 1956.
Toops, H. A. *Ohio State University Psychological Test.* Columbus, Ohio: Ohio College Association, 1919–1958. (Form 21, 1940, published by Science Research Associates.)
Winer, B. J. *Statistical principles in experimental design.* New York: McGraw-Hill, 1962.

DISCUSSION

William G. T. Douglas: This is a truly ambitious and impressive study in its scope and methods,* yet—as in all studies of this sort—there is at points lack of clarity of the theoretical concepts related to the empirical variables one is getting at, on the one hand, and the indicators (evidence) of these variables on the other hand. Samuel Klausner's discussion of concept-indicator relationships† would help Father Carroll on this point.

I am concerned particularly about the clarity of the concepts of "the clergyman," "the effective clergyman," "success in the ministry," and "perseverance in the vocation." Many unspecified concepts are mixed into the predictor (independent) variables as well as the dependent (criterion) variables. Throughout, I wonder: "Who is the clergyman?"

If I consider this question empirically, my response is that there are many kinds of people who are clergymen. We need to have a discriminative discussion, not simply a global one, with regard to different kinds of *people* with different kinds of *outcomes* in different kinds of *situations.* Therefore, I find the question: "Who is the effective clergyman?" rather meaningless, since there are differ-

---

* At the time of the Conference (1966) Fr. Carroll was in the process of analyzing his data and was consequently unable to report on his results. Dr. Douglas was, therefore, responding to the preliminary paper presented at the conference, not to the finished paper in the published proceedings. In view of this fact, his attention to "theoretical concepts" is understandable. —Ed.

† A presentation of some of Dr. Klausner's views on this point may be found in the Fifth Academy Symposium, held in 1961, when Dr. Klausner served as discussion leader for a session entitled Methods of Data Collection in Studies of Religion. This material is found in *Research in religion and health: Selected projects and methods.* New York: Fordham University Press, 1963. Pp. 1–17.—Ed.

ent kinds of effectiveness, in different kinds of situations with different kinds of requirements.

Similarly, I would respond negatively to the phrase "the future effective clergyman." I wonder what kinds of future effectiveness there are in candidates? The phrase "predictive criteria of success in the ministry" is rather slippery and ill-defined.

When you take a careful, controlled look at those who were tested in a screening program, as is the goal here, do you have a *homogeneous* group in terms of who enters training over a long period, such as fourteen years? Also, I would be as much concerned with those *not* accepted, and the *basis* for non-acceptance, and the *outcomes* in their future careers.

I also question the criterion of perseverance in the vocation, which has been an implicit criterion in much of our discussion. People may *get out* of a religious vocation for very good reasons, as well as for reasons that we would regard as less healthy. I question, in this connection, the criterion of "very good adjustment to the religious life." In psychological theory, we seem to be moving from emphasis on "adjustment" to emphasis on "coping." I would hope that we would move past "coping" into "initiating and influencing." But certainly "adjustment"—whether to religious life or anything else—does not seem an adequate kind of criterion at this point.

In terms of the tests that are used, such as the ACE, Ohio State, Bier's version of the MMPI, Sentence Completion, Figure Drawing, I get the sense, as with most of our research, that the selection of these particular instruments to provide predictive data is as much opportunistic in terms of what is available, as it is theoretically defensible in terms of the particular questions of research that are being raised.

We still seem to need appraisal techniques related to the specific questions that are being raised and for which we are seeking answers. And I am not clear how these tests or portions of tests contribute to a total diagnostic portrait. We need to develop total profiles, with predictions as to specific behavioral outcomes of particular profiles. These predictions should then be empirically tested over a sufficient period of time for the relevant variables to operate. I have been working along these lines for about the last ten years, in careful longitudinal studies of developing patterns of ministry in relation to psychological "life styles" of Protestant clergymen from a wide range of denominations.*

With respect to the rating system employed in the research, it seems to me that Father Carroll is in danger of reinforcing present patterns. He is really getting a picture of what is valued by those who are already ecclesiastically established. And I wonder what is the empirical, operational definition of "promise" or of "desired behavior." When we select people who are judged as good people by those already established, we are implicitly reinforcing present patterns.

These, then, are some of the issues of which we should be aware in research of this sort. Most of the criticisms I have made would apply to my own research as well as to that of Father Carroll. But, it is at the point of this hard theoretical specification of theoretical concepts related to empirical variables, and of indicators which are defensible in terms of these concepts and variables, that most of our research is weak. It is at these points that research must be strengthened if more solid knowledge is to be developed, and more adequate decisions made on the basis of that knowledge.

GENERAL DISCUSSION

Another Study with Peer and Faculty Ratings. Dr. Arnold, speaking from her experience in supervising two studies (Burkard, 1956; Quinn, 1961), on the correlation predictions made on the basis of the Story Sequence Analysis Test and faculty ratings (Arnold, 1962a, 1962b), noted that the chief difficulty encountered was that the seminary faculty were the ones who had the notion of what is a good characteristic. The researchers thought that the faculty had nothing more than their own guesses to go on. They finally did a global rating. Both peers and faculty were asked to

---

* This refers to an on-going career development study being conducted by Dr. Douglas. There are, as yet, no published results from the study. —Ed.

rate on this basis: if the religious order were abolished and started all over again, who would be the people you would pick to start the new group? Whom would you consider expendable and whom could you not do without? This was not a selection procedure—these people were all in the novitiate or the scholasticate. It was a blind prediction; there was a score on the basis of the Story Sequence Analysis. The researchers got a correlation of about .63 with peer ratings (Lucassen, 1963), which Dr. Arnold considered fairly good.

In the case of the novitiate, Dr. Arnold added, they have since found out that in the cases in which the examiners' scoring did not agree with faculty ratings in the intervening four years, the scoring was proving correct, because the faculty rating was chiefly on the basis of docility rather than on initiative and promise.

Mr. Kling, observing that one has to start somewhere, said he was glad that Dr. Arnold and her colleagues had started and wished them success. Within the limitations of the question, he believed they would find some valuable answers, although they can be discounted considerably on the basis of the "Why didn't you do something else?" kind of question.

Points about Fr. Carroll's Rating Scale. As for long items on a questionnaire, a point raised by one of the participants, Mr. Kling said he was not sure whether they were objectionable or not. Short ones are more precise because they do not allow a respondent to think of only part of a question. David Saunders* is using single words and finds that he is getting just as reliable information as with the longer items in the Myers-Briggs Type Indicator (Myers, 1962). But there should be qualifications, Mr. Kling said; there are some things that cannot be said by a single word or sentence.

Father Carroll explained that items on his questionnaire for faculty and peer ratings were broken up into several parts. For example, the item about docility was represented by three questions: 1.) Does the person have docility? 2.) Is he one who can

* David R. Saunders, currently at the University of Colorado, did this work while at the Educational Testing Service, Princeton, N.J. As far as can be ascertained, this material has not been published.—Ed.

question traditions and customs without losing his basic willingness to learn from the past? 3.) Can he follow directions and accept correction without losing initiative? Father Carroll agreed with Mr. Kling that one cannot get items down to too much brevity, because it impairs accuracy.

In response to a question about an attempt to determine whether the responses to these items could be grouped on a logical basis, Father Carroll replied that the analysis is still in process, but he thought the responses would come together. For example, if a person got an average rating on one question, he would probably get an average on the others.

Dr. Dittes wondered what the experts mentioned by Father Carroll thought they were doing when they made up the 203 items, their suggestions of required characteristics for effectiveness in the ministry. Protestants doing something of the kind might have thought they were expressing some kind of personal preference about the kind of people they like to have around them or in their order. Or they might have thought they were making a prediction that people who have docility are more likely to perform in certain specific ways when they assume the function of their role. Or they might have seen their task as a deductive procedure from a theological or other kind of criterion leading to the idea that one might derive normal docility. He himself liked the third possibility.

Other Observations on the Study. Asked whether there had been any attempt to find out why forty-two persons approached had declined to participate in the study, Father Carroll said that there had been. One of the things he thought it important to determine was how the forty-two would have come out in the original predictions. It turned out that they were distributed among the three groups just the same as were those who had accepted the invitation to participate in the study. Hence, whatever their reasons for non-participation, this group by withdrawing from the study did not create a bias in the experimental sample.

Expressing his conviction that the kind of study Father Carroll was doing is much needed, Brother Dondero said there should be more focus on the fundamental qualities of the criteria that are coming out of the study—the test assessment instruments. There is too much attention being paid, he thought, to the development of performance criteria and not enough to the predictive criteria other than that people are making the clinical judgment of high promise, low promise, or something in the middle. He believed one should relate performance criteria with the test instruments being used.

Dr. English thought that Father Carroll's study, when complete, would have considerable influence on the Jesuit Order. A similar study completed by the Office of Personnel in the United States Public Health Service of its young physicians in an attempt to find out who is a competent medical officer used criteria of effectiveness developed by senior officers, many of them close to retirement. The picture of the effective officer they produced confirmed past performance patterns. Instead of "docility," they talked about a kind of passivity that makes for good working relationships and a certain style of operation associated with certain Public Health Service programs. There is a tendency to reinforce one side of the feeling within the system as a result of the study.

The reaction of the students described by Father Carroll, Dr. English suggested, might reflect some of the tension between faculty and students on some of the issues.

Perhaps the faculty was involved in another kind of thing, Dr. English said—a kind of reactionary attitude to some of the things going on in seminaries now. Some of the criteria are being redefined as a certain interpretation of the Christian virtue of obedience and how it is manifested today. He asked Father Carroll what he was doing about this problem in a study that could have great significance in the order.

Father Carroll replied that a number of the peer raters had discussed the questionnaire with him in advance. They agreed to participate because they hoped that many of the things the study would reveal would bring about a change in the training of the Jesuit.

Criteria of ministerial effectiveness. Dr. Mills asked for general discussion of the time problem involved in follow-up studies. Dr. Brown had spoken of the ten-year period being used in his research. Father Carroll had men who were tested at different stages of their studentship during the fourteen-year period of a testing program, with two classes now out in the ministry. Dr. Mills wanted to find out how valuable or valid is the procedure of testing and follow-up testing without regard to the stage at which the testing happens. One may cover very different five-year periods in a person's life. It is a consistent problem, though Dr. Mills did not know whether anything could be done about it. Dr. Kildahl suggested that one could at least statistically determine whether there are significant differences between what happens in different segments of the training.

Another difficulty, Dr. Arnold remarked, is that the success of the prediction is still a matter of success only in the seminary. One still does not know what these people are going to do in the ministry. Another point is that often the peer and faculty ratings are similar because the peers have gone through the indoctrination process that the faculty prescribe. Whether or not the student may protest against the notion of docility, every order has its image of the good member, which has been given to the seminarians. "Sometimes it is the tests that are right and not the criteria—the peer or faculty ratings—but this may become clear only much later."

Reinforcing the remarks of both Dr. Mills and Dr. Arnold, Dr. Douglas said that once he had listed 146 possible studies he could do if he followed the advice of all his consultants. One must decide, as Mr. Kling had said, what one was trying to do. But he thought the question of culture as it changes with time was important. Seminary students today are a different crop from those of four years ago. Test profiles show differences in that time. Students as seen from their profiles also differ among the seminaries. He thought it possible that there might be equal differences among various Jesuit training centers. But he still thought one had to begin where he was and with the available material.

"Much of the Catholic research on religious personnel," Father

D'Arcy said, "consists of M.A. theses and Ph.D. dissertations. My impression is that some of these studies have been over-ambitious. The authors have seen some big problems they have wanted to study and have tried to do too much. One small part of the work has been to develop tests or scales to measure the variables. The development of a valid and reliable test or scale is itself a major undertaking. Unless the tool is good, all the other work is in vain. This holds for the problem we are discussing. Unless these instruments are carefully developed and their reliability and validity evaluated, no number of correlations will prove anything.

"Father Carroll has spoken of having effectiveness in the ministry evaluated by a group of experts. Who is an expert in this area, in which so little is known? What are the criteria of an expert? A lay person would be better at evaluating effectiveness as it relates to him than would anyone else. One might do better to think of ratings by different reference groups, i.e., authority, peers, laity, etc. It would be interesting to see the relationship among the different ideas of effectiveness of each reference group. Even within a group such as a seminary faculty, how much agreement or consistency would there be in their ideas of priestly effectiveness?

"Are there other criteria of effectiveness besides ratings? These might include prominence, positions held, and number of transfers."

Dr. Mills asked whether anyone in the conference group had ever brain-stormed on the subject of the identification of criteria of effectiveness, throwing out everything that comes to mind and pooling two or three hundred items on a wide variety of experience, both in relation to research and involvement in theological education. He thought it might be worth the effort.

Concluding Comments. Speaking of ratings, Dr. Ashbrook recalled that in the Protestant seminaries it appears that grade point average coincides with faculty-rated potential above .70. Also, in relation to peer and faculty ratings, in two of his samples the correlations of these two kinds of ratings were .85 in one group and .83 in the second, both significant at the .01 level. The second group was a consistently performing group on tests. The first was composed of inconsistent-pattern kinds of people apparently influenced by personality factors as measured by the MMPI. There is some differentiation, but there is also a tremendous convergence toward a shared image of the "potentially scholarly pastor." In his studies he had used the total faculty in rating, rather than selecting only a few of them. This requires a special kind of statistical analysis, converting rank order into a paired comparison matrix and then securing a composite rank order from the resulting matrix. Then he had gone back into the faculty ratings to find the men who had clearer perception than the others to observe the differences among faculty perceptions. This sharpens what had been said about bringing one's own value judgments to his reactions and differentials. In some cases, they even get cancelled out.

Commending Father Carroll for the scope of his study, Dr. Kildahl noted that the caution being expressed by participants was all about how to interpret his data and correlations. He thought that the cautions would sharpen Father Carroll's interpretations. All concerned would be waiting eagerly for the published study,* because of the fallibility of faculty and peer ratings.

Dr. Golden mentioned the research on creativity that Calvin Taylor is doing at the University of Utah,† working with NASA to test Air Force scientists and medical personnel. The investigators have come to the conclusion that the grade point average and IQ are good predictors in high school for college and graduate school performance, but not for adult performance. Dr. Taylor believes that the instrument he has developed, which he cannot release because NASA forbids it for the present, has tremendous potentialities in other occupational groups. He has written a number of books. Dr. Golden thought his work has possibilities for ministerial candidates and students.

* As already noted, at the time of the conference Father Carroll had not yet analyzed the results of his study. He has since done so and his paper, updated for the published volume, reports on these results. Significant relationships were found both with predictions and with current test scores for faculty ratings, but not for peer ratings.—Ed.

† There has been a series of Creativity Research Conferences, the first having been held in 1955 and the sixth in 1964. The proceedings are available in four published volumes edited by Taylor (1963, 1964a, 1964b, 1966). —Ed.

REFERENCES

Arnold, M. B. *Story Sequence Analysis: A new method of measuring motivation and predicting achievement.* New York: Columbia University Press, 1962. (a)

Arnold, M. B. A screening test for candidates for religious orders. In V. V. Herr (Ed.) *Screening candidates for the priesthood and religious life.* Chicago: Loyola University Press, 1962, Pp. 1–63. (b)

Burkard, Sister M. Innocentia. Characteristic differences, determined by TAT Sequential Analysis, between teachers rated by their pupils at the extremes of teaching efficiency. Unpublished doctoral dissertation, Loyola University (Chicago), 1956.

Lucassen, Sister M. Rosaire. Appraisal of potential leadership qualities among young women religious. Unpublished doctoral dissertation, Loyola University (Chicago), 1963.

Myers, I. B. *The Myers-Briggs Type Indicator: Manual.* Princeton, N.J.: Educational Testing Service, 1962.

Quinn, T. L. Differences in motivational patterns of college student Brothers, as revealed in the TAT, the ratings of their peers, and the ratings of their superiors. Unpublished doctoral dissertation, Loyola University (Chicago), 1961.

Taylor, C. W. (Ed.) *Creativity: Progress and potential.* New York: Wiley, 1964. (a)

Taylor, C. W. (Ed.) *Widening horizons in creativity.* New York: Wiley, 1964. (b)

Taylor, C. W., & Barron, F. (Eds.) *Scientific creativity: Its recognition and development.* New York: Wiley, 1963.

Taylor, C. W., & Williams, F. E. (Eds.) *Instructional media and creativity.* New York: Wiley, 1966.

VALIDITY OF PSYCHOLOGICAL TESTING WITH RELIGIOUS*

CHARLES A. WEISGERBER, S.J.

AS THE CONFERENCE PROGRESSED, a division of opinion became apparent: some felt, with Dittes, that the validity of psychological testing for the ministry had not been proven; others, and perhaps the majority, maintained that tests make a definite contribution to the selection process, although their value should not be exaggerated or accepted uncritically. Among the participants, many had some research in progress or newly completed, but had not come prepared to present specific data. Hence the deliberations of the conference lacked "closure" in this regard; and for this reason the editor requested the following summary as a sort of companion-piece to Fr. Carroll's paper.

Research on a screening program was carried out over a period

* This summary of a follow-up study of a testing program was prepared by Rev. Charles A. Weisgerber, S.J., who was a conference member, at the editor's request. This study, which has just been completed, is published by the Loyola University Press (Chicago, 1969), and the tables which are included are reproduced with the permission of the Loyola University Press. —Ed.

of years. Much of it dealt with the evaluation of the Minnesota Multiphasic Personality Inventory (MMPI) and other tests or methods. Only the findings of more general interest can be reported here. As it is, the account has had to be curtailed in order to keep it within reasonable length, and many questions of procedure and interpretation may have been left unanswered. The reader is referred to the fuller presentation in book form (Weisgerber, 1969).

PROCEDURE

This study concerns the success of psychological screening methods used in two provinces (administrative units) of a large religious order of men. Before a psychologist was called in to assist, the order had employed traditional means of assessment of candidates, according to Canon Law and its own constitutions. These depended heavily on interviews and the judgment of the interviewers, who, although not psychologists, were professional men in their own sphere. The main additions made by the psychologist at first were Bier's 1949 modification of the MMPI, a more systematic use of a previously existing reference and rating form, and a follow-up of doubtful cases by means of other tests and a psychologically oriented interview. In addition, the psychologist involved had a summary of the scholastic record and scores on the American Council on Education Psychological Examination (ACE) and English and Latin achievement tests. The MMPI was administered by the vocation directors in the various localities served by the order; and the further tests and interview were often delegated to a local psychologist; but all the interpretation was done by the one psychologist in charge. Among the further tests were the Rorschach, Thematic Apperception Test, Wechsler Adult Intelligence Test, Form I, and the Draw-a-Person Test. Some minor changes of procedure were made, but the approach remained fundamentally the same for the first five years, 1950–54.

In the sixth year, illness forced the psychologist to look for a successor and virtually to suspend the program. The successor took full charge in the seventh year. Because of this break in continuity and some later changes in procedure, an earlier study was restricted to the first five classes, and it is preferable to keep this group distinct. The pertinent changes will be mentioned later.

The psychologist's report contained a judgment of the candidate's fitness and a more or less brief comment or personality description, followed by appropriate recommendations. The aspect of interest to us here is the judgment of fitness, which was expressed under three headings: satisfactory, doubtful, or unsatisfactory. The major emphasis in making this judgment has been on mental health. But attention has also been given to personality characteristics which would help or hinder adjustment to the demands of the religious life, even though there may have been no indication of a weakness conducive to mental illness.

EARLIER STUDY

The earlier study, then, involved 211 men who had been admitted to the novitiate in 1950–54 (Weisgerber, 1962). These were candidates for the priesthood. Those who did not actually enter the novitiate were excluded,* except for one phase of the research, as will be seen later. No doubt this makes it a little more difficult to show strong positive evidence for the value of the screening, since the great majority of those who entered had been judged satisfactory—the problem, familiar to personnel psychologists, of cutting off the lower end of the range on the predictor variable.

The criteria for determining the correctness of the psychologist's judgments were: perseverance, mental health, and overall adjustment. Perseverance is a much used and much criticized norm, but it has the advantage of being objective and can be defended on the grounds that those who persevere over the years are for the most

---

* The exclusion of the most unsuitable is, however, an important factor in admissions and one of the reasons why psychological screening appeals so strongly to ecclesiastical and other officials responsible for the decisions on admissions. This is also the reason why follow-up studies, which usually are able to work only with those *admitted* (as in the case of the two studies reported in this volume), do not fully reflect the value of psychological testing in ministerial selection. To the "modest" results shown by follow-up studies must be added the contribution made by psychological testing in the initial exclusion of the truly unsuitable candidate.—Ed.

part well-adjusted to the religious life, while those who drop out have at least found that they do not fit into this sort of life. Certainly, it is not inferior as a criterion to such indices as long-time employment vs. turn-over in industry. To assess mental health and adjustment, a quasi-rating form was used. For those men still in the order, it was filled out by two persons in official positions which would permit them to know the men reasonably well; for the dropouts during the novitiate, this was done by the master of novices. The form used had the structure of a rating scale but it was really intended to obtain certain critical points of information in a uniform and systematic way, so that it could more readily be used statistically. And the emphasis was, as much as possible, on objective facts, external behavior, or qualities that could be inferred from behavior with a minimum of interpretation. For example, under mental health there were the following items: 1.) no emotional difficulties of any significance; 2.) tense, nervous, anxious, moody, emotional, hypochondriac, or similar troubles; 3.) has had or has illness ostensibly physical but diagnosed as psychosomatic, i.e., primarily due to emotional difficulties; 4.) has been or is under psychiatric or psychological treatment; 5.) hospitalized, left, and/or sent home because of mental illness or impending mental illness. Details were requested. Under the heading of social adjustment the steps were: 1.) well-liked, cooperative, respected, a leader; 2.) in-between; 3.) does not get along, quarrelsome, uncooperative, unadaptable. The other areas similarly covered were: religious discipline, and adequacy of work as a student or as a teacher.

The information was gathered in 1961–62 and the men were classified for mental health and overall adjustment, according to a definitely specified system. The principles were carefully spelled out in order to reduce, if not avoid, the play of subjectivity. The final categories were simply: satisfactory, doubtful, and unsatisfactory —to correspond with those initially used by the examining psychologist. This was done separately for mental health and overall adjustment—although, of course, the interdependence of the two had to be recognized.

In preparing the later summary of this work (Weisgerber,

1969), the results were brought up to date as of early 1967; that meant a follow-up interval of 16½ years for the first class and 12½ for the last. No new rating forms were sent out, but a check was made with the religious superiors regarding those who had meanwhile left the order, and their classifications were changed in accordance with this information. At this time an attempt was made to add the criterion of ordination to the priesthood, for the 1950–53 classes, which had reached that phase of training. The results were very promising—in fact, statistically quite significant (.02 level). However, during the lag between preparation of these data and publication, the class of 1954 had also reached this stage, and a recalculation seemed called for. Unfortunately, the results now failed to be significant (.20 level). In point of fact, there is no difference between this criterion and simple perseverance in the order. Hence no mention of ordination will be made in the subsequent account. The perseverance data were again brought up to date.

For some subjects the original records of the psychologist or the subsequent information was not adequate for classification, sometimes in one regard, sometimes in another. Of the original 211, there were 195 who could be classified regarding mental health; 199 for overall adjustment; 200 for perseverance.

The percentages of correct predictions according to the three criteria are listed in Table 1. Of those subjects declared satisfactory in regard to mental health, 75 percent proved actually so; 60 percent of those labeled doubtful or unsatisfactory failed to persevere. Other percentages are lower. The base rates indicated in the table are the percentages of the entire group who actually proved satisfactory (in the left half of the table) and doubtful or unsatisfactory (in the right half). Encouraging as a percentage like 75 may be, it is of little meaning if it is not much better than the base rate. Even a relatively low percentage may be good from this viewpoint. Hence, the figures for improvement over the base rate provide an estimate of the extent to which the psychological examination contributes to the success of the admission procedure. This statement must, however, be qualified. Unless the testing was completely ineffective, the results are biased to some degree against

TABLE 1
EARLIER GROUP: SUCCESS OF PREDICTIONS
COMPARED WITH BASE RATE

	Prediction					
	Satisfactory			Doubtful or Unsatisfactory		
Criterion	Percent Correct	Base Rate	Improve-ment	Percent Correct	Base Rate	Improve-ment
Mental Health	75.3	72.1	3.2	37.9	27.9	10.0
Adjustment	57.7	54.5	3.2	54.8	45.5	9.3
Perseverance	54.1	51.2	2.9	60.0	48.3	11.7

Note—When the data for both types of prediction are combined, Chi squares are: Mental Health: 2.210 ($P = .20$); Overall Adjustment: 1.800 ($P = .30$); Perseverance: 2.037 ($P = .20$). (Modified from Weisgerber, 1969, p. 24.)

the psychologist: for the base rates were obtained from the screened group and not from unselected control subjects. The Chi squares given in the footnote to the table show that it is not impossible to attribute these results to chance. However, the data to be given later constitute a repetition of the research and provide some degree of confirmation.*

If one considers the favorable predictions, the improvement is only about 3 percent. However, the situation is better for the unfavorable predictions, in which the gain is roughly 9 to 12 percent. In neither case does this rather modest success remotely realize the high expectations with which the psychological screening of religious was begun some years ago; yet it is something.

* The reader will detect a little ambivalence in regard to tests of statistical significance. The reason is that the application of sampling statistics in this instance is questionable, to say the least. The data are taken from a definite, circumscribed population, and the whole population is included except for cases of incomplete information. If there is sampling in any sense, it is that we hope the data from these groups will hold true more or less for future groups; but then we do not have random samples but relatively intact groups. The statistical techniques for handling intact groups, for example in analysis of variance, are not readily applicable because the data are in the form of frequencies and percentages. Nor is generalization to groups from other religious orders intended. Replication of research seems to be the only sound approach.

Since the impetus of the screening movement was derived from the hope of determining in advance those candidates who are unfit for the religious life, it is appropriate to ask how many of the unfit were actually detected. The figures are given in Table 2. From this

TABLE 2
EARLIER GROUP: IDENTIFICATION OF THOSE
WHO WERE NOT SATISFACTORY*

Criterion	Not Satisfactory	Identified	Percent
Mental Health	52	11	21.2
Adjustment	88	17	19.3
Perseverance	86	18	20.9

* I.e., doubtful or unsatisfactory in mental health or adjustment; in regard to the last criterion: failed to persevere. (Taken from Weisgerber, 1969, p. 26.)

it appears that the psychologist is catching only about 20 percent of the problem cases, regardless of the criterion. This, again, is something, but it is rather disappointing. Certainly it suggests the need of improvement.

LATER CLASSES, 1956–62

Besides the fact that a different psychologist had been put in charge, the screening procedure with later classes underwent some changes. Bier's 1955 revision of the MMPI was adopted, a Sentence Completion Test was added, and, from 1957, all candidates were interviewed by a psychologist except in the extremely rare case in which distance made this impractical. There were additional changes from time to time which were of minor importance: for example, replacing the ACE with the School and College Ability Tests, dropping the achievement tests, further changes in the reference and rating forms, and a progressively greater reliance on the interview to clear up doubts rather than such tests as the Rorschach and Thematic Apperception Test. Mention must also be made of a brief autobiography, but this was used with only about one-half of the men in the last two classes.

The follow-up was made toward the end of the novitiate. At first this consisted in getting from the master of novices a brief personality description of the men. Later it was done by means of the quasi-rating form used in the earlier study with the 1950–54 classes. With those who persevered, no further information was obtained; with those who left after the novitiate, the major superior was asked to indicate the reason for leaving. As before, the religious were rated for mental health and overall adjustment, and according to the same principles as much as possible. (There was some difficulty with the free descriptions.)

In the original account (Weisgerber, 1969) from which this summary is taken the subjects were divided into two groups. For one of these the writer had done all the psychological interviewing, and the follow-up interval was 4½ years for the last class and 10½ for the first; for the other group there were several different interviewers, and the interval was 5¾ to 11¾ years. The slight differences in results between the two groups were overshadowed by the similarities; hence, only the combined data are given here. Again there were problems with incomplete records or inadequate information in some instances. The original pool of cases was 413, but the usable subjects were: 368 for the mental-health criterion, 378 for overall adjustment, and 379 for perseverance.

The data concerning the success of the predictions are to be found in Table 3. In comparison with the previous results the percentages correct are somewhat lower for the favorable predictions, somewhat higher for the unfavorable. The improvement over the base rates is a trifle better for both: 3½ and 15 percent respectively. Whether this difference may be due to a shorter follow-up interval is a moot question; it is a distinct possibility. On the other hand, there had been some changes in procedure which were intended as improvements.

As far as the prior detection of the unsatisfactory is concerned (Table 4), there is again a slight advance over the earlier work: 24 percent as against 20. If one may be permitted in this instance to appeal to the data for the subgroup in which the same man

TABLE 3
LATER GROUP: SUCCESS OF PREDICTIONS
COMPARED WITH BASE RATE

| | Predictions | | | | | |
| | Satisfactory | | | Doubtful or Unsatisfactory | | |
Criterion	Percent Correct	Base Rate	Improve-ment	Percent Correct	Base Rate	Improve-ment
Mental Health	67.8	64.3	3.5	50.8	35.7	15.1
Adjustment	48.2	44.7	3.5	71.8	55.3	16.5
Perseverance	48.7	44.9	3.8	68.5	55.1	13.4

Note—When the data for both types of prediction are combined, Chi squares are: Mental Health: 7.690 ($P = .05$); Overall Adjustment: 9.387 ($P = .01$); Perseverance: 7.023 ($P = .01$). First two from 3 × 2 tables; the last from 2 × 2 table. (Modified from Weisgerber, 1969, p. 32.)

interpreted the tests and conducted the psychological interview, the percentage is close to 29. (This is not given in the table.) However, in any event the picture is not greatly changed, since it is clear enough that far too many of the unsatisfactory slip by.

TABLE 4
LATER GROUP: IDENTIFICATION OF THOSE
WHO WERE NOT SATISFACTORY*

Criterion	Not Satisfactory	Identified	Percent
Mental Health	130	31	23.8
Adjustment	210	51	24.3
Perseverance	207	50	24.2

* Cf. note to Table 2. (Modified from Weisgerber, 1969, p. 33.)

Some far more encouraging data were provided by a happy accident. For about half of the men in one year and practically all in the following year (a total of 50 cases), one master of novices began his description by saying: "You were right in this case," "You were wrong," or some such remark. With the exercise of a little skepticism, it was possible to distinguish instances in which the psychologist had been quite correct (64 percent), mostly correct (16 percent), and wrong or only partially correct (20 percent). Combining the first two categories makes a percentage of 80 substantially correct, a fairly respectable figure. No doubt the influence of suggestion has to be reckoned with, since the judgment was made by the master of novices with the reports actually before him. Perhaps what we have in our data are several diverse estimates of accuracy, with the 80 percent forming the upper limit and the rest of the distribution represented by Tables 1, 3, and later 5. One hesitates to accept the present figure at face value, but it is a tenable approach to the matter.

"CLEAR HITS" *vs.* "CLEAR MISSES"

One of the considerations which prompt superiors to call for the help of a psychologist in selection of candidates is the occurrence of breakdowns or of serious emotional problems, particularly when they happen in the early years of training. Accordingly, the data were searched for clearcut instances of mental illness among those who had been admitted. These, in the jargon of psychometrics, are called "misses," and the adjective "clear" has been added to signify that they could hardly be doubted. "Clear hits" are those cases in which the psychologist's opinion was confirmed by a psychiatrist or by subsequent behavior which definitely indicated instability. For this side of the ledger, it was necessary to dip into the cases of applicants who were not admitted. Obtaining such information about these men is not easy, and most likely the lack of systematic follow-up prejudices the data against the psychologist's "batting average" to some degree. However, enough cases were found to make the effort worthwhile.

The data for the first four classes of the earlier group showed 6 clear hits and 9 clear misses, which would average 1.5 hits a year and 2.25 misses—if it is permissible to speak of a person-and-a-fraction. The records of those rejected in the fifth and sixth years were so inadequate that they could not be used. But it was possible to resume with the later classes, 1956–62. In this seven-year span, 9 were caught and 17 missed, for yearly averages of 1.3 and 2.4 respectively. With this group there was some evidence in the files that the psychologist did better than the bare numbers reveal: there were a few cases of undoubted mental disturbance which, although they were clear in the case history or obvious during the examination, could not be included without contaminating the criterion, which had to be subsequent behavior.

Since the records of the other group were more complete and there are other troublesome conditions which fall short of frank mental illness—such as psychosomatic complaints, need of psychological treatment, pronounced indecision, instability, and so on—a further count was made of such cases. In this the record was: 34 caught and 57 missed; the averages: 4.9 and 8.1 respectively per year. To make a rough compromise between the various figures, the screening manages to identify just a little better than one out of three problem cases. This is not remarkably good. Nevertheless, one such person a year can cause so much trouble that the reaction of some superiors is favorable to screening if it accomplishes no more than that.

BROTHERS

The screening of brother candidates was begun somewhat later in this religious order. Because of the late start and the investment of time in research on the candidates for the priesthood, the brothers were not followed up regularly. Some data, however, are available on 83 of them admitted in 1956–63. Particularly, we can pit the psychologist's predictions against the criterion of perseverance and can examine the record of clear hits and misses. It is unfortunate that the brothers were not included in research plans from the start: they constitute a more heterogeneous group in age, background, and life experience, with the consequence that they show the wide scatter of aptitude for the religious life that one needs for a good test of the screening process.

It appears (Table 5) that those judged less than satisfactory by the psychologist tend to leave—roughly 75 percent of them. (That

TABLE 5

PSYCHOLOGIST'S JUDGMENTS OF BROTHER CANDIDATES
AGAINST CRITERION OF PERSEVERANCE

Judgment	Persevered	Left	Total	Percent Persevered
Satisfactory	22	26	48	45.8
Doubtful	8	24	32	25.0
Unsatisfactory	1	2	3	33.3
TOTAL	31	52	83	37.4

Note—Chi square (2×2 table): 3.501; $P = .10$. (From Weisgerber, 1969, p. 148.)

the Chi square is not significant is due partly to the fact that 54 percent of the satisfactory also leave, and perhaps also to the relatively small number of cases.) Of those who left and were from that standpoint unsatisfactory, exactly half were identified in advance; with the other candidates the percentage was at best 29. Hence, the value of the screening is more apparent with the brothers.

One also gets a more favorable picture of the hits and misses. As for mental illness, there were 3 hits and 2 misses (0.4 and 0.25 per year); for the other troublesome conditions, 14 hits and 3 misses (1.8 and 0.4 per year). In contrast to the data for the seminary candidates, there are more hits than misses, at a ratio of about 3:1.

SHORT- *vs.* LONG-TERM PREDICTION

Implicit in the argument for the screening of seminarians is the assumption that it is possible to detect at this early stage those who are likely to prove unfit even in the long run. After some preliminary investigation, the hypothesis had been formed that the best one can do is to predict for a period of four or five years, i. e., to determine with at least some degree of accuracy who will prove satisfactory and who will have problems within that time but not beyond it.

To put the matter to the test, examination was made of the records of 200 men who entered the novitiate in 1950–54, and of 352 who entered in 1956–61. These comprise all the men in these classes except for a few whose records were incomplete and one who could not be followed up. There was also a problem with those required to withdraw because of academic failure or poor physical health, reasons which do not reflect unfavorably on mental health or personal-social adjustment. These men were excluded, not in the original count, but in the tabulations for the year in which they left the order. Perseverance—or, perhaps more accurately, dropping-out—was the criterion; under the circumstances, a yearly check on adjustment was impossible.

The two groups have been kept separate primarily because of a difference in approach. With the earlier group the psychologist's judgment was based on the MMPI and other written information, except for a small number of men who were interviewed or tested further. Although the great majority of the men in the later group had been interviewed, the judgment based on the tests and other documents was the one used here; not the judgment after the interview. Because of the lapse of time between analysis of the data and publication of the book, the figures have been revised to make them current. The data for 1950–54, presented in Table 6, have been carried up to the 14th year. In computing the percentages, the question arose: what to take as the divisor? The solution chosen was to use the number of men in the given category who were present at the beginning of the year. These are the totals listed in the table. The last column gives the differences in dropout rate between those originally judged satisfactory and those judged doubtful or unsatisfactory, the minus sign being used when a greater percentage of the satisfactory had left.

Because the number who leave each year after the first is small, the data for the 1956–61 group (Table 7) are given by way of a replication study, despite the fact that some of these classes are comparatively recent. The 1961 men have been religious for eight years, and that is the limit to which we have figures entirely comparable to those of Table 6. In order to avoid contaminating the data for years beyond the eighth by including men who had not

TABLE 6
JUDGMENT OF FITNESS AND DROP-OUT RATE BY YEAR OF TRAINING:
1950–54 CLASSES

| Year | Judgment | | | | Difference |
| | Satisfactory | | Doubtful or Unsatisfactory | | |
	Total	Left	Total	Left	
1	169	13.6%	31	35.5%	21.9%
2	146	5.5	20	.0	−5.5
3 & 4	138	3.6	20	5.0	1.4
5 & 6	133	3.0	19	.0	−3.0
7 & 8	129	7.0	19	.0	−7.0
9 & 10	120	6.7	18	5.6	−1.1
11 & 12	112	8.9	17	11.8	2.9
13 & 14	102	2.0	15	13.3	11.3

Note—Totals are the number who began the year. The total underlined (18) was adjusted because one case was excluded, since the reason for leaving was academic failure. (Table modified from Weisgerber, 1969, p. 105.)

yet reached the given stage of training, adjustment had to be made. For the ninth year and beyond, the 1961 class was dropped from the count; for the tenth year and beyond, the 1960 class; and so on for the rest. This entails a successive reduction of the number of cases and consequently the reliability of the percentages.

The results from Tables 6 and 7 suggest that the screening shows its principal effectiveness in the first year: a greater proportion of the doubtful or unsatisfactory leave—28 and 35 percent as against 14 and 17 for the satisfactory. In the second year the two tables are not in agreement, but the greater numbers of cases in Table 7 make it the more dependable. One tends to conclude that the span of prediction should be extended to the second year. For the third and fourth years the matter is still more uncertain, while for the following six years it is the satisfactory who leave in greater proportion. However, a change again occurs, and during the eleventh to fourteenth years the balance shifts in favor of the

TABLE 7

JUDGMENT OF FITNESS AND DROP-OUT RATE BY YEAR OF TRAINING: 1956-61 CLASSES

| Year | Judgment | | | | Difference |
| | Satisfactory | | Doubtful or Unsatisfactory | | |
	Total	Left	Total	Left	
1	231	17.3%	121	28.1%	10.8%
2	191	12.6	87	17.2	4.6
3 & 4	167	9.6	72	5.6	−4.0
5 & 6	150	12.7	68	8.8	−3.9
7 & 8	131	16.8	62	12.9	−3.9
9 & 10	99	16.2	50	16.0	−.2
11 & 12	59	11.9	26	15.4	3.5
13	13	7.7	9	11.1	3.4

Note—Numbers underlined have the same meaning as in Table 6. The eighth year is the last one completed by all of the classes. From the ninth year on, those have been excluded who had not yet completed the year in question; hence, the pronounced decrease in the totals. (Table modified from Weisgerber, 1969, p. 106.)

psychologist once more. It is at this period that the men are engaged in theological studies and facing a decision about ordination to the priesthood. Perhaps the special strains of these years bring out personality weaknesses which the psychologist correctly noted in the beginning. At any rate, there is an indication that some of the predictions, which had appeared incorrect during some years of apparent good adjustment, are finally verified.

It may be contended that the small number of cases involved in the years after the first prevent accepting the reliability of the later drop-out rates, particularly in Table 7 after the eighth year. One thing seems reasonably clear: that the major success of the screening is in reference to the first year. However, the two sets of data agree regarding the last few years, and this lends some credence to the results. At any rate, they fail to confirm the hypothesis that the best one can do is predict for a period of four or five years. Much more data are needed, and a replication would be welcome.

MOTIVATION AND OTHER FACTORS

Although the following material does not precisely concern the question of the validity of screening procedures, it is presented here in the hope that it will prove helpful to the psychological examiner. It is concerned with motivation, family relations, and scrupulosity.

The importance of these factors should have been anticipated and records should have been kept accordingly. Unfortunately that was not the case. The pool of subjects used in this aspect of the research was the 413 in the 1956–62 group; but adequate information could be obtained for only 113 for motivation, 139 for home life, and 34 for scrupulosity. Motivation was classed as good if it was sufficiently supernatural and firm; poor, if merely natural, selfish, or hesitant; doubtful, if the candidate was vague in describing his motives or if the master of novices, after conferences and observation, doubted the sincerity or strength of the motivation. Home life was considered good if there were unity, closeness, family loyalty, reasonable discipline, and so on; fair, if there was too much possessiveness or domination, notable sibling friction, disunity or disorganization, or little show of love and attention; poor, in cases of divorce, impending divorce, constant quarreling between parents, alcoholism or psychosis or serious neurosis of a parent, serious resentment against one or both parents, or failure to get along. A man was reckoned as scrupulous if he was obviously thus afflicted at the time of assessment or had been for an appreciable period, i.e., more than a few months; doubtful, if the indications pointed to scrupulosity but not clearly enough; tending to scrupulosity, if the history showed brief episodes of anxiety about matters of conscience or similar manifestations. At the time of this phase of the research the follow-up interval was 9½ years for the 1956 class and 3½ years for the 1962. The criterion chosen here was perseverance.

Table 8 presents the results in abbreviated form, i.e., by listing

TABLE 8
RELATION OF MOTIVATION, HOME LIFE, AND
SCRUPULOSITY TO PERSEVERANCE

	N	Drop-out Percent	Chi Square*	P
Motivation Poor or Doubtful	36	91.7	17.852	.001
Home Life Poor	44	65.9	2.330	>.30
Scrupulous	25	68.0	——	—

* Chi square was, of course, computed from the complete distribution and from the frequencies, not percentages. In the case of scrupulosity small numbers prevented its use.

only the unfavorable categories. The drop-out rate associated with poor or questionable motivation is striking, and the relation is statistically significant as judged by the Chi square of the complete distribution. The high percentages of drop-out connected with poor home life and scrupulosity are also worthy of note, although statistical significance is lacking in one instance and not readily calculable in the other. Poor home life can be detected fairly well in the Sentence Completion Test; and, in a study of that instrument (Weisgerber, 1969, Ch. 6), the above finding is confirmed. What is surprising in regard to scrupulosity is not that it is undesirable, but that so many of the scrupulous leave the religious life. It seems clear that these three factors must be given great weight in judging the fitness of a candidate. However, the assessment of motivation is far from easy. In a single interview one often finds the applicant vague in describing why he wants to be a religious; as for tests, it is questionable whether they can reveal the hierarchy of a person's motives and to what extent unselfish and supernatural elements prevail.

CONCLUSIONS

The validity of the psychological assessment of religious is best approached from the standpoint of improvement over what can be done without this additional help. This is estimated by calculating the improvement over the base rate. The improvement is small: roughly 3½ percent in those instances in which the psychologist had pronounced favorably on the men; from 9 to 16 percent for the unfavorable predictions. Thus there is some validity, but it is rather modest. From the standpoint of identifying those who will prove more or less unsatisfactory, the data for those studying for the priesthood indicate that only some 19 to 29 percent are detected. For the brother candidates, 50 percent are correctly identified. This again is some improvement, but scarcely as much as had been expected.

If we consider only the more serious cases—mental illness or persistent, serious emotional disturbances—we find approximately 1.4 clear hits and 2.4 clear misses per year with the seminarians, and 0.4 hits and 0.2 misses with the brothers. As to other serious conditions short of mental illness, the results show 4.9 hits annually and 8.1 misses for the seminarians, 1.8 hits and 0.4 misses for the brothers. The most favorable of all the results is a figure of 80 percent substantially correct, in the sense that the master of novices agreed with the psychologist's report. But this is with a small group, is most likely inflated by suggestion, and seems to be too good to be true.

The final conclusion is that the screening has some validity but leaves much to be desired.

A study of drop-out rate over successive years of training reveals that the best prediction record is for the first year. Lines cannot be drawn very precisely, but the psychologist's judgments have little relation to perseverance from about the fifth to the ninth year. In the tenth to fourteenth years there is again some limited evidence in support of the psychologist's predictions. But more data are needed.

Motivation is a critical factor: the vast majority of those insufficiently motivated drop out. Unsatisfactory family relations and scrupulosity are also unfavorable indicators.

REFERENCES

Weisgerber, C. A. Survey of a psychological screening program in a clerical order. In M. B. Arnold, *et al. Screening candidates for the priesthood and religious life.* Chicago: Loyola University Press, 1962. Pp. 107–148.
Weisgerber, C. A. *Psychological assessment of candidates for a religious order.* Chicago: Loyola University Press, 1969.

PSYCHOLOGICAL PROBLEMS OF THE CLERGY

Edward S. Golden

INTRODUCTION AND PERSPECTIVE

In order that you understand my observations and concerns, you must first understand the polity of my church, The United Presbyterian Church, i.e., the way a particular church *calls* its minister; secondly, you must understand the peculiar role I occupy in my church—that is, as a personnel officer in charge of one of the personnel offices of my denomination. We are familiar with some denominations which have invested power in a bishop who assigns clergymen to a particular function in a particular locale. This is not the method of my denomination—where the local congregation *calls* the person to be its minister. Therefore, it follows that a person, to warrant a call, must either have the potentiality to fulfill the expectations of his call or have established a record of success or effectiveness. On the other hand, a person who has been neither effective nor successful in ministry has little likelihood of obtaining a call, and may be frozen out of whatever position he may hold. If a person becomes a psychological casualty, given the mind-set of our day, he may have very little hope of continuing

209

at all in the ministry if it is known, or he may be shunted off to a side track to await hopefully some miraculous event or some political changes that might catapult him back into the mainstream.

Given this type of polity structure, we are faced with an increasing pressure upon those in ministry to prove to themselves and to others that they can be effective and/or successful. We are noting an alarming increase of restlessness among our clergy to move from one church to another, or into new or different forms of ministry, or even out of the ministry. Within recent years, the number of ministers seeking change of positions has more than doubled, and the possibility of being called to a new position is lessened. There are many possible reasons for this restlessness and disease. Here are only a few: changing role of the ministry which conflicts with role expectations of their people; financial needs which continue to increase; lack of interpersonal skills and emotional resources which enable them to continue to handle others and themselves.

Now, as secretary of one of several personnel offices of our denomination, I am in continual contact with clergymen and professionally trained directors of Christian education. In order to be responsible for those who are in various crises, we have attempted to develop procedures and structures which might be described theologically as redemptive—healing—or maximally therapeutic. In the course of providing such services, we become intimately involved in the lives of our constituency. We have collected many observations and have formed a few conclusions. We regret that we have not conducted research, but we are now beginning to do this. In the fulfillment of our personnel assignment, we have a responsibility both to the individual and to the institution. It is no easy task to be mutually responsible, but it would be equally immoral to favor either one over the other.

In the course of providing our personnel services, we have focussed upon the term "Career Evaluation" as a neutral and, we hope, non-threatening definition of what we are attempting to do. In this effort we are attempting to help a person think through his experience, himself, and his goals. Out of this process, recommendations are made and strategies considered to assist these folk. Yes, we use a *battery* of tests and are also experimenting with a variety. We give the Strong Vocational Interest Blank, and MMPI, and then a projective battery consisting of Rorschach, TAT, House-Tree-Person (Buck & Jolles, 1956), Sentence Completion, and Bender-Gestalt.* This battery is given by a clinical psychologist. It should be made clear that we do not consider this to be a psychiatric service, though we have a psychiatric consultant. It is primarily a career evaluation service that employs psychological skills and procedures to assist those in their career development, whether they are in a crisis or not. Ideally, we would like to assist those in ministry to have enough knowledge about themselves, and an understanding about their experiences and their goals, that they might avoid many of the crises we see in the ministry. At some later conference, we would like to report on our progress and whatever findings we uncover, and whatever conclusions we might possibly reach.

Let us conclude this section by saying that whatever psychological problems a minister might eventually have will influence his professional performance and fulfillment. Therefore, in the interest of the stewardship of human resources within the ministry and the mission of the church in our society, we must find new ways and utilize every resource to assist. This should be done not only in behalf of the church and its goals, but also in behalf of those in ministry as persons. In our particular church, it is of necessity that we assist those in ministry, because we have no way to care financially or occupationally for them and their families if they become psychological casualties with the result that their ministerial positions are jeopardized.

THE RESULT OF FAILURE TO EXPERIENCE SATISFACTION IN THE MINISTRY

There are many factors which apparently contribute to the crises about which I have been speaking. Let me mention a few which

* References have been provided in previous papers to all the tests mentioned here except the House-Tree-Person Test for which a reference is supplied.—Ed.

I consider to be important. First, there appears to be, in many of our religious traditions, a real and subtle contempt for ourselves as persons and as psychological beings. In my tradition, I perceive such an attitude among laymen and clergymen. It has been revealed in our theological education process. Only recently, and even then only partially, has there been any attempt to assist students in understanding themselves, their motivations, self-concepts, anxieties, guilts, strengths, and weaknesses. By inference, this traditional process implies that ministry can be achieved without regard —responsible regard—for the selves involved in ministry. As a result, many of our clergy do not understand how to make use of themselves as persons. Many have a haunting suspicion that they are no good and carry an impossible burden of guilt about their humanness. It seems to me that we must somehow influence our traditions so that we accept the fact that it is good in the Biblical sense to be human, and that we acknowledge the responsibility which each of us has to know and fulfill our humanity creatively and responsibly. For instance, would it not be helpful to assist our ministers and seminarians in accepting the fact that they are emotional beings? Only a limited attempt is made in our seminaries, to my knowledge, to assist students to understand the influence of negative emotions, frustration, etc. I observe among many of our clergy a constricting of their emotional range, frequently resulting in the inability to express either positive or negative feeling. These negative feelings then become translated into self-destructive behavior of either a physical, emotional, interpersonal, or theological sort. Many of our clergy are unaware that they can be human beings and are relieved to discover that it remains a possibility, and indeed a necessity.

On the other hand, our clergy are frequently perceived by their parishioners in non-human terms. They are expected to communicate positive effects, but when and where can they reveal their negative ones? By perceiving themselves as some non-human Christ-figure, many clergymen are locked in a double bind. To themselves and to others they are not allowed the privilege of being human.

Another factor, which contributes to psychological problems in the ministry of today, is the fact that the ministry, as a role, is undergoing change. We are caught in a period of transition, at least in the United Presbyterian Church, where old forms and new forms are in conflict. Our congregational constituency has one set of expectations and many of our clergy have another. For instance, the civil-rights issue is a case in point. By and large, our laymen are conservative politically, but many of our clergy are liberal. To be prophetic in our day does not endear one to one's congregation. Harry Levinson of the Menninger Foundation in a private conversation last August said that, in his judgment, the clergy as a profession or as an occupational group was probably under greater stress than any other occupational group, including the unemployed. Only a very secure person can long endure these stresses without crippling himself emotionally or physically or spiritually.

A third factor which plays upon this crisis today has been the neglect of the minister's wife. Here, our Roman Catholic brethren have reason to be relieved. As human beings, the wives of clergymen have a significant role to play. We have all known this, but we have not initiated steps to help *him* or *her* in understanding their mutual effect upon one another or upon his ministry. A wife can be either the making or the undoing of a minister's health or his professional career. The minister's family should be seen as a unit and more attention must be given among denominations which allow for married clergy to nurture husbands and wives. We have seen many couples, both of whom are ill to some degree and each needs attention. To deal only with the clergyman's pathology or problems would be a partial solution.

PSYCHOLOGICAL PROBLEMS OBSERVED AMONG THE CLERGY

Since ministers and their wives are human beings, it should not be a surprise that they manifest the entire range of human behavior. Since we are frequently consulted about the physical and emotional dilemmas of our people, we see at least a sample of many dimensions of clerical life. I would like now to sketch out briefly a few broad types of psychological problems which in themselves are over-simplified, and which are never seen as isolated entities.

1. *Depression Resulting from Crisis of Faith.* From the diagnostic study program conducted at the Menninger Foundation for the United Presbyterian Church, the report comes back that many of those seen have no undergirding faith to support them. One psychiatrist said that it was strange for them to note this frequent phenomenon, for to them it would be like a psychiatrist having no acceptance of the unconscious. What is observed in a small sample under psychiatric evaluation does, apparently, exist in a larger number. For many, God is dead—or at least whatever they affirmed earlier now has no meaning. We have been in a period of theological revival with many schools contending for influence. With such a plethora of possibilities, some ministers and ministerial candidates may have difficulty sorting through them. Others may have difficulty resolving the conflict between the adolescent theology and their acquired theological formulations.

Again, some ministers are victims between what they believe and what their people profess, but they resolve this dilemma by denying their integrity and preach and profess what their people want to hear. Naturally, they compromise out of fear, but one wonders if one can long serve as a minister when one lives the difficult role of a double-agent.

2. *Problem of Over-Constricted Emotionality.* We have already touched upon this problem before, but it appears quite common to our experience. I will draw a short diagram, over-simplifying to be sure:

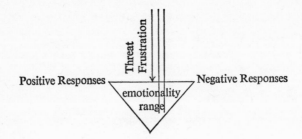

The straight line represents the emotionality continuum extending between two extremes, positive and negative responses. I define negative as aggressive-hateful responses, and positive as loving-tender responses. In my judgment, the potentiality at both ends of the continuum exists in every man, i.e., men have the potentiality for both positive and negative responses, and clergymen are no exception. Furthermore, it is my opinion that whenever we experience frustration or threat there is an immediate negative response. It is as natural as breathing and quite automatic and involuntary. People handle this negative response in a variety of ways, consciously and unconsciously, but clergymen, by their role and concept of themselves, are not allowed some expressions available to others. When faced with many frustrations in their work, clergymen are supposed to grin and bear it, or transcend their frustration in some divine manner. But as I understand this process, it is not so easily resolved. Instead, we observe a constricting process emerging where many, not being able to express their negative feeling appropriately, discover their positive responses unavailable or alienated from them. This results in a constriction of the emotional range, as illustrated in the diagram below:

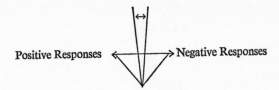

Thus we find that many under our observation, because of themselves or because of the community's expectations, are constricted emotionally, being unable to express either positive or negative emotions. Thus, they lose their humanity; they become castrated, losing their creativity, flexibility, spontaneity, warmth, and naturalness. Thus, they become rigid and fragile. What concerns me is the loss of their positive emotions. They lose the capacity to care, to love, to be sensitive. I have a theory that unless we can assist persons to deal appropriately with their negative feelings, they may lose their capacity to respond favorably—at least to some degree.

As a result of a process like this, we observe a frightening amount of apathy, inertia, and vegetating among persons with greater potentiality than they are exhibiting in their work. Their interpersonal lives are routine, mechanical, and unimaginative. These persons are generally suppressed. They may by far outnumber all those who suffer other kinds of debilitating disorders. They become the occupational conformists and frequently the ecclesiastical misfits.

3. *Problems Resulting from the Occupational Demands of the Ministry.* We know that it is imperative that persons find satisfaction in their work. Once upon a time it was clearer what the objectives in ministry were. The objectives are neither as clear nor as simple today. As one minister recently said to me (and he was relatively successful and effective), "If the next twenty-four years are like the past twelve, to hell with it."

In our society we are confronted with a pervasive tendency to measure our work performance. In the ministry, this is very difficult to do, unless one refers to those measurable statistics like numbers or finances, which most clergymen decry.

Furthermore, in spite of the increased competence of clergymen in their interpersonal skills, many still do not possess the capacity to give themselves personal assurance and confidence. One frequently hears clergymen speak of their disillusionment over their preaching. Among some of our clergy, one continues to encounter expressions of frustration and despair over their administrative responsibilities. With the growth of particular churches and the multiplication of church activities, there is an irresistible demand for administrative and management knowledge and capability. Very frequently, one hears complaints of too much to do and very little time for oneself and one's family.

On the other hand, clergymen live in a society in which success is honored by financial rewards. In our denomination, salaries are above the norm for most other denominations, but many of our clergy find their economic rewards sparse and inadequate for their family's needs.

All these factors can influence a clergyman's performance as well as his emotional life. Many would consider leaving the ministry, but after so many years of preparation and service, they find that they are not trained for other options—they are not marketable.

4. *Problems Resulting from Inability to Entrust Themselves to Other People.* It is a common saying that there are three kinds of people—men, women, and ministers. As ridiculous as it is, the saying has an element of truth. This viewpoint is seen in the act of ordination, which is frequently misinterpreted as separating completely, rather than as designating for function. Many who enter the ministry seek its authority, isolation, and separateness (among other reasons).

Nevertheless, many in the ministry abhor this separation and its resulting isolation. They want relationship apart from function and are frustrated over their inability to break through the barriers that keep them separate. Living in a fish bowl is not a modern convenience for most ministers. Furthermore, one hears ministers say that they abhor being associated with other ministers. They try to avoid social occasions when they are thrown with them. For many, then, they are isolated from others by their role, and they then avoid contact with their ministerial colleagues. One gets the impression that there are many who are indeed isolated. There is some evidence to believe that some of those who enter the ministry have difficulty in developing relations of trust with others. Some entrust themselves to God or Jesus Christ, but build walls around themselves and others. It can become a very lonely existence. Those who flail against their imposed separateness by their religious tradition and social mores frequently develop adolescent forms of rebellion which can eventually be very destructive—such adolescent forms as drinking inordinately or immaturely, cursing, sexual obsessions, etc. Of course, all of these may be a reflection of more serious behavioral problems.

It follows, then, that related to this inability to establish trusting relationships is the apparent inability of some to enter into meaningful personal relations of any kind except in the performance of their duties as clergymen. In the fulfillment of such responsibilities, they can function fairly adequately, but there is a longing to develop greater contact with more meaning. Even in their marriages, one frequently finds psychological distance and lack of meaning. Within the past seven months, there have come into our office eight couples, who are either breaking up their marriages, or involved emotionally with others. In some cases, it has been the wives who have either thrown in the towel or have found relationships outside the home. In other cases, it has been the husband.

OBSERVABLE SIMILARITIES AMONG MINISTERS
WITH PSYCHOLOGICAL PROBLEMS

We are aware that all types of persons enter the ministry. There is great diversity of talents, intellectual abilities, physical resources, etc. However, there are sufficient observable similarities among some of those we see to warrant further study and research. Let me mention a few.

We observe that many enter the ministry because of their need to be loved and accepted, and because of a corresponding inability to love and to accept others. This need to be loved may be one of the major motivations for selecting the ministry as an occupation. If this is true, then the decision to enter the ministry may be an act of saving. However, this is basically no different from other occupational decisions that offer persons the possibility of fulfilling their lives.

The ministry does offer a great deal of promise for positive response from people. Among God's people it is indeed a joyful day when a person makes a decision to enter the ministry. God favors those who make such a decision. Among our religious traditions, we tend to perpetuate the belief that the decision to enter the ministry is the greatest of all possible occupational choices. I have no doubt that most men who enter the ministry have such an aura cast around their decision. Now, I am aware that the need for love and acceptance is a need which each person has a right to claim, but in our work with clergymen of our denomination we find that this goal is frequently mentioned. It appears to be conscious. This fact does not appear serious in itself, except that this need may go unmet in a time of social change, when the church and its clergy are preoccupied with developing progressive steps. For instance, some of our clergy were faced with extensive inner stress a few years ago, when the civil-rights issue broke upon the public scene. To support the civil-rights movement would definitely bring them into conflict with their people, who were threatened by such issues and by the church's stand.

One of the more frequent complaints our ministers voice is their inability to set limits to their work. To set limits or to say "no" to demands made upon oneself might be related to the above-mentioned need for acceptance. To set limits in behalf of one's responsibility to oneself might conflict with the interests of others and thereby cause conflict.

We have observed some interesting similarities in the developmental histories of the clergymen who seek help from our office. First, many of these ministers seem to come from homes where they have had defective paternal relationships. Either their fathers were absent because of death, divorce, separation, or work, or, if present, were psychologically distant, being either strong and removed, or weak and removed. In any case, the youngster had an inadequate paternal figure with whom to identify. This fact might be responsible for the lack of confidence that they manifest in their own masculinity, and their own self-image, and might be the basis for problems related to masculine authority. It is also observed that in many ministers with psychological problems their mothers are dominant identity figures. She fills the vacuum created by the absence or distance of the father and compensates by over-relating to the children. The youngster who enters the ministry from this kind of family background also identifies with his mother's interest. At the same time, another process is at work, probably as a result of the two already mentioned—i.e., an under-socializing process with one's peer group. This process might begin early and continue through late adolescence. Without adequate heterosexual experiences, many tend to marry the first or second girl they date.

These factors are not necessarily indicative of a negative developmental history, even though there are possible factors which later might have serious adjustment problems. However, some of these factors might be decisive in selecting the ministry as an occupation. For instance, the identification with a maternal figure might be a plus, if the ministry is considered a nurturing, sustaining, and caring occupation. In fact, these qualities are desirable in a shepherding concept of the ministry. On the other hand, having had such an early identity figure does not in itself prepare one for such a calling. These observations are presented as possible handles by which we might help those in ministry to understand themselves and their behavior.

CONCLUSIONS

1. It appears that ministers are experiencing greater stress today—running the entire gamut of adjustment problems. There does not appear to be an alarming increase in serious psychotic cases, but there are definite signs of increased tension and stress which influence the ministers of our denomination and their work.

2. There appears to be a need for preparing those entering upon and engaging in ministry to know themselves, so that they may maximally use themselves as persons in their work. This requirement might mean preventing a few from entering the ministry, if evidence should prove their deficiency in self-knowledge, but everyone needs to understand his personality. To say this does not imply that each minister should have a personal analysis, but it does underscore the need for more self-understanding in order that they may be more effective as persons and that they might be more effective in their work as ministers.

3. For those religious groups which allow marriage in the ministry, such a concern should be extended to wives of ministers, since they play a central role in their husbands' lives.

4. Many resources must be employed in assisting ministers in psychological need, including the use of psychological tests. Psychological tests have reached a high level of sophistication and we are grateful for all those who have labored in their development. However, we must move beyond their use for diagnostic purposes and utilize them within a larger context.

5. Those of us concerned with the adjustment problems of our clergy must somehow address ourselves to the inhuman attitudes that persist that clergymen should not have such frailties. The article in the *Saturday Evening Post* entitled Fallen priests (De Gramont, 1965) should help many to view the problem more realistically and sympathetically. Unless we address ourselves to the context (which contributes somewhat to the problem) we are focussing on a very narrow field. Ministers, priests, and rabbis are human, and as such are vulnerable to all of humanity's ills. This context is created, not merely by the laity, but by those within the church who frequently control our educational structures and their curricula. We have all contributed to our malaise, out of fear and overprotectiveness, and now we must ask what we can do to dispel the clouds of anxiety hovering over us as a result.

REFERENCES

Buck, J. N., & Jolles, I. *H–T–P: House-Tree-Person Projective Technique.* Los Angeles: Western Psychological Services, 1956.
De Gramont, S. Fallen priests: Via Coeli refuge in New Mexico. *Saturday Evening Post,* 1965, *103,* 288–299.

DISCUSSION

Paul F. D'Arcy, M.M.: What relevance does the topic "Psychological Problems of the Clergy" have for the theme of this Conference which is "Psychological Testing for Ministerial Selection"? In other words, what is the connection between post-seminary problems and pre-seminary testing?

When you stop and think of it, the underlying concern of this conference is to provide the church and the world with a clergy who are better able to function and who can be happier in their work. Dr. Golden shows in his paper that there are many dysfunctions in the life of the clergy. He quotes Dr. Harry Levinson of the Menninger Clinic to the effect that the clergy as a profession are under greater stress than any other occupational group. To achieve the goal of a more effective clergyman and one who is more personally fulfilled, we need to know much more about the strains in his life so that we can either do something about their causes or make him better able to meet them.

We must put psychological assessment into its proper perspective among the various factors promoting a healthy clergy and be careful not to make it responsible for too much. It is only one of several equally necessary avenues of attack on the problem of providing an effective clergy. Its main impact is felt early in the process at the time of application to the seminary, but selection continues to occur throughout the period of training and some individuals require further professional assessment in the light of developments after their acceptance.

Other important factors besides selection are training, placement, personnel services, and structural renovation. The whole broad program of training is obviously of central importance in preparing an effective clergy. Those who are eventually ordained are by that time a carefully selected and trained group, but still it is important for their optimal functioning that they be correctly placed and that there be a program of personnel services to look out for their interests, develop them further, and tide them over in times of crisis. Finally, in the organization of the church itself there are antiquated structures which no longer work and which are chronic obstacles to clergy effectiveness and happiness. These need to be re-examined and renovated. No exclusive emphasis on any one of these suffices. Only a multifaceted approach can achieve the goal of a clergy who effectively minister to men and who thrive on this service.

Psychological assessment is ordinarily thought of as promoting a healthy clergy by the rather negative means of screening out the unfit. This is its selection function which it does in two ways. It detects those who are too psychically deprived either to adequately minister to the people or to cope with the strains of such ministrations. It also helps those who are stable enough, but for whom it would be an unrealistic vocational choice, in which they would not be happy.

But assessment has a number of positive values for developing the candidates who are admitted. In the first place it can help seminarians to face up to and get counseling assistance with problems brought to the fore in assessment interviews. Furthermore, interest, ability, and personality testing can help the individual find his right function and setting within the ministry.

Assessment data can help the administrator too. General norms and profiles of the student population of the seminary help the staff design a program fitted to meet the individual and group needs of the seminarians. On the long-range side, through research which utilizes such assessment data, we come to understand relationships between characteristics which candidates have at the time of admission and their perseverance to ordination, their later problems and accomplishments, and their effectiveness in the ministry.

Thus far we have explored the relationship between assessment and later strains, showing how assessment helps negatively by elimination and positively by helping the survivors and the program.

Now I would like to explore further the state of our knowledge about the strains themselves. There are seven published studies about mental strains of Catholic clergy and religious (Kelley, 1958, 1959, 1961; McAllister & Vanderveldt, 1961, 1965; Moore, 1936; Vanderveldt & McAllister, 1962), but, generally speaking, from the Catholic's point of view, the clergy and those in authority especially have a sort of implicit experiential knowledge of what is going on in others of the cloth; but there is very little careful analysis and research of these problems. Even bare data on the number of defections, breakdowns, alcoholics are nonexistent. All is by prudent estimation. Why is this? I suppose there is a fear of scandal should such data become public. It is certainly difficult to get accurate information, even about the number of dropouts in seminaries. There is no doubt that researchers in this field will encounter severe opposition, and some who have been interested and capable of doing the research have thought prudence the better part of valor. Yet, data and research into such problems would, as in any other area, help us more accurately to understand and interpret the situation, and take positive steps to improve it. Barriers to research on their problems hold up progress on providing the world with a more effective and happy clergy.

Dr. Golden has given us some of the conflicts which have come to his attention in the Protestant ministry. It would help to outline the major strains found in the Catholic priesthood. These could be compressed into five categories. In the first place let me put problems of faith, since these are devastating for a vocation centered in faith such as the priesthood. Secondly, there are problems of role, function, and status of the priest and his relevancy to the world, accentuated by the changes going on in the world and in the Church itself. Thirdly, there are problems of authority, partly due to structure and partly due to factors within the individual. Fourthly, are sexual problems. Included here are "acting out" behavior, unresolved relationships with women, and incapability of adequate response to another person. Finally, there are problems of addiction, notably alcoholism.

It would help to define some of the conflicts with which the Jewish rabbi is confronted. What we want is a taxonomy of the problems of the clergy, Jewish, Protestant, and Catholic.

In devising this classification it is important to bear in mind that there are many varieties of religious personnel. These will experience different conflicts because of their different situations. The strains are specific. Let me illustrate the point that by making distinctions among religious personnel, we will be able to make distinctions about their conflicts.

In the Catholic clergy we have the diocesan clergy on the one hand and the religious clergy, i.e., the Jesuits, Dominicans, Trappists, etc., on the other. There is a difference in the authority problems which both have. Nuns have some different strains from priests, especially in the area of freedom. Women religious are much more confined and are fretting under this. Those with different work functions have different problems, e.g., priests in the pastoral ministry and those in the intellectual ministry, teaching brothers and lay brothers, nursing sisters and teaching sisters.

Obviously there are tremendous strains now among the diocesan clergy in major urban centers, where, because of a system of promotion by seniority, a curate has no chance of being a pastor until he is well on into his fifties. It is not until he is ordained 25 to 35 years that he has his first hope of being in a responsible position. This problem does not exist in rural dioceses.

I have tried to clarify the connection between the strains of the ministry and pre-seminary assessment, which is one among several necessary approaches to providing a healthy clergy. We need to know more about the variety of strains experienced by the clergy of all faiths. There is an unfortunate lack of precise knowledge on such questions and there are also attitudinal barriers to conducting such research. All here are involved in research and know the power of truthful and accurate knowledge to lead the way to constructive changes.

Paul M. Steinberg: Father D'Arcy's discussion of the paper was most illuminating. Rather than seek to add to his excellent introduction for this discussion, I should like to make some comments on several aspects of Dr. Golden's paper as they relate to the problem of screening candidates for the Jewish ministry.

A major emphasis in our program is the utilization of test findings in order validly to determine the kind of training program we should have in our College–Institute's human relations program.

A student making application for admission inevitably is asked the question: "Why do you want to be a rabbi?" There are several kinds of responses we receive. Most students will usually say: "I feel that Judaism has something to say to the world. I am interested in the survival of the Jewish people and Jewish culture. I like working with people."

He is then introduced to a curriculum which is essentially a professional curriculum. He is exposed to the language and literature of the Jewish people. He studies Hebrew, Bible, history, rabbinical literature, homiletics, education, and human relations. And it is in the human-relations training-program at our school that we try to develop his sensitivity to people and their needs. But where do we begin? How shall we begin?

The story is told of a rabbi who said in his later years: "When I was young I sought to change the world. As I grew older, I limited it to my community. Now that I am older and wiser, I see that I should have begun with myself." Beginning with one's self means gaining self-understanding.

We seek then to begin with the man himself. We try to get him to gain an understanding of himself, his motivations, his concerns, and his anxieties. The best way of summarizing it is perhaps in the question, "What on Earth is he doing for Heaven's sake? For man's sake?" Moreover, what meaning does his training in the seminary have for him when he goes out into the active ministry? Is there any real preparation? Is there any relevancy?

Relevancy is indeed the critical question confronting graduates of the Jewish seminaries in America. Marshall Sklare, who has made an invaluable contribution to our understanding of Conservative Judaism (Sklare, 1958), has noted that the problem is even greater for the tradition-trained and tradition-oriented Conservative rabbi than it is for the Reform. His knowledge of Judaism does not, in the eyes of his congregation (or himself), relate to many of his activities in the active rabbinate. The position of the rabbi today is in sharp contrast to the classical role of the rabbi— i.e. a "scholar-saint" in a sacred society who served as an expert and arbiter in the history, doctrines, and practices of Judaism.

We meet some very interesting contradictions in the Jewish ministry. The times have catapulted the rabbi into living new roles and he has emerged with enlarged activities. Not only is he concerned with the duties and functions which parallel those of his Christian counterpart in the community; he has also expanded the scope of his rabbinical activities to include education, community relations, resistance to anti-Semitism, synagogue administration, and philanthropy. Scholarship and teaching, once a primary concern, have become secondary.

The Role of the Rabbi Today: The definition of the Rabbi's role is crucial to the effective functioning of the synagogue or temple. There are multiple forces shaping the image that a local congregation has of its rabbi. This image is derived from the concept of the rabbi or minister in present-day culture, which is often reinforced by the portrayal of the rabbi or minister on television, radio, screen, and stage. Norman Vincent Peale, Bishop Fulton J. Sheen, Bishop James Pike, Stephen Wise, Billy Graham, and other clergymen have helped maintain and shape the image of the clergyman through the mass media. The image is also reinforced by the general orientation and perception that the public has of the Catholic priest, the Protestant minister and the rabbi. A rabbi's predecessors in a community and the image they projected will influence the community's perception of him as a minister and their expectations of him. Knowledge about other clergy, or observation of them in some communal activity, will also influence their image of their rabbi.

Each rabbi, each minister in a community helps shape the image people have of the rabbi or minister. The rabbi has become a priest, preacher, pastor, parson, and rector. As a priest he will lead the congregation in prayer and ritual observance: he will, as a preacher, deliver addresses on the sabbath and holy days; as a pastor he will give counsel and guidance to his people in their hours of crisis; as a parson he will serve on committees and boards concerned with community welfare; and as a rector he will administer the synagogue and temple. Within the Liberal-Reform synagogue the rabbi may follow his personal predilection based upon his self-image as a rabbi and devote himself to preaching, teaching, counseling, or community relations. His self-image consists of ideas, beliefs, and opinions that describe and explain his position in the culture and community. The rabbi reveals something of his self-image through his role behavior and by the way he describes himself to others.

It has been said that "the rabbi is just like everyone else—only more so." What is true for the average person is even truer of the rabbi. The rabbi too is exposed to cultural contradictions, pressures, and conflicts.

A study by Fleishman (1955) evaluating a leadership training course for supervisors after they returned to their industrial situation also has implications for the rabbi who is often placed in the role of exemplar and wonders why he fails as a rabbi. The influence of the supervisor's own boss was demonstrated in this evaluation of foreman training at the International Harvester Company. Foremen had been sent to a supervisory training program in which the emphasis was on human relations training as well as on content related to planning and organizing. The general finding was that the effect of such training was not great in actually changing behavior back on the job except for some initial decrease in "consideration behavior." This was, of course, opposite to one of the objectives of the training program. One reason for this turned out to be the influence of the "leadership climate" in the plant—that is, the attitudes and behavior of the foreman's own supervisors. It was found that those foremen who worked with a supervisor who ranked high in "consideration" tended to be also more considerate of their subordinates than those foremen who were subordinate to supervisors who were less considerate. This is a "chain reaction" effect of leadership climate which is exceedingly important in determining the leadership behavior of the foreman. It might be stated that an individual learns to behave in a certain way according to the reinforcement he receives. So, too, the congregant who is constantly exposed to the leadership of the rabbi will react not only to the preachment or words but to the action of his rabbi.

How the rabbi handles himself in life situations may at times be confusing and disconcerting to his congregants:

—A rabbi is supposed to be spiritual and eschew material gains and pleasures. What then is the result when he speaks of an increment in salary?

—A rabbi speaks of cooperation and deplores competitive activities. What is the result when the congregation embarks upon a membership and building fund campaign, and the rabbi, as "promoter," pushes them toward the goal?

—A rabbi is supposed to be humble, kind, understanding, and like unto Moses of old, meek. What is the result when the rabbi loses control at a board meeting and "flies off the handle"?

—A rabbi gives counsel to a parent whose child is difficult in

religious school. What happens when the rabbi's own children mis-
behave at a congregational function?

The rabbi and his family live in an exposed fishbowl, ever subject to the scrutiny of the community. A rabbi's wife and children
are constantly under scrutiny. The clothes she wears, the kind of
home they have, the behavior of their children are often the subject of discussion.

Through our testing program we try to select the people who
are able to take the strain of living this rewarding and yet taxing
life. We try to help the student to learn to cope with the many
problems and challenges. We seek to do this through a variety of
techniques. In addition to the formal course-work on personality
and counseling, we utilize the case-method, role-playing, and observation of students in a congregational setting as training methods. In our program of supervising students, a faculty member is
assigned to several student-congregations. He visits these congregations, observes the student-rabbi in action, and immediately
after the visit gives feedback to the student. Our goal is his growth
as a person.

The Ultimate Role of the Rabbi: The rabbi becomes the exemplar in the tradition of the Hassidic rabbi. His people look to
him for guidance as they seek to cope with anxiety and as they
strive to express their potential. The rabbi is not interested in
helping the individual to become good for something, as in industry. The rabbi is interested in helping the individual to *become,* to
realize *himself.*

If the rabbi is to have meaning and be of assistance to the congregant in both the crisis situation and the daily desperations that
are the human lot, he must then weave himself into the fabric of the
congregant's existence and *share his life.* The rabbi must use his
daily contact with the congregant to prepare him for the inevitable
tragedies of life. He must share in the trivial as well as the dramatic
in the congregant's existence.

He is with his congregants not only in the moments of dramatic
crisis when they may be subjected to the shock of disaster, whether
in the form of serious personal illness, the loss of a loved one, or

similar personal catastrophe. He is with them also in the prolonged yet perhaps less dramatic crisis of their lives of quiet desperation. He participates in their life.

It is through the seemingly unimportant daily association that the rabbi builds his relationship with his people. He must listen to the commonplace if he wants to comprehend truly how their lives are lived; he must learn of their discontents as well as their joys.

To begin the comforting of the bereaved only after the tragedy and after the heavens have crashed is to have foregone the opportunity to fortify the soul against the ultimate grief. Even when he merely listens to the person, he shares in his life and is already helpful to him. As a symbol of religion and as a symbol of the human species, the rabbi can often gratify the hope of the sufferer by simply demonstrating that if there is one person in the whole wide world who has the interest and capacity to give comfort and to stir hope, there must be others. Thus the rabbi becomes a source of support, even when the individual's whole world seems to be cold, rejective, or punitive. By his concern for him, the rabbi makes clear the central theme that Judaism conveys to the individual: You count! You make a difference! You are important to me!

If the individual believes in the rabbi, respects him, sees him as the person who can help him, and as one who responds to him, even without giving specific answers, then the rabbi will be able to be of assistance to him in achieving his goals.

With regard to the problem of placement I should like merely to note the following.

The average age of a graduating senior is about 28. He then serves for two to three years in the chaplaincy. He then may make two moves in his career. By the time he is forty he has to be with the congregation that he really wants or else he may find that he will be forced to remain where he is.

Most of our congregations want men in the age-range of twenty-five to thirty-five. When a good position opens up, and this means a large congregation with a large budget for educational and religious activities, the congregation is not interested in a man who may have acquired wisdom through the years. They are interested, they say, in a young, dynamic person, about thirty-five to forty. This is the time when the rabbi may run into problems, emotional problems with his wife and with his children. If he is forced to remain in a very small community but would really like to relocate to Memphis, New York, Los Angeles, or Chicago (notwithstanding the fact that he has told us prior to ordination that he will serve *anywhere at all* when he is ordained as a rabbi), when he comes to the Placement Committee, he will insist on any opportunity to make a change.

Secondly, there are men who are out in the field who tell us that we are over-producing in the rabbinate. We are not over-producing. Within the Reform rabbinate we need at least fifty or sixty rabbis a year. At present we are ordaining only about thirty to thirty-five rabbis. There are enough positions on the beginning level, but there are not enough positions on the higher level. There really is not enough room at the top. This, of course, also creates a great deal of frustration and anxiety among the men.

GENERAL DISCUSSION

A Dual Role. Expressing sympathy with the Presbyterian minister, whose problems Dr. Golden had described, Dr. Brown said that he did not agree with Father D'Arcy that the crucial matter here is selection. Rather he regarded the congregation as having moved far beyond the minister, who, perhaps because of his idealism, may be attempting a kind of imitation of Christ. The congregation places the minister in a difficult position. On the one hand they say, "Be our shepherd, our spiritual leader," and on the other they say, "Don't rock the boat. Be a good guy." In other words, they ask him not to take literally his moral and ethical commitments. This is the source of the depression Dr. Golden had mentioned. If the minister attempts to be Christ-like, he is pilloried in many subtle ways. He does not know how to maneuver so as to place himself in the right position because he does not know what the right position is.

He has two choices: 1.) to lower himself to the level of the congregants and be a good guy, renouncing in effect his fundamental commitments based on an ideal that goes back 2,000 years; 2.) to raise the level of his congregants, partially by preaching, by teaching religion, which will make people uncomfortable. As for selection, no matter how well it is done, the clergyman will be confronted with this painful dilemma.

Agreeing with Dr. Brown that congregations often take the "don't rock the boat" attitude, Dr. Steinberg said he did not know how effective sermons are in changing behavior; but the students at Hebrew Union College are not misled into thinking that behavior can be changed by the sermon itself. The college tries to show them that it is their role as exemplars that will influence behavior patterns of their congregants.

Another point about the confusion of role, Dr. Steinberg continued, is that in all three branches of Judaism the religious-school teachers are often paid rather well. Therefore a member of the rabbi's congregation who also teaches in the religious school is in an employee-employer relationship with the rabbi. Her husband may serve on the board and will pass on the rabbi's contract when it comes up for renewal. The rabbi may be involved in counseling the wife of the vice-president of the congregation; she may report to her husband that "the rabbi agrees with me." Then the husband volunteers to become chairman of the rabbi tenure committee.

Irrevocability of Decision. Father Bier said he wished to qualify somewhat his earlier remarks about the difference between the priest on the one hand and the Protestant minister and the rabbi on the other in the irrevocability of their commitment to their calling. Before hearing Dr. Golden's paper, he had not been as aware as he is now that the minister and the rabbi may be in a situation somewhat analogous to that of the priest in the sense that after a certain age they have no good alternative to the ministry or the rabbinate to which they have committed themselves. Does it make any difference that the priest has made his commitment antecedently? The minister and the rabbi do not make the same kind of full commitment in advance. But they may find themselves in situations from which they cannot well extricate themselves.

The irrevocability for them may come as a later development. Therefore, as he had said before, Father Bier thought that selection may be more crucial for the priest because he makes his irrevocable commitment earlier in life.

Dr. Golden commented that when the young men in his denomination make their commitment they are likely to do so with a great deal of fantasy, with much unrealism that is undependable. The personnel office tries to help them so that they do not need to stay in the ministry if they have not proved to be effective. In that event, it tries to help them leave the ministry, retraining them for other employment and helping them get relocated. The personnel office, however, tries equally to help them if they wish to stay in the ministry, or if their skills do not suit them for other vocations.

Were there possible differences, Dr. McCarthy asked, between Jesuits, who are ordained relatively late in life—in their thirties—and priests in general, who are ordained in their twenties, in their ways of perceiving the consequences of their choice, and a resulting greater need for more attention to selection? Within his experience, the candidates for entrance into the seminary do not really understand the consequences of making a permanent vocational commitment until they have been in the seminary for some time. Dr. McCarthy did not mean to understate the importance of selection—it is critical, but support is important, too. This is especially true for men who reach their late thirties and early forties without having been given a pastorate or any other advancement.

Dr. Steinberg said he did not want Father Bier to retreat from his earlier statement about the irrevocability of the priest's decision, because of anything he had said. He thought that the Orthodox rabbi often is able to move from the rabbinate into a secular vocation without much difficulty. The college, however, has had very few dropouts from the Conservative or Reform ministry after the men have completed their studies. Those who have dropped out have gone into related fields, such as psychology or medicine.

Dr. Mills remarked that he had been struck recently by the fact that many priests refer to their training as "formation." While it is true that selection is made and the decision of the priest is more far-reaching and irrevocable than that of the minister or the rabbi, he wondered whether the nature of the educational processes for the three is significantly different, and whether perhaps differences in the selection and educational processes may account for some of the dropouts among Protestants. The education of the Protestant minister is theological. There is little in it approaching the formation of character that is the ideal of the Catholic training.

Emotional Problems of the Clergy. Recalling that Dr. Golden had alluded to the church as a subculture in which some of the attitudes of the young men he mentioned are born, Dr. DeWire observed that students come out of churches which have this kind of restriction to begin with. When they come to the seminary, this restriction often constitutes the entire range of their emotional possibilities. Only in the seminary do they wake up to the fact that there is space on both sides of Dr. Golden's chart. It follows, then, that while this conference has been looking at the man as he stands over against the congregation, the members should look also for some sociological interpretation of the church and the parish. The man who suffers from the restriction Dr. Golden was talking about comes out of what is essentially a conservative and constricting environment. Protestants face the same problem as the one Dr. Steinberg had in mind when he spoke of the congregations that send no men into the rabbinate. It would be interesting to find out whether or not men with broad emotional capacity come from churches that do not send men into the ministry. Some allied disciplines should be called upon to help study this problem, to bring forth some kind of idea of what these congregations look like, and what kind of social and religious settings sponsor the kind of people who go into the ministry.

Dr. McCarthy suggested that perhaps, as Dr. DeWire had said, the base from which clergymen are drawn should be broadened, as they now come from a segment of the population that is characteristically restricted in its ability to manage emotions. And if vocations to the ministry are going to continue to come from populations in which there is more than the usual degree of emotional restriction, someone will have to help the prospective clergymen learn how to express emotions properly. Otherwise the effectiveness of their personal services will be limited.

Suggestions for Research. Commenting on the great value of Dr. Golden's paper because he is immersed in the data it contains and in trying to help ministers deal with their emotional problems, Dr. Mills said he had drawn from it a number of hypotheses that he considered testable. He mentioned a few of them and urged research on them. First was the relation between theological orthodoxy or piety in the Protestant tradition and self-rejection. In connection with an occupational decision, this is important for theological education, for recruitment, and for maintenance of the ministry. Second, tying together three or four concepts—faith crisis, compromise of integrity, psychological depression, and other psychopathological problems—brings out many research possibilities. Third, the problems of those entering the ministry who have the need to be loved but are unable to love, who have defective paternal relationships, who are socially underdeveloped especially in peer relationships and heterosexual development, who are involved in unrealistic fantasy rather than realistic planning for occupational decisions, call for special research. Anyone who has anything to do with theological schools, Dr. Mills said, could find a long list of hypotheses emerging from the statement of a man like Dr. Golden who has been dealing with these problems.

The Clergyman's Need for Support. Dr. Steinberg, recalling Dr. Golden's remark about ministers' finding the company of other ministers difficult to take, spoke of the clergyman's need to build up his own resources for moral support. His primary source of affection and attention is his family. The second is his colleagues, with whom he can air and discuss his problems. At Hebrew Union College the Alumni Day observed during the past four years, when some fifteen rabbis meet to discuss some of their problems, has proved very valuable. For the past five years the college has conducted an orientation program, on a voluntary basis, for the wives of its students. Wives of men active in the rabbinate and of the college staff have also been involved. It has been a particularly good experience for the young women who are going to serve as helpmates to the rabbis-to-be.

Dr. Dittes suggested that the acceptability of fellow-clergy for support might be one of the fruits of ecumenism. He suspected that a priest and a rabbi are much more compatible psychologically, once they get past the barriers; there is not the sibling rivalry that keeps the Protestant clergy away from one another.

Present-day Restlessness of the Clergy. The restlessness of the clergy that Dr. Golden had mentioned, Dr. McCarthy thought, could be better understood if it was seen within the context of contemporary American values. In this country today, no one wants to be caught standing still. For example, people seldom buy a house nowadays with the intention of sinking roots for a lifetime. They usually buy it as a place from which eventually to move as their financial position improves. This commitment to constant change is reflected in the attitudes and behavior of all, including the clergy.

Dr. Arnold observed that perhaps part of the difficulty of the married clergy is the fact that they commit not only themselves, but their wives and children as well. A man may be willing to put up with a low salary and various difficulties, but when he sees that his wife has to share all this and that his children lack some of the advantages that other men's children have, that may add to the restlessness that has been noted.

Satisfaction. The concept of satisfaction in his career, Dr. Ashbrook said, can be an independent predictor or a dependent criterion, according to the way it is regarded. The research that has been done by Katz and his associates at the University of Michigan using satisfaction as a criterion or as a predictor has proved to be relatively worthless. The results have shown that there is little relation between satisfaction and performance in work (Katz, Maccoby, & Morse, 1950; Katz, Maccoby, Gurin, & Floor, 1951). In his own work, Dr. Ashbrook said he had found that those who were most satisfied on functional designations, such as administration or something of that nature, or in the overall situation, were likely to be the least effective in the least successful churches. Where the minister feels some degree of dissatisfaction with his functional roles or overall performance, he is likely to be more effective and more successful in operation. Dr. Ashbrook thought the concept of satisfaction was a useful one in the professional category of the ministry.

The Cross-cultural Approach to the Ministry. Mr. Anderson observed that many of the things Dr. Golden had said about the role and problems of the minister are quite true of the minister living within the American culture. But they may not be true or relevant to the situations of clergy in other parts of the world. The Academy is an international organization.

Dr. Golden remarked that studies made by the World Council of Churches indicate that at least the Protestant denominations around the world are experiencing the same things as are those in America.

Mr. Anderson considered this fact highly important. He thought there should be differentiation between the points that are characteristic of American culture and the problems that are faced by clergy in other cultures. There is an enormous opportunity for studies aimed at finding out whether one can test some of the hypotheses we find here on a cross-cultural basis.

REFERENCES

Fleishman, E. E. Leadership climate, human relations training and supervisory behavior. *Personnel Psychology*, 1955, *6*, 205–222.

Katz, D., Maccoby, N., & Morse, N. *Productivity, supervision and morale in an office situation.* Ann Arbor, Mich.: Institute of Social Research, 1950.

Katz, D., Maccoby, N., Gurin, G., & Floor, L. G. *Productivity, supervision and morale among railroad workers.* Ann Arbor, Mich.: Institute of Social Research, 1951.

Kelley, Sister Mary William. The incidence of hospitalized mental illness among religious sisters in the United States. *American Journal of Psychiatry*, 1958, *115*, 72–75.

Kelley, Sister Mary William. Maladies mentales des religieuses. Supplement, *Vie Spirituelle*, 1959, *12*, 295–305.

Kelley, Sister Mary William. Depression in the psychoses of members of religious communities of women. *American Journal of Psychiatry*, 1961, *118*, 423–425.

McAllister, R. J., & Vanderveldt, A. Factors in mental illness among hospitalized clergy. *Journal of Nervous and Mental Disease*, 1961, *132*, 80–88.

McAllister, R. J., & Vanderveldt, A. Psychiatric illness in hospitalized Catholic religious. *American Journal of Psychiatry*, 1965, *121*, 881–884.

Moore, T. V. Insanity in priests and religious: I. The rate of insanity in priests and religious. *American Ecclesiastical Review*, 1936, *95*, 485–498.

Sklare, M. Aspects of religious worship in the contemporary conservative synagogue. In M. Sklare (Ed.) *The Jews: Social patterns of an American group.* New York: Free Press, 1958, Pp. 357–376.

Vanderveldt, A. J., & McAllister, R. J. Psychiatric illness in hospitalized clergy: Alcoholism. *Quarterly Journal of Studies in Alcoholism*, 1962, *23*, 124–130.

IV
Conference Summary and Recommendations

SUMMARY OF FINDINGS

WALTER J. COVILLE*

BEFORE I GET TO THE MATTER OF SUMMATION, I would like to make by way of introduction some general remarks for which there might otherwise be no opportunity.

On behalf of the Committee—and I am sure on behalf of all the participants in the conference—I wish to extend to Rev. Anderson, his Executive Assistant and the Academy, our warmest feelings and sincere thanks for making this conference possible. I believe this is an historical occasion. To my knowledge, this is the first meeting of a group of priests, ordained ministers, educators, psychologists, and a psychiatrist, joined together by a common interest in an atmosphere that promotes warmth and easy relationships to discuss openly and in an understanding but spirited fashion the many and complex variables involved in the assessment of candidates for the religious ministry by means of psychological testing.

We are privileged, and I am pleased, to participate in this process of identifying, inspecting, analyzing, and evaluating what

* The summary of findings was prepared by a Committee consisting of Magda B. Arnold, Walter J. Coville, and Edgar W. Mills. As Committee Chairman, Dr. Coville presented the report, and the two remaining Committee members were given the opportunity of speaking first in the discussion period which followed.—Ed.

has been done, what is being done, and what should be done in this broad area of psychological testing for ministerial selection.

This series of sessions represents an enlightening, stimulating, and inspirational experience that on the one hand supports our interest in this area, and on the other hand prods us to push forward in our efforts to secure the hard, empirical data necessary to insure the reliability and validity of our various approaches.

I also want to say that the comments I am about to make reflect the combined deliberations of Dr. Arnold and Dr. Mills, each of whom will supplement my summation in an attempt to achieve a more complete coverage. Further, because of our own processes of selective attention, prejudice, or interest, these summary comments do not constitute a complete or definitive statement of psychological testing for the ministry. My aim, here, is rather to identify the current or recurrent general categories discussed in our sessions, to repeat some of the hypotheses and cautions with regard to each category, and then to offer them to you for further consideration and discussion. Actually, I hope that these summary comments will serve as a kind of memory-jogging experience for the general discussion that is to follow.

In our review of the somewhat overwhelming amount of material presented during this conference, it seems feasible to classify it under given general categories. The order in the following list does not signify relative importance.

First, there are the approaches to psychological testing for ministerial selection, and the various supplementary activities that are necessary to insure and maintain the effectiveness of these approaches. Second comes the study of the various instruments of measurement that comprise the testing approach. In third place are the experiences of the programs or disciplines that contribute to a further understanding of the effectiveness of psychological testing; fourth is a review of the research that has been done and needs to be done; and fifth, there is the consideration of the varied psychological problems of the clergy. The last-named category might easily have been listed first, since it is out of these problems that the need for testing and selection programs evolves.

Although we would like to say that we as psychologists providing a service in this area see the need for psychological assessment for positive reasons—that is, to identify strengths and weaknesses for the benefit of an individual—we have to face the fact that the religious administrators who are charged with the development of these students have a pressing need for these assessment programs in order to identify and eliminate the mentally and emotionally sick or weak, and the so-called misfits who might, and so often do, become burdensome responsibilities in one way or another for their administrators. However, since the discussion of clergy problems appears last in the sequence of papers, we will let it remain there for the purpose of reporting this conference. But now, to get on with identification of some of the salient points of this conference, as they fall within one or another of these categories.

APPROACHES TO PSYCHOLOGICAL TESTING

In the first category—the approaches to psychological testing—we refer to the use of psychological techniques. These, of course, include the use of tests and interviews to bring together certain information about an individual, analyze it, interpret it, and present it in an organized fashion designed to provide us and the decision-makers with a dynamic description of the personality. This is something that was not done before, nor could the administrator learn so much about a candidate in so short a period of time. In practice, however, the level, reliability, and validity of these dynamic descriptions of personality is a function of the tests themselves, the testing procedure, and the setting in which the candidate is to function, as well as of the training, interest, and experience of the psychological examiner. Parenthetically, I might point out that, at least in the case of Catholic psychologists who are doing this work, the need for examiners is quite large. Thus, we have scheduled for this summer a workshop for the training of psychologists who are interested or currently engaged in this work.*

* This workshop was held at St. Vincent's Hospital and Medical Center, New York City, August 31st and September 1st, 1966. The proceedings have been published (Coville, D'Arcy, McCarthy, & Rooney, 1968).—Ed.

KINDS OF PSYCHOLOGICAL TESTS EMPLOYED

Next we discussed the kinds of tests, and several phrases kept recurring. One was "positive selection." This would refer to the use of psychological testing to identify characteristics of personality that may predict effectiveness in the ministry or in some phase of it, in the same way that tests of scholastic ability predict effectiveness in academic endeavors, or the patterns of interest and motivation predict perseverance in any vocation.

Another recurring phrase was "negative selection," used to identify pathology, from the point of view of seeking to eliminate such individuals from the training program. It seemed to me that there was consensus that the acting-out psychopath, the homosexual, and the pre-psychotic personality represented three major kinds of personality disorders that need to be identified and screened out.

PROGRAMS AND DISCIPLINES CONTRIBUTING TO AN UNDERSTANDING OF SELECTION

In the third category our comments turned to the notion of testing for guidance and counseling. Testing here is used to identify the strengths and weaknesses in the personality of the individual for his benefit. Once the candidate has been accepted into a training program, this information can be used by guidance counselors and psychotherapists for the purpose of supporting an individual through the program. Actually, the way a testing program is applied in this respect differs from one group to another. In the testing of candidates in Catholic institutions, for example, where the commitment is different from the commitment in other groups, the role of testing is, perhaps, more important in making a decision for selection. On the other hand, we have other groups which do not use test results for purposes of selection but rather for the purpose of understanding the total personality and for developing a follow-up training program with provisions to provide counseling or psychotherapy in individual instances as needed. Here the emphasis is more on treatment of psychologically disturbed students than on identifying or eliminating them from a program.

For all practical purposes the consensus is that psychological testing should be used to understand the make-up of accepted candidates and to develop follow-up training programs for their benefit. The aim, then, is to use this material gained through testing to help the individual know himself. The assumption is that the degree to which he knows himself will determine the degree to which he will know others, and to that degree he will be able to function more effectively in his role as a minister.

I want to take this opportunity, also, to thank Dr. Steinberg and Dr. Brown for their perception of our needs and for providing such thorough and basic historical information, enabling us thereby to understand the needs and the status of testing for the Jewish ministry.

Some groups apparently test a large number of candidates, while others test smaller groups. Necessarily, a distinction must be made in these cases between the group-testing and individual-testing approaches. Some of us—and I am one of these—initially began by using individual tests in the examination of candidates. Because of pressure of time and the large numbers that were to be examined, it became uneconomic to continue examinations on an individual basis, and so group techniques were developed.

Throughout the various discussions, a number of cautions were raised with regard to testing. Many of these cautions were pertinent implications for research. For instance, we do not know what really constitutes effectiveness or success in the ministry. It is generally agreed that successful graduation, ordination, or profession does not necessarily imply adequacy of performance or success in the role expectation. This result can only be determined in time. In many instances, also, we are not sure of what the tests are measuring, and we need to think through what these tests mean and why we are using them.

Factors of variability that are inherent in the examiner, the testee, the testing situation, and in the interpretation of test findings were highlighted throughout the discussions as significant influences that tend to distort our prediction. A further point concerned the importance of seeing test data in terms of developmental stages of the individual as well as in terms of the immediate setting or environment. We were also cautioned that we must attempt to match the potentials of a candidate to the unique requirements of the situation that he will have to deal with.

From time to time the point was emphasized that predictions based on psychological testing are probabilities and by no means certainties, and that responsible recommendations made on these bases must reflect this fact. With regard to the various instruments that comprise a test battery—and here we overlap with the preceding comments and some of the comments that will follow with regard to research—most of the discussion dealt with the need for establishing worthwhile criteria and the problems inherent in such a venture. With respect to criteria of effectiveness in the ministry, there appears to be a tendency to rely on perseverance data and the use of peer ratings. The weaknesses of the latter were discussed to some extent. It was noted that we often use tests because they are available, and not because they are measuring what we want to measure.

A recurrent note concerned the multiplicity of roles thrust upon the clergyman. It is often difficult to identify these roles, and, even when identified, they are subject to change. The job of developing or adapting tests to measure these elusive variables as they apply to the unique aspects of the ministry is not an easy one, and yet it is something that must be done.

The problem of different groups and of the effect of changing times also calls for the development of local and current norms. One cannot assume that what was appropriate for one group a year or two ago is appropriate for that same group today, or appropriate for another group.

Another distinction that was made concerned objective and projective tests, from the standpoint of their utility in an assessment program. Objective tests would seem to be substantially influenced by past and current attitudes in predicting future behavior; some of the participants expressed the opinion that projective tests are more effective in predicting future behavior.

The observation was made that to develop a model for prediction of future ministerial performance, we would need to know what is going on in time, in space, and in a particular setting. Although the idea for models has attractive possibilities on the theoretical level, it is also evident that the transition from the theoretical to the concrete level would be most difficult to achieve.

One point which received emphasis several times was that it must be remembered that testing is but one tool in the total process of assessment, and that the effectiveness of assessment is in turn dependent on how test results are used by those responsible for making decisions with respect to admission. Admission policies differ sharply from one group to another.

Finally, we come to the contributions which other programs and other disciplines can make to the understanding of the selection of candidates for the ministry or the religious life. More specifically, the reference here was to the abundant experience of the Peace Corps and its effective use of psychologists and psychological testing in the selection of candidates. Seemingly the effectiveness of this selection program is determined by the leadership that is furnished for the individuals accepted into the program, the follow-up that is also provided, and the fact that at every level of training the staff people, in effect, are counselors.

RESEARCH NEEDED

The fourth of our categories was research: what has been done and what needs to be done. In this area, T. V. Moore's (1936) study was reinterpreted, and it was sobering to learn that the priests reported on in this study were actually healthier than initially indicated. However, Father Moore was the first to bring out and put on the table for inspection and consideration a set of facts that disturbed him, just as some of the facts that we are confronted with today are disturbing to us.

These troublesome facts precipitated and stimulated the study of psychological problems in the clergy, and the use of tests to identify them early. Most reported studies seem to be cross-sectional and descriptive. Although studies of this type have fulfilled a need, comments of participants in this conference indicate that what is required at the present time are longitudinal studies, which would enable us to test our various tools and our hypotheses at different stages of the individual candidate's development and performance.

These longitudinal studies eventually, it is hoped, would lead to a definition of success or excellence in the ministry, and to the development of more appropriate measures for their prediction. One such study was reported by Father Carroll. This study, based on the candidates to the Society of Jesus over a fourteen-year period, involved 350 men who persevered in the vocation. The study is promising, and we look forward to the results.*

PSYCHOLOGICAL PROBLEMS OF THE CLERGY

The final category was concerned with the psychological problems of the clergy. Of course, these were implied throughout the conference at times subtly and at times more directly. However, Dr. Golden in his paper removed the lid, so to speak, and described the various kinds of personal problems that occur in the Presbyterian Church, and indicated some of the things being done to identify and to help the people involved.

Dr. Golden's experiences are paralleled in other religious groups as well. The problems are diverse and include all types of pathology, ranging from obnoxious personality traits to severe personality disorders. Generally, it is agreed that psychopathology occurs frequently enough to require continuing concern and study. Some of the specific psychopathologies mentioned as being found among the clergy included personalities whose basic needs compel the individual to exploit the ministry for his own benefit rather than to function in it for the benefit of others. Reference was also made to the passive-dependent, the weak, and the ineffectual personality type that could be a potential problem in a religious community, or the psychosexually immature or confused individual with a defective background in interpersonal relationships. Other problems listed revolved around authority relationships, sexual adjustment, addiction, problems of faith, and problems of status.

The point was made that it is important to know oneself, in-

* As already indicated, these results are now available: Carroll (1968); see also Fr. Carroll's updated comments in the present volume.—Ed.

cluding, of course, one's limitations, but it is equally important to strengthen areas of weakness, so that the individuals in question might be able to handle stresses as they arise. It is likewise important to alert candidates in training to the problems that they might be expected to face in the future.

Obviously, it is not easy adequately to cover the many areas of discussion touched upon during the conference. I hope that what I have presented is sufficient to jog our memories and provide a basis for further discussion. Dr. Arnold and Dr. Mills will supplement my summary remarks.

DISCUSSION

Basic Optimism Expressed. Dr. Arnold added her strong impression that the most encouraging thing about the conference had been that the participants, like most professional people, had started out by questioning what they were doing, whether they were using the right instruments, cautioning themselves that they ought to be able to explain why they were using certain tests and what the tests were supposed to accomplish. As the conference had proceeded, it had become clear that, in spite of their doubts and difficulties, these people are achieving something, their selection procedures do get at some important and interesting points.

Then there had gradually emerged the fact that the clergy and other religious personnel are in the same situation. They are apologetic about their functions. But toward the end of the sessions the psychologists had found out that the clergy are in better mental health, compared to the general population, than often seemed to be the case, that they could be helped by counseling— in fact, they could be helped to do an excellent job. The initial questioning had given way to the certainty that much can be done in the field. The outcome of the conference was altogether on the side of optimism.

Caution Injected. Dr. Mills thought that, in spite of the general optimism, the criterion problem still loomed like a cloud over the heads of the group. Failure to dispel the cloud was due in part to the fear of doing something unpsychological—probing the normative, the level of criterion selection and decision. Attempts to solve the problem of selection or to define criteria for predicting performance always resulted in a failure to push the question into a vivid and illuminating discussion.

Closely related to this perhaps wise caution was the comment frequently made that selection at the beginning of an education or career may be less important in relation to total performance than are placement and support.

Two questions still unanswered, Dr. Mills continued, are, first, how testing is used to enrich the placement and support processes, and, second, what the function of feedback from testing data in the total process of education, training, and career development is.

A third point calling for attention is the importance of contextual elements surrounding test data from the standpoint of interpretation of testing rather than from that of technique. Dr. Douglas and Dr. Dittes had made valuable comments about test interpretation as necessarily involving the individual's own life setting and stages. What are the responsibilities of the tester for the growth of the person being tested at this point?

The importance of drawing hypotheses out of the empirical situation rather than from the variables that a test offers to measure or from the theoretical framework out of which test development has occurred was a final point that had impressed Dr. Mills. Dr. Golden's paper had emphasized the fact that whatever instruments one uses and whatever theories the tester brings to the seminary setting, the questions he has to answer have to come out of experience in schools, personnel offices, and the like.

Dr. Douglas expressed concern about a possible oversimplification represented in the frequent use of the word "support" in the discussions. Perhaps the professional personnel spend too much time nursing the sick in the seminaries and among the clergy instead of doing more to help the most able candidates, determining what their optimum career development is, at what point they can make their most appropriate contributions, and what supplementary growth opportunities they should have. How, he asked, does one do diagnostic studies, not only relating to what is wrong with a person, but also aimed at finding out what supplementary growth opportunities at what points in his total professional and personal development can help a candidate make the most of his total human and ministerial potential?

Misgivings Voiced. It may be a necessary ritual to begin a conference with misgivings and to end it with an upbeat, Dr. Dittes said. It is undoubtedly possible to psychologize away cautions and reservations as the symptoms of an insecure profession. It is also possible to psychologize away optimism and confidence and positive feelings as a necessary rationalization for what one is doing. He hoped these things might be recognized as rituals, so that the way could be left open for pursuing some of the issues.

Remarking that he had not been convinced by the discussions that predictions, recommendations, and selective procedures can be validly made in ways in which psychologists do make them, Dr. Dittes observed that psychologists who share this doubt nonetheless do administer tests and make little predictions about who will become a good minister or little recommendations based on the tests. They do not make the big recommendations about accepting and encouraging candidates on the grounds of the tests, but they do two things that assume some confidence in the tests: 1.) they give the descriptions to others for use as the basis on which to make decisions. They hide behind a kind of scientific neutrality, like the physicists who say, "We just make the atom bombs—whether to use them or not is for somebody else to decide." This may be all right for a physicist, but a psychologist is too sophisticated. Knowing how such things are used by administrators, he should not be comfortable with this retreat into neutrality; 2.) they also use the test results for counseling. Sometimes this means that in the counseling they subtly and indirectly make recommendations to a student. They alert and guide him toward a decision based on some confidence in the test results, decisions that the psychologist is not ready to make, but the effect is the same as if he had done so.

Concurring with Dr. Dittes' insistence that psychologists should look more carefully at their tests and try to validate them, Dr.

Arnold suggested that perhaps there had been too much concern with the effectiveness of the whole battery. Maybe it would be better to find out what each of the tests contributes to the battery. Although she has the advantage of using a test (the Story Sequence Analysis Test) that has not been used in any battery, she and her colleagues have found that, on comparing their ratings with those of faculty or other authorities and then following up the various positives and negatives, they get much information showing why the faculty rating was different from that produced by the tests. Eventually this procedure will show a great deal more about their tests, why they use them, and in what situations a certain test will be particularly helpful.

Dr. Ashbrook cited three investigators with extensive experience in the field of assessment (Philip Vernon [1964], Gotthard Booth [1963], and Molly Harrower [1964]), all of whom expressed considerable pessimism about the value of testing for screening purposes because the material is highly complex and should be held loosely and matter-of-factly despite the great professional and personal investment psychologists have made in it.

Different subcultures in different parts of the country, Dr. Douglas said, have rituals relating to the respective values of certain tests. He believed that tests are useful therapeutically for psychologists as a means of giving them some sense that they know what they are doing. Psychologists pick up clues and hunches from the data and proceed in a complicated process to a pattern of clues and hunches, thence to an interpretive scheme, and from that to decisions.

Dr. Douglas agreed with Dr. Dittes that psychologists have moral responsibility for the use of information acquired about another person and for the way in which the information is transmitted in relation not only to decisions made by others, but to change processes within the person himself. Not only do psychologists sometimes abdicate responsibility by saying "Let somebody else decide; we only describe." They also, like people in group dynamics, occasionally manipulate by means of the use of test results. Caution should be used. Perhaps it is important to discover what sensitivities are involved in picking up clues and hunches and structuring them in a way related to a theoretical system and to the empirical data, moving from this to interpretation and decisions. Perhaps it will turn out to be not so much a matter of the tests used as of the human factor of the psychologist.

Some Positive Expressions. In defense of testing and making decisions on the basis of the results, Dr. Kildahl cited a case from the records of the Peace Corps reported in the *American Psychologist* for November, 1965.* Use of the MMPI had prevented the sending overseas of a person for whom the experience would have been disastrous. Pathology was revealed and the person received helpful counseling. Dr. Kildahl believed many participants in the conference could report similar instances.

It is often difficult to handle test data statistically and still make the fullest use of them, Father Weisgerber said. For example, he may report that a candidate should be accepted, but that certain weaknesses revealed by the tests should be counseled for and watched. His original estimate may not be confirmed, but the reason may be that the master of novices, taking the report seriously, has counseled the candidate for the weaknesses mentioned. Was the original estimate wrong, then? The statistical answer is not easy to find.

Although participants evidently felt that one cannot predict accurately who will make a good clergyman, Dr. McCarthy said, they had not looked carefully at the other side of the question—who will *not* make a good clergyman. Studies done on this point, such as Father Weisgerber's follow-up (Weisgerber, 1962), show that it is easier to make this negative prediction, which should be kept in mind in the evaluation of the psychologist's contribution to assessment work. Father D'Arcy's work on the SVIB (D'Arcy, 1954) proves that one can identify people who lack the interests of the clergyman. On this basis, one can make predictions about the candidates who are not likely to be successful ministers. But one cannot do the opposite—predict who, among those with high clergy interests, will be successful.

* P. 922. Example given by Abraham Carp, Chief, Selection Division of Peace Corps, in testimony before the Senate Subcommittee on Constitutional Rights, June 9, 1965.—Ed.

Dr. McCarthy believed that assessment work can and often does have several purposes. One is to screen out people. Another is to elicit information that can be used to help a person develop the qualities he needs to be successful. Although, as Father Weisgerber had said, the use of information from the assessment to counsel candidates or to help their development toward desired goals creates serious research problems that make it difficult to check predictions, it is a genuine contribution that should not be overlooked.

Community Contributions to the Clergyman. The community into which the seminarian is to go needs study, too, Dr. Brown suggested. Psychologists have focused their attention on the personality integration of the seminarian. Attention should be paid to attitudinal factors along various lines, not just to those of the individual. For example, a study of medical students reported a few years ago (Becker & Geer, 1958) showed that they pass through a hardening process, changing from the idealism characteristic of the first year to cynicism in their last year. The analogy with seminary students may not be exact, but one should know what attitudinal changes do take place and what the values and expectations are from the first year to the last on the part of seminarians and those who teach them. But the community into which the seminarian goes should be approached from a psycho-sociological point of view. A wide range of the factors, values, and expectations would probably be revealed. With developing understanding of communities, it may be possible to eliminate stress factors so that there is support in a different sense from that of the nurturing function that had been mentioned.

Dr. English added a strong recommendation that mental-health people try to see their skills more widely used in the total organizational structures they serve. Although their initial role in the area of selection is of critical importance, they can also reinforce their contribution if their skills are extended into such areas as training, and the psychological preparation of people for the rigors of seminary training and for the predictable problems that psychological studies may make apparent. This would be support in the broader sense that Dr. Douglas had spoken of.

All of this implies a general awareness on the part of administrators that psychologists and psychiatrists represent primarily the human dimension—the way in which people are handled in the organizational structure. This great vested interest on the part of the mental-health professions requires more contact with the organizations in which they work than just that of testing and counseling. They must have access to the total population of seminarians—and of seminary faculties—so as to find out what their problems and expectations are.

Conclusion. "It is agreed that the sensitivity of the therapist in psychotherapy is a critical factor in the effectiveness of that therapy," commented Dr. Coville. "Ideally, one tries to match a therapist with a patient and his problems. We may find that certain psychologists who have a feel for assessing candidates for the ministry or the religious life are more effective in their examinations and predictions than are other kinds of psychologists. The divergent backgrounds of psychologists, some of whom are clinical, others counseling, and others experimental, seem to me to be important variables in determining the effectiveness of our work in this area of assessment for the ministry. The question requires further study."

REFERENCES

Becker, H. S., & Geer, B. The fate of idealism in medical school. *American Sociological Review*, 1958, *23*, 50–56.

Booth, G. Tests and therapy applied to the clergy. *Journal of Religion and Health*, 1963, *2*, 101–124.

Carroll, D. W. Initial psychological prediction as related to subsequent seminary performance. (Doctoral dissertation, Fordham University), Ann Arbor, Mich.: University Microfilms, 1968. No. 68–3682.

Coville, W. J., D'Arcy, P. F., McCarthy, T. N., & Rooney, J. J. *Assessment of candidates for the religious life*. Washington: CARA (Center for Applied Research in the Apostolate), 1968.

D'Arcy, P. F. Constancy of interest factor patterns within a specific vocation of foreign missioner. *Studies in Psychology and Psychiatry*, 1954, *9*, No. 1. Washington: Catholic University of America Press.

Harrower, M. Mental health potential and success in the ministry. *Journal of Religion and Health*, 1964, *4*, 30–58.

Moore, T. V. Insanity in priests and religious: I. The rate of insanity in priests and religious. *American Ecclesiastical Review*, 1936, *95*, 485–498.
Vernon, P. E. *Personality assessment: A critical survey.* New York: Wiley, 1964.
Weisgerber, C. A. Survey of a psychological screening program in a clerical order. In M. B. Arnold, *et al. Screening candidates for the priesthood and religious life.* Chicago: Loyola University Press, 1962. Pp. 107–148.

CONFERENCE RECOMMENDATIONS

HARRY A. DEWIRE*

THE COMMITTEE ON FINDINGS and our Committee on Recommendations sat together, and it was agreed that we would follow a similar procedure in dealing with our reports. After I have presented what stands to be the corporate wisdom of the Committee, I will ask Father Charles Weisgerber and Dr. Victor Benson to fill in the empty pockets which I have left. Then, after their additions or modifications, we will open this report to general discussion.

I have one or two preliminary remarks about the framework of these recommendations. First, there is some question to whom these recommendations should be directed. As it turns out, there are at least three "audiences" to whom we could be and undoubtedly are speaking. The first is the Academy of Religion and Mental Health. The second audience is the group of participants in this

---

* The Conference Recommendations were also prepared by a Committee consisting of J. Victor Benson, Harry A. DeWire, and Charles A. Weisgerber. Again, the Chairman, this time Dr. DeWire, presented the report, and the two remaining Committee members were afforded the opportunity of speaking first in the discussion period.—Ed.

conference. The third audience is the broad field of researchers and scholars who devote significant time to ministry studies.

My second preliminary point is similar to one stated by Dr. Walter Coville in the findings report, and has to do with a word of profound appreciation to the Academy for providing the format and content of this conference, and for bringing together persons of high-level concern for the problem of testing in relation to the ministry and an equally high-level competence in this area.

One of the most heartening observations about this conference is the demonstration it provides that we are getting to a point in the ecumenical conversation where more than the superficial exchange and defense of ideas are being accomplished. We have been looking at the goals and procedures in psychological testing specifically, and the matters relating to ministerial candidate guidance and education generally, with free discussion and probing to the important areas of research procedure, priority of concerns, and even methods of cooperation in subsequent programs.

As this is being said, it is also true that we are probably still at the stage of idea-sharing. All of us would agree that in this conference we have uncovered more issues than could be dealt with. Nearly every question raised required more attention than a preliminary conference like this one is able to provide.

With these preliminary remarks concluded, let us turn to the recommendations which the Committee desires to present for the consideration of the conference participants. We found, after we had compiled a list of potential recommendations, that they clustered around three general ideas to which we have given the following headings: 1.) Future conversations and studies; 2.) Research collaboration; 3.) Communication with church authorities. The report will deal successively with these three headings about which the Committee recommendations cluster.

FUTURE CONVERSATIONS AND STUDIES

We ought to begin, the Committee thought, by recognizing and assessing the total effort being made in the area of ministry studies. Currently, in addition to the Academy, there are a number of

other national organizations and religious denominations interested and active in the field. Groups such as the National Council
of Churches, Department of the Ministry, Ministry Studies Board,
Society for the Scientific Study of Religion, Catholic Psychological
Association, and religious denominations—especially the United
Presbyterian Church, the Lutheran Church in America, and others
—are deeply involved in one or another phase of ministry studies.

It would seem to the Committee that among these higher-level
groups which function on a national, and even on an international,
basis, there should be continuing conversation about their intentions, and perhaps even some staking-out of certain areas of responsibility. However it is dealt with, we should make sure that
the difficulty in dealing with the problems of research in testing
and use of tests is not compounded by a lack of communication
among the agencies engaged in the task.

The first recommendation of the Committee in this respect
would be that initiative be taken, probably by the Academy or by
some of these national groups in informal conversation, to determine how these groups can function at least in cooperation and
at most by working jointly in areas mentioned later on in this
report. With this in mind, then, it is strongly urged that the
participants in this conference, or a group similarly constituted
that has the advantage of knowing what this group has done, be
brought together again for the consideration of one or more specific areas to which this conference could give only passing attention. It would appear that we have gone probably as far as we
are able in sharing ideas and placing in front of each other our
particular interests and the nature of our work. Future conferences
should focus more sharply upon the tasks rather than upon ideas
about the tasks. Case data, research design, research in progress,
completed research, or a particular instrument dealt with in depth
could, in each instance, provide such a group with the means of
making ministry studies useful to the churches. Following Dr.
Arnold's suggestion that a conference be called to consider the
value of particular tests for ministry studies, we might also explore
ways of cooperating with test-distributing agencies in the study of
those instruments used widely in the evaluation of candidates.

But even if such long steps cannot be taken, it does mean that we have reached the point at which we can best function by narrowing the focus of our concerns by undertaking specific activities within areas discussed by the conference, rather than by simply speaking out of our own experiences.

A further recommendation for future conversations would be that we bring together again the collective competence represented in this conference, to raise the critical questions about research needs and what research should have high priority. We have focused heavily on the criterion problem, and undoubtedly this is most crucial. However, little has been done to list subsequent problems which could be explored along with the criterion studies. What are the second and third most important problems, and is it necessary to wait until the criterion problem is solved before the others are dealt with?

This raises a further possibility. Such a conference could deal with the procedures of research as they apply to ministry studies. Sometimes we are stymied because we are dealing with a value-oriented profession and value-oriented people. It is recommended that a future conference deal with the manner in which empirical methods relate to the issues that may on the surface seem to be out of the reach of our existing tools.*

A third recommendation in this cluster has already been alluded to in the discussion on findings—namely, that we look at the assessment of men by the use of psychological tests as simply one among many resources available to assist the candidate toward a productive career. We have discussed the need for what Dr. English has called "support," and it may be that our total job is one

---

* The Academy has taken some initiative along the lines recommended, although with a somewhat broader focus. A Conference on Research in Relations between Religion and Health was held under the sponsorship of the Academy at the Nassau Inn, Princeton, N.J., November 17–19, 1968. Present were researchers, research directors, and foundation representatives. A principal purpose of the conference was to determine the need for co-operative efforts among researchers and research organizations so as to facilitate research, communication, and funding, and to propose specific means to achieve these ends. A follow-up conference is planned which would be devoted to a consideration of specific research proposals, so that something along the lines envisioned by the Committee seems to be in the process of development.—Ed.

of education: in some persons we have to reach back further to start this process than we do with other people.

Can tests be used and interpreted for this purpose? How can they be incorporated into the curriculum structure of our various training programs? How are teachers in training institutions drawn into a discussion of the meaning of tests and their place in the curriculum?

You will want to add other possibilities for future conversations. But, broadly speaking, these seem to be areas where the focus of future conferences can be narrowed, in our opinion, with a great deal of profit.

RESEARCH COLLABORATION

The second cluster of recommendations has to do with the whole question of research assessment, and for lack of a better word I have selected the word "control" to describe the attempt to prevent waste and duplication in ministry studies. There is a vast proliferation of work being done as is attested to by the bibliography produced by the Ministry Studies Board and the Lutheran Church in America, and edited by Robert Menges and James Dittes (1965). At the present time there are across the country— even across the world—a great many research projects in various stages of completion. Some place along the line we need to establish some responsibility for using this research, developing useful research, and at the same time exercising an economy of time, effort, and money. Here again the national groups interested in ministry studies should be alert to the fact that they are in a strategic position to assist in this process.

Two broad recommendations grow out of this concern. First, that someone be responsible for providing a clearing house for the purpose of listing and consolidating the gains and knowledge that we have acquired in the use of tests, with a view to being able to look for an extension or replication of research, rather than simply the duplication, or near-duplication, of it.

Beyond this stands the very delicate question, who eventually decides that a specific research design is legitimately and properly conceived. I think a good case in point is the discussion which grew up around Father David Carroll's presentation. This is an excellent example of how his research is rightfully related to previous studies, and the natural outgrowth of something that has already been done. The comment was made that this now raises a host of questions. How can we get other people to proceed from Father Carroll's findings and move in a reasonable direction toward the full exploitation of what he is doing?

In other places, especially among graduate students, pre-doctoral students, and even professors who have both the opportunity and money for research, there is no easy access to the kind of help which would assure them that the research they are about to undertake will meet the most pressing needs.

It must be recognized, of course, that the person in research is pretty much a law unto himself, and may in the final analysis decide to do what he thinks best, or merely wants to do, regardless of these kinds of controls or suggestions that might be available to him. On the other hand it has been my experience, as I have worked with the Ministry Studies Board, that researchers are generally interested in knowing where they can function to serve the best interests of the broader field in which they are working. I can remember two instances involving pre-doctoral students with whom I discussed dissertation plans. After they had a clearer picture of the kind of research that was going on and what was needed, their pre-doctoral studies were changed, in one case quite radically.

Therefore, the second recommendation in this second cluster is that there be established an agency where help be made available for people who may have difficulty finding their way through the kind of studies they have in mind, or may have difficulty with the particular designs they have in mind or who may have difficulty with carrying through specific parts of their research on testing, and other phases of ministry studies. As a start we might determine what facilities are now available. If no agency is currently equipped to perform such a function, steps should be taken to alert national organizations to the need for such research assistance.

COMMUNICATION OF TESTING AND RESEARCH RESULTS
TO CHURCH AUTHORITIES

The third cluster has to do with communication about which Dr. English spoke. It is good to know that what one is going to say has some approval before it is said. It is increasingly important that the rather wide gulf be bridged between the professional and what might be considered the consumer.

Church administrators, candidate committees, and parish ministers are the persons who can not only eventually make use of research findings, but should also provide increasing assistance in many phases of research such as data-gathering and field-testing. These persons eventually make the important decisions about the candidate's ordination and placement. If research is to be helpful, it must be translated into terms readily understood and usable by persons unfamiliar with the process and language of research.

One of the reasons why this conference came into being is that there were inquiries from the heads of churches asking about the availability of tests and how reliable they are. Assuming that is correct, I am quite interested to know what Rev. Anderson is going to tell them, or what they are going to do when they receive a report of the findings of this conference.

At present, research findings are usually made public by the individual researcher who receives support from other individuals familiar with his work. Regardless of their validity, the layman may be unimpressed by the findings unless they have support from recognized authorities or from research groups in which they have confidence. On the other hand, he may be overimpressed by the work of a researcher who happens to be a friend or who is over-persuasive.

If research results are to be communicated to the church with consistency and clarity, it probably cannot be done best by the researcher himself. He needs the support and direction of agencies which have won the confidence of the church and whose competency can be trusted. Such a procedure will help to put research results in their proper perspective, and, at the same time, help to break down resistance to the use of empirical methods in the study of the ministry.

The members of the Committee have no ready answer how this can be done, but we encourage responsible groups not to lose sight of the fact that research may have a great deal to offer the church which will not be useful until it can be implemented through training sessions, institutes, and other media of communication.

DISCUSSION

Comments of Committee Members. Dr. Benson called attention to the need for improvement in communication among the people concerned with testing and evaluation of candidates, coming as they do from different professional backgrounds. For example, he had felt the need to know more about Dr. Ashbrook's definition of a working model. What do people mean about a criterion, which is one thing, and about criteria, which are many things? There is a general assumption that everybody knows what is meant by these and other terms, when actually this is not the case. Simplicity and clarity of expression are essential if the messages of a conference of this kind are to be made understandable to the people who need them, especially the denominational leaders.

Another tendency in discussions of this kind, Dr. Benson continued, is the reluctance to pick out the most important interests that are present all the time. When people talk about enigmas of their work or themselves, they often really mean that they have misgivings about the way tests are being used and the way the reports from the tests are handled by ecclesiastical officials. The basic concern is for the people with whom the psychologists are working—the greatest enigmas of all. These people are so enigmatic that they are unpredictable; and the psychologists themselves, members of the great class of human beings, are enigmatic, too.

It is likely that both psychiatry and religion will proceed through mutations and transmutations that will produce new and better forms. In one's concern for the modification of human behavior, it is well to be mindful of the fact that evaluation will not be coerced. "The God of Abraham, Isaac, Jacob, Jesus, Paul, Augustine, Calvin, Luther, Freud, Jung, and William James is also a cosmic clock."

Therefore, Dr. Benson concluded, perhaps the people working in this area should not take themselves too seriously, but should get on with their work, which involves dealing with the crowning glory of God's creation—the fascinating human being, especially those who are interested in becoming leaders in the church.

In making its recommendations, Father Weisgerber said, the Committee had felt that it would not be doing justice to the trend of much of the discussion if it did not make a recommendation about thorough study of the criterion problem.

Information about Research. To provide a clearing house for information, Father Weisgerber wondered whether it might not be feasible for the *Journal of Religion and Health** to have a section or a column in which it would provide information about what various people in the field are doing. It might be just a list of research in progress, or a series of abstracts of research. It might overlap with a book like that of Menges and Dittes (1965), which might consider publishing an annual supplement, but a periodical that would commit itself to such a function would be most helpful.

Dr. English added that either the Academy or representatives of this conference could use the services of the NIMH clearing house, which is still in evolution, to gather this kind of information for publication in the *Journal of Religion and Health*. The clearing house has categories for which one can apply. One will then receive regular listings of all the new reports that come out in the categories selected.

A further suggestion along this line came from Father Weisgerber, who spoke of the comparatively new Medical Literature and Analysis System, a computerized search and bibliographic system of the National Library of Medicine. It is used in preparing

* Published quarterly by the Academy of Religion and Mental Health, 16 East 34th Street, New York, N.Y. 10016. Intended "for all who are interested in the indivisibility of human well-being: physical, emotional, and spiritual," its editor is Harry C. Meserve, D.D., and 1969 was its eighth year of publication.—Ed.

the *Index Medicus* and can provide regular bibliographies on subscription or on demand (Karel, Austin, & Cummings, 1965). One would have to have the System's list of Medical Subject Headings in order to specify the "descriptors" to be used in the search. One would then make a request through a library. The usefulness of the service for our purposes would depend on whether or not the service regularly searches the appropriate journals and adds the appropriate headings to the program.

In regard to research consultation facilities, Father Weisgerber continued, a good illustration of what can be done was provided here in the discussion of Father David Carroll's plans. A good example of research evaluation had come out in the analysis of Father Moore's data. The thinking behind one of the recommendations reported by Dr. DeWire was the possibility of holding conferences for the discussion of case material, particularly research.

Dr. Steinberg suggested the possibility of similar conferences dealing with the whole question of the training in the seminary itself—what the seminary can do to strengthen, support, and guide the students. Related to that would be the question of periodic testing, of what goes by the name of mid-career review within the seminary or after the man is out of the seminary.

Another suggestion, from Dr. English, was that the Academy consider another meeting centering completely on the psychological problems, the growth and potential of clergymen at certain periods of their training and their service. With that kind of information, plus more of what Father D'Arcy had presented from the Catholic point of view, such a conference might encourage many other psychological resources that would become available to all kinds of community organizations besides religious communities. This would move away from a concentration on the troubled segments of the religious population. Peace Corps experience shows that 90 percent of the volunteers go through significant psychological crises. The 10 percent who do not are the ones to be most concerned about, because of the denial involved in the absence of crises.

Concluding Comments. To Brother Dondero, the main thing was to decide what is to be the thrust and purpose of this conference group: to be a stimulant to others? to present and air problems? to bring problems to the attention of others so that they may mobilize their forces and attack these problems? or should the group narrow its efforts to specific things? He approved Dr. English's suggestion, but he did not want to see the group drop too soon the things it had started in order to go on to new horizons prematurely.

A purpose of this conference that had not had enough attention, Dr. Douglas said, is the continuing education of the participants themselves, a broadening of their perspectives and development of their sensitivity of interpretation. He wondered how members of this group could spread the kind of training they had given one another in assessments, interpretation, guidance, and evaluation to others who perform these functions in seminaries, denominations, etc., and who are inadequately trained.

Mr. Bergman ended the conference with a request that the participants send the Academy letters containing their evaluations, criticisms, and analysis of this conference with suggestions how conferences of this kind can be structured more meaningfully. The Academy also would like to know what the members of the group would think of holding annual conferences to keep abreast of contemporary developments in testing—to continue this dialogue on a current basis perhaps for several years. The Academy would also welcome suggestions for projects, studies, programs not related to the conference.

REFERENCES

Karel, L., Austin, C. J., & Cummings, M. M. Computerized bibliographic services for biomedicine. *Science*, 1965, *148*, 766–722.
Menges, R. J., & Dittes, J. E. *Psychological studies of clergymen: Abstracts of research*. New York: Nelson, 1965.

Participants

Rev. George C. Anderson, D.D.
Honorary President, Academy of Religion and Mental Health, New York, N.Y.

Magda B. Arnold, Ph.D.
Professor of Psychology, Loyola University, Chicago, Ill.

Rev. James B. Ashbrook, Ph.D.
Professor of Psychology and Theology, Colgate–Rochester Divinity School/Bexley Hall, Rochester, N.Y.

Rev. J. Victor Benson, Ph.D.
Secretary for Psychological Services, Board of Theological Education, Lutheran Church in America, New York, N.Y.

Charles C. Bergman
Executive Vice-President, Academy of Religion and Mental Health, New York, N.Y.

Rev. William C. Bier, S.J., Ph.D.
Professor of Psychology, Fordham University, Bronx, N.Y.
Chairman, Conference Committee

Fred Brown, Ph.D.
Head, Division of Psychology, Department of Psychiatry, Mount Sinai Hospital, New York, N.Y.
Member, Conference Committee

Rev. David W. Carroll, S.J., Ph.D.
Director, Counseling Center, Fordham University, Bronx, N.Y.

269

WALTER J. COVILLE, Ph.D.
Consulting Clinical Psychologist, St. Vincent's Hospital, New York, N.Y.

Rev. PAUL F. D'ARCY, M.M., Ph.D.
Director of Education, the Maryknoll Fathers, Maryknoll Seminary, Maryknoll, N.Y.

Rev. HARRY A. DEWIRE, Ph.D.
Professor of Psychology and Pastoral Care, United Theological Seminary, Dayton, Ohio

Rev. JAMES E. DITTES, Ph.D.
Professor, Psychology of Religion, Yale University Divinity School, New Haven, Conn.

Brother E. AUSTIN DONDERO, F.S.C., Ph.D.
Chairman, Department of Psychology, La Salle College, Philadelphia, Pa.

Rev. WILLIAM G. T. DOUGLAS, Ph.D.*
Associate Professor, Psychology of Religion, Boston University School of Theology, Boston, Mass.

JOSEPH T. ENGLISH, M.D.†
Chief Psychiatrist, Medical Program Division, Peace Corps, Washington, D.C.

Rev. EDWARD S. GOLDEN, Ed.D.
Secretary, Inter-Board Office, Personnel Services, General Division of Vocation and Ministry of the Board of Christian Education, United Presbyterian Church, Philadelphia, Pa.

JOHN P. KILDAHL, Ph.D.
Chief Psychologist, Lutheran Medical Center, New York, N.Y.

Rev. FREDERICK R. KLING
Research Associate, Educational Testing Service, Princeton, N.J.

THOMAS N. MCCARTHY, Ph.D.
Professor of Psychology and Director, Counseling Center, La Salle College, Philadelphia, Pa.

---

* Currently, Pastor of West Parish Congregational Church, West Barnstable, Mass., and Professor of Psychology in Cape Cod Community College.
† Currently, Assistant Director, Office of Health Affairs, Office of Economic Opportunity, Washington, D.C.

Rev. EDGAR W. MILLS, Ph.D.
 Executive Director, Ministry Studies Board, National Council of the Churches of Christ, Washington, D.C.
 Member, Conference Committee
PAUL M. STEINBERG, Ed.D.
 Dean, Professor of Human Relation and Education, Hebrew Union College, New York, N.Y.
Rev. CHARLES A. WEISGERBER, S.J., Ph.D.
 Professor of Psychology, University of Detroit, Detroit, Mich.